MIGRANT FUTURES

Duke University Press   Durham and London   2018

AIMEE BAHNG

MIGRANT FUTURES

Decolonizing Speculation in Financial Times

© 2018 DUKE UNIVERSITY PRESS. All rights reserved
Text designed by Courtney Leigh Baker and typeset in
Whitman and Trade Gothic by Tseng Information Systems, Inc.

Library of Congress Cataloging-in-Publication Data
Names: Bahng, Aimee, [date] author.
Title: Migrant futures : decolonizing speculation in
financial times / Aimee Bahng.
Description: Durham : Duke University Press, 2017. |
Includes bibliographical references and index.
Identifiers: LCCN 2017025278 (print) |
LCCN 2017041274 (ebook)
ISBN 9780822373018 (ebook)
ISBN 9780822363644 (hardcover)
ISBN 9780822363798 (pbk.)
Subjects: LCSH: Speculative fiction. | Finance in
literature. | Future, The, in literature. | Speculation.
Classification: LCC PN98.F56 (ebook) | LCC PN98.F56
B346 2017 (print) | DDC 809.3/876—dc23
LC record available at https://lccn.loc.gov/2017025278

Cover art: Sonny Liew, art from *Malinky Robot*.
Courtesy of the artist.

for Dara

CONTENTS

Preface · ix   Acknowledgments · xiii

INTRODUCTION. ON SPECULATION
Fiction, Finance, and Futurity · 1

1. IMPERIAL RUBBER *The Speculative Arcs of
Karen Tei Yamashita's Rainforest Futures* · 25

2. HOMELAND FUTURITY
Speculations at the Border · 51

3. SPECULATION AND THE SPECULUM
Surrogations of Futurity · 79

4. THE CRUEL OPTIMISM OF THE ASIAN CENTURY · 119

5. SALT FISH FUTURES *The Irradiated Transpacific
and the Financialization of the Human Genome Project* · 146

EPILOGUE. SPECULATION AS DISCOURSE,
SPECULATION AS EXUBERANCE · 168

Notes · 171   Bibliography · 201   Index · 217

PREFACE

This project emerges in many ways from my particular affiliation with Pasadena, California—longtime home not only of the Jet Propulsion Laboratory of the National Aeronautics and Space Administration (NASA) and the California Institute of Technology (Caltech), the science and engineering powerhouse, but also of the black speculative fiction writer Octavia Estelle Butler (1947–2006). In an obituary for this "Sister from Another Planet," Jervey Tervalon describes Butler's hometown as a "racially explosive community, where blacks and whites frequently encounter each other—unlike so much of Los Angeles where freeway distance gives a false sense of security."[1] Against the backdrop of Los Angeles's suburban sprawl, filled with gated communities that would inform the postapocalyptic terrain of Butler's Parable series, Tervalon tells the story of a "racist Pasadena that Jackie Robinson, another native son, hated and never wanted to return to." Though this black-white polarity had already been complicated for many years by steady migrations of Latinos and Asians to the San Gabriel Valley, the Pasadena I came to know during my upbringing nonetheless remained a racially tense and divided environment. In official settings (such as school and sponsored activities), I often found myself pulled into a strained narrative of multiculturalist assimilation—the token Asian poster child in a rainbow delegation for Pasadena's self-promotion as a diverse city that manufactured model minorities in every shade, even as it doled out routine servings of racist messages scrawled in shaving cream on our driveway, or flung xenophobic "Go back to China!" calls from neighborhood bullies on bikes.

Los Angeles, more broadly, was a place that, as Mike Davis has pointed out, witnessed the conjuncture of a postwar, science-based economy (Caltech and NASA) and the "imagineering" ethos of Disney and Hollywood in the second half of the twentieth century.[2] In *City of Quartz*, Davis suggests that this convergence of an expansive community of scientists and engineers and the commercial film and television industry produced a hotbed of science fiction. My own interest in science fiction, no doubt influenced to some degree by the reasons Davis gives, also happened to take shape alongside my earliest formations of racial consciousness and feminist-queer community. I sought and found a sense of outsider commiseration in the video arcades and comic book stores. While there was no shortage of the more stereotypical white, suburban geeks who turned to what was then still a subculture as a place they could dominate—a smaller pond in which to be a big fish—the realm of science fiction was also a bustling contact zone for urban youth of color whose interests in popular media affiliated with science fiction (film, television, comic books, and video games) constituted one of the few opportunities for cross-ethnic solidarities in an otherwise segregated and gender-normative landscape. Science fiction, which constituted fugitive reading in my household, offered not only a break from more canonical, achievement-oriented reading regimens, but also a place for many people to take refuge from the social realities of racially unequal systems of housing, fissured with decades of redlining practices and the dismantling of public transportation, libraries, education, parks, and other meeting places in a period of relentless privatization. In the context of experiencing geeks of color in queer, playful assembly in the literary, gaming, and role-playing worlds affiliated with science fiction, I began to wonder why this genre, some of which has facilitated an off-world repository for Orientalist, imperialist, and misogynist desires in an era of political correctness, might nonetheless harbor a set of alternative possibilities for antiracist, feminist, and queer critique.

Reading science fiction also performed a certain work on me—work for which I had already been primed. Most of the books I was asked to read in school required that I step into the shoes of the usually white, male, prep-school protagonists of works like *A Catcher in the Rye* and *A Separate Peace*. I certainly felt a tinge of injustice (Where were all the female protagonists? Even the animals seemed to have names of boys I knew), which meant that I also recognized how powerful the act of reading could be. In being repeatedly asked to relate to these unfamiliar social positions, contexts, and problems of the East Coast boarding school; comprehend homosocial hazing environments; and understand the brooding psychic landscape of those teenage boy characters, I developed a capacity to reach beyond my immediate frames of reference in order to grasp at someone else's sensorium. These classic novels of adolescent angst presumed a reader's familiarity or identification with the protagonist. That presumption worked through the tacit presentation of these works as realist fiction, whereas my experience of those worlds was one of utter alienation. The literary canon's unspoken promise to deliver universal human experience imposed a narrow field of feeling, relating to, and being in the world that felt to me more like science fiction than the books I kept stashed between my mattress and box spring at home. In this sense, my experience was similar to that of other people of color who have reflected on being drawn to reading materials characterized by their otherworldliness.[3] The authors of the science fiction to which I was drawn (such as Octavia E. Butler, Ursula K. Le Guin, and Samuel R. Delany) took pleasure in catching the reader jumping to conclusions about what was familiar and what was strange. The reader who was willing to set aside her assumptions of how the world worked would often be rewarded with an easier acclimation to alternative ontologies, epistemologies, and universes. Reading science fiction became for me a practice of unlearning hegemonic principles.

I began writing *Migrant Futures* many years ago as a project that identified the potential in science fiction to do antiracist and antinormative work. My understanding of speculation as praxis became all the more charged when I began to push my thinking about speculation beyond the framework of genre. When I began to see forms of speculation all around me — most significantly in the ever-burgeoning financial sector, but also in the insurance industry, histories of imperial expansion, and generally the crafting of futurity across a wide array of platforms — I resolved to broaden the scope of what could have been a fairly narrow literary study to an examination of a wider culture of future-telling. This initial impulse to take my original questions to the field of economic and financial speculation was spurred on by the provocative claim that it is "easier to imagine the end of the world than the end of capitalism."[4] What follows might be considered a "starter archive" of attempts to imagine if not the end of capitalism, then an alternative to it, by way of those who may find themselves mired in capitalism or displaced by it, but who continue to speculate beyond its logics.[5] What I have assembled here is a promiscuous set of cultural texts, often paired in ways that highlight a tension between fortune-telling in the service of capitalism and migrant futures that dare to imagine a world beyond it.

ACKNOWLEDGMENTS

If speculation is a practice of world making, completing this book similarly required the cosmological aggregation of many generative thinkers. My earliest teachers, who first grabbed hold of my imagination and shook off my assumptions of how the world could be, were the aforementioned writers of science fiction: Octavia E. Butler, Samuel R. Delany, and Ursula K. LeGuin. Though their works of fiction are not the objects of analysis in this project, the force of their fabulations rewired my brain early on and instigated a whole lifetime of critical inquiry. I am also deeply grateful to the convivial and critically acute group of thinkers called an uncertain commons, whose collaboratively written and collectively published *Speculate This!* serves as a sort of companion manifesto to *Migrant Futures*. It has been thinking in common with folks like these as well as the inimitable Donna Haraway and all of the feminist-queer science and technology studies students who have been inspired by her work, that has made this book a possibility.

Migrant Futures began as a doctoral dissertation at the University of California, San Diego (UCSD), where I not only received crucial guidance and support but also found the best models of bringing scholarly pursuits, teaching practices, and political commitments together in meaningful ways. First and foremost, I want to acknowledge Shelley Streeby, whose steadfast encouragement and level-headed focus on political work (and the politics of work) sustained a whole cadre of students, myself included, who would take to heart her daily practice of showing up when it mattered and growing a sense of solidarity too rarely experienced in our line of work. My heartfelt thanks also go to Lisa Bloom, Lisa Cartwright, Michael Davidson, Page duBois, the late Rosemary Marangoly George, J. Jack Halberstam, Nicole King, George Lipsitz, Lisa Lowe, Eileen Myles, Roddey Reid, Winnie

Woodhull, and Lisa Yoneyama. It was at UCSD that I encountered some of the most lasting teacher-interlocutor-friends. Neel Ahuja, Kyla Schuller, and Elizabeth Steeby: I am so lucky to have you in my corner. I would be remiss not to acknowledge also the solidarity and mentorship I received from several women of color in the cohort who graduated just prior to me, including: Neda Atanasoski, Jinah Kim, Su Yun Kim, and Gabriela Nuñez. There are many more I would like to name, but suffice it to say that I feel honored to count myself a part of an extensive UCSD intellectual family.

I have had strong and caring teachers all along. Among those who helped show me a path of scholarly and political commitments are teachers from my time at Princeton University and the Bread Loaf School of English: Wendy Chun, Gina Dent, Diana Fuss, Martin Harries, Claudia Johnson, Tom Keenan, Arthur Little, Wahneema Lubiano, Emily Martin, Jeff Nunokawa, D. Vance Smith, Claire Sponsler, Cornel West, and Hertha Sweet Wong.

This book's engagement with finance culture was significantly enriched from my time with the University of California Humanities Research Institutes Residential Research Group, "Speculative Globalities." This space of convivial collaboration brought me into a new set of reading, thinking, and writing practices that has expanded what I thought possible in academe. To Cesare Casarino, Bishnu Ghosh, Colin Milburn, Geeta Patel, Rita Raley, Bhaskar Sarkar, and Sudipta Sen: I thank you for all you taught me in intellectual spheres as well as in culinary appetites.

More recently I have had the great pleasure of reading and thinking in common with Kiran Asher, Jennifer Hamilton, Rebecca Herzig, Banu Subramaniam, and Angie Willey. Together, we have constituted a feminist science and technology studies research group based in New England, and that camaraderie has been tremendously inspiring and productive for this work. Banu and Angie have extended their caring attention to me when I needed it most, and I hope to be able to keep reciprocating that care for the rest of our lives. A little farther afield, I have found other feminist-queer-geek-confabulators, such as Alexis Lothian and Rebekah Sheldon, who remind me that sometimes the best critics are also fans.

Much of this work evolved over the course of presenting its component ideas as talks given at the Five Colleges; Stanford University; Seoul National University; the University of California, Santa Cruz; and, on several occasions, the annual Futures of American Studies Institute. Being invited into international and transdisciplinary scholarly arenas has been rewarding, and I want to thank the generous audiences at the national conferences where I have presented this work, including the annual meetings of the American Studies Association, the Association of Asian American Studies, the Modern Language Association, the National Women's Studies Association, and the Society for Cinema and Media Studies.

Asian American Studies has over the past decade become an increasingly important intellectual community for me, and so many folks have gone out of their way to engage my scholarship and support my career in multitudinous ways. For their intellectual and emotional labor, I owe a great debt to: Jason Oliver Chang, Kandice Chuh, David Eng, Christopher Fan, Catherine Fung, Tammy Ho, Betsy Huang, Jinny Huh, Joseph Jeon, Rachel C. Lee, Sue J. Kim, Martin Manalansan, Anita Mannur, Christine Mok, Lisa Nakamura, Cathy Schlund-Vials, Stephen Sohn, and Min Hyoung Song.

During my time at Dartmouth, I was lucky to find an intellectual community that carved out a space for coalitional and communal living and thinking. Though many of us are now part of a Dartmouth diaspora, our overlapping time together laid the groundwork for friendships that outlast the vicissitudes of institutional affiliation. Special thanks to: Laura Braunstein, Adrienne Clay, Mary Coffey, Soyica Diggs Colbert, Reena Godlthree, Christian Haines, Max Hantel, Rashauna Johnson, Eng-Beng Lim, Abby Neely, Tanalis Padilla, Julia Rabig, Russell Rickford, Naaborko Sackeyfio-Lenoch, Jeff Sharlet, Craig Sutton, Derrick and Stephanie White, and more generally, the Ferguson Teaching Collective.

Dartmouth College also provided various forms of structural support for the production of this manuscript. Thanks to the Walter and Leslie Center for the Humanities, the Walter and Constance Burke Research Initiation Award, the Gender Research Institute, and the Dean of Faculty's Junior Faculty Fellowship. Several senior colleagues (Colleen Boggs, Andrew McCann, Don Pease, Barbara Will, and Melissa Zeiger) also read portions of the work, and I thank the English department and Women's, Gender, and Sexuality Studies program in particular for providing the space and time to grow this project among you. Dartmouth also became an institutional member of the National Center for Faculty Development and Diversity. I have found valuable mentorship, commiseration, and guidance in my Faculty Success Program alumnae group there, as well as among the many women and nonbinary people of color in academia on social media.

Thanks, too, to Ken Wissoker and the entire editorial team at Duke University Press, including Elizabeth Ault, Sara Leone, and Jeanne Ferris. Ken has believed in this work for many years, and without his unwavering support and care manifested in many ways, it would never have come to fruition. Sincere thanks also to Sara, who peeked out from behind the project editor's track changes to share an uncommon level of empathy during a particularly rough patch. Before the manuscript arrived at Duke, I was able to have the incisive, generous, and witty Josh Rutner, my freelance friend-editor, prepare it for more official eyes. It is a pleasure to work with such attuned and deeply committed editors.

Sometimes, extraordinary measures taken by a tightly knit fabric of friends and family are the only way a project gets completed. Among all those who held my hand or helped drag me across the finish line, Bill Boyer has probably had to shoulder most of this loving labor. One could not dream of a more steadfast partner across so many terrains, and I am deeply grateful to be facing the world with the best of teammates.

This book is for my families, who are listed above in porous groupings, but in many ways, it is a book that comes out of my first family. For this reason, I want to acknowledge most tenderly Joon, Jaisoo, and Gene Bahng, who instilled in me a love of critical inquiry that sustains the speculations that follow.

Some of the individual chapters listed below were previously published in different versions. "Extrapolating Transnational Arcs, Excavating Imperial Legacies: The Speculative Acts of Karen Tei Yamashita's Through the Arc of the Rain Forest," "Alien/Asian," edited by Stephen H. Sohn, special issue, MELUS 33, no. 4 (Winter 2008): 123–44; "The Cruel Optimism of Asian Futurity and Reparative Practices in Sonny Liew's Malinky Robot," in *Techno-Orientalism*, edited by Betsy Huang, Greta Niu, and David Roh (New Brunswick, NJ: Rutgers University Press, 2015), 163–79; "Specters of the Pacific: Salt Fish Drag and Atomic Hauntologies in the Era of Genetic Modification," "Fictions of Speculation," edited by Hamilton Carroll and Annie McClanahan, special issue, *Journal of American Studies*, 49, no. 4 (Fall 2015): 663–79.

INTRODUCTION

ON SPECULATION
Fiction, Finance, and Futurity

We need visions of the future, and our people need them more than most.
—SAMUEL DELANY, "The Necessity of Tomorrows," 1978 address at the Studio Museum in Harlem

You've got to make your own worlds. You've got to write yourself in.
—OCTAVIA BUTLER, "Octavia Butler on Charlie Rose"

We must organize our methods to illuminate the relation between culture and economy, thus refusing to separate, as has been the practice, the operational and mathematical techniques of the derivatives markets from their social implications.
—EDWARD LIPUMA AND BENJAMIN LEE, *Financial Derivatives and the Globalization of Risk*

As of December 2014, approximately $710 trillion of the world's capital was circulating in the global financial derivatives market, a metamarket of trading in commodity futures, options, and swaps.[1] It is a statistic designed to stagger. Economists call it a "notional figure," as it serves as more of a placeholder of value than actual money changing hands; it is alien currency from another time, from a time out of joint, from the future anterior.[2] This notional figure of future-refracted value shimmers in the distance like a desert mirage, with social factors such as risk and optimism flickering across its screen of projection. Even as economists apply mathematical algorithms to render their extrapolations more supple, accurate, and complex, the market in financial derivatives—tethered notionally to its underlying assets—relies on an engine of speculation, extrapolation, and projection to render value out of the not yet. Derivatives function as insurance policies, working to hedge against the uncertainty of speculative futures. What Marx termed "fictitious capital" emerged notably out of the national debt and credit systems of his day in the form of promissory notes with no link to underlying assets.[3] Characterizing these financial claims on debtors as predatory lending, Marx described usury capital as parasitical on money wealth: "It sucks its blood, kills its nerve."[4] Marx's figuration of fictitious capital as vampiric[5] and the "notional figure" of the financial derivatives market point to the central role of fiction crafting and figuration in the production of finance capitalism.

This book puts into conversation speculative finance and speculative fiction as two forms of extrapolative figuration that participate in the cultural production of futurity. To put these two seemingly disparate arenas of narrative production into conversation, I largely use the methodologies of an emerging field that could be called critical finance studies in conjunction with a longer standing field called feminist science studies, which trained me to beware of the "god trick of seeing everything from nowhere" purveyed by the seemingly pure, objective vision of scientific and capitalist realism.[6] It is indeed a god trick to get people to mistake prophecy for truth, notional figure for value, or futurity for the future. As a lifetime student of the power of narrative to alter reality, or at least perceptions of it, I have often been awed by fiction's nearly magical actuarial potency. By approaching both speculative finance and speculative fiction as narrative productions, I emphasize the performativity of economics and therefore the potential power of the literary imagination to call forth new political economies, ways of living, and alternative relational structures; and different sorts of subjects into the world.

I use the term "futurity" to highlight the construction of the future and denaturalize its singularity, while maintaining an emphasis on how narrative constructions of the future play a significant role in materializing the present. "Extrapolation," for example, is the name for the mathematical modeling practice economists use to predict future commodity prices and investment trends based on data compiled in databases such as the

CRB *Commodity Yearbook*, Wharton Research Data Services, as well as Global Financial Data Solutions. At the same time, science fiction studies might first associate extrapolation with the eponymous academic journal, which publishes scholarly essays on science fiction (also called extrapolative or speculative fiction). *Migrant Futures* investigates how we narrate futurity across various platforms, from speculative fiction to financial speculation. How do our stories of the future chart the ways we invest—financially, politically, ideologically, and intellectually—in the present? How do the logics of preemption break across the shores of financial securitization, military preparedness, and scientific projection? These are some of the questions taken up by anthropologists, sociologists, historians, cultural theorists, and other scholars contributing to an interdisciplinary examination of financialization.[7]

Most notably, Edward LiPuma and Benjamin Lee assert the social construction of financial derivatives—a social construction that, like race, nonetheless has profound material effects on people's livelihoods, state politics, and international conflicts. LiPuma and Lee call derivatives "socially imaginary objects" and assert "the social construction of the various types of derivatives."[8] They also emphasize the *"abstract symbolic violence"* that speculative capital wreaks on the world—"symbolic in the sense that it is not accomplished physically by means of military force or colonialism, though it may, of course, engender the conditions (such as impoverishment) that precipitate violent crime and warfare" and "abstract in the sense that it never appears directly; rather it mediates and stands behind local realities—such as interest rates, food costs, and the price of petroleum."[9] One poignant example that LiPuma and Lee provide is the effect of presidential elections on the global economy. In the case of the 2002 Brazilian presidential election, for example, when Luiz Inácio Lula da Silva of the Worker's Party was projected to win, "the principal players in the Latin American financial markets started to sell and short the Brazilian currency."[10] Electoral projections produced economic reality. As *Migrant Futures* headed into the final stages of production, the United States has witnessed the election of Donald Trump as its president. On the evening of November 8, 2016, as people watched the results come in, they also noted the Dow Jones falling precipitously. By morning, though, markets seemed to have leveled out, and the futures markets in U.S. Steel and private prisons in particular were looking quite good, indeed. This last example, when read through the burgeoning body of critical work in prison abolition movements, yokes the abstract violence of finance capitalism to more overt manifestations of state violence as exacted through the police force disproportionately on black and brown, queer and trans bodies in the United States.

Predicated on prediction, the algorithmic models used in the financial sector as well as by insurance companies often count on the movements of legible and calculable subjects. Financial speculation, extrapolation, and prediction rely on mathematical models and probabilistic logics to transform quantitative data into a narrative arc. By plotting points along a line on a graph and deriving meaning from those data, these narratives require a rendering of a trajectory. Though that rendering often takes shape in the visual field of graphic representation, financial forecasters produce extrapolative fiction when they functionally convert data into an interpretive arc, to be articulated and narrativized in and beyond the graphic form. Econometrics extrapolates from data collected by the University of Michigan Consumer Sentiment Index and Index of Consumer Expectations, for example, which reduce sentiment and expectation to numeric values in an attempt to measure and then advise for or against hedging uncertain futures. This "datafication" is also a rendering of data into fiction or statistical narrative, which Kathleen Woodward has characterized as "the preeminent expression of late capitalism."[11] Financial speculation produces a kind of speculative fiction, and despite its overtures to fact over fiction, it both contributes to and is affected by a broader cultural production of futurity. By reading the social construction of financial derivatives alongside more readily recognizable forms of speculative fiction, *Migrant Futures* asks if another mode of speculation is possible, one that is not immediately captured by the anxious gatherings of risk.[12] If finance is, as Max Haiven characterizes it, "capitalism's imagination," wherein neoliberal financialization "comes at the expense of the radical imagination," I locate a primary site of radical imagination in migrant futures that shift the site of emergency away from terror toward deportation, attend to alternative pockets of wonder such as feminist fabulation rather than defense strategy think tanks, and speculate worlds that demand new onto-epistemological ways of being and thinking.

Launching this examination are fundamental questions about who narrates these futurities and what kinds of subject positions play out in these projected temporal landscapes. Implicitly, the project interrogates who stands to profit from and who risks extinction in prevailing narratives about the future. The principal players in the derivatives markets are multinational corporations, international agencies such as the World Bank and the Asian Development Bank, investment banks, and hedge funds that pool the investments of wealthy clients—basically, everyone but individuals and nations.[13] The funds of the four largest U.S. participants—JPMorgan Chase, Citibank, Bank of America, and Goldman Sachs—represent more than 30 percent of the total global derivatives market.[14] Furthermore, the fundamental governance of the global financial system has been dominated entirely by U.S. and European economic interests, though countries with clearly emerging market economies, such as China, India, and Brazil, have demanded a seat at the rule-making table.[15] The financial colonization of the future builds on preexisting disparities of wealth held over from earlier histories of empire and neocolonial enterprises that break at the fault line between what has been called the Global North and South.

Meanwhile, mass migrations of the undocumented, unbanked, and state-less workers move in and out of geopolitical spaces, the nuances and histories of their displacement and precarity flattened by statistical aggregation. They are migrant noncitizens, outliers, most of whom hail from the Global South and have slipped beyond even "dividual" statistical legibility.[16] In the calculus of risk, the unmeasurable uncertainty of this statistical undercommons generates some friction, some disruption of the would-be-unflappable promises of securitization. The economist Frank Knight, in his interrogation of risk, distinguishes calculable probability (risk) from the "absolute unpredictability of things" (true uncertainty).[17] In the risk-uncertainty dialectic, sheer uncertainty invites profit seekers to convert profoundly unknowable states into probabilistic forecasts, to fold uncertainty back into risk practices—yet uncertainty cuts loose from risk discourse's capture, eluding containment and quantification. While true uncertainty might refuse the grid of intelligibility that securitization would foist upon it, it remains knowable as lived experience, felt and negotiated perhaps most profoundly by those held in "the waiting-room of history." As he describes this imaginary waiting room in *Provincializing Europe*, Dipesh Chakrabarty suggests that the "modern, European idea of history . . . came to non-European peoples in the 19th century as somebody's way of saying 'not yet' to somebody else."[18] In the context of finance capitalism, though, the inhabitants of the waiting room are in fact being written out of the future. What would it mean to reconfigure that marginalization from European notions of progress, modernity, history, and futurity? What alternative futurities emerge from those living beyond the purview of statistical projection?

If the abstraction of populations into calculated risks and algorithmic approximations of lived experiences produces for state and international regulatory institutions "a legible and administratively convenient format,"[19] queer and trans theorists have been particularly helpful in thinking through a politics that does not simply demand inclusion in that system. A 2015 special issue of *Transgender Studies Quarterly*, for example, takes aim at the *"imperative to be counted,"* which becomes "another form of normativizing violence that trans subjects can encounter."[20] Census Bureau and National Health Statistics data that feed U.S. biopolitical regimes of population regulation work to regularize a population and "flatten its zoetic confusions of movement and form, of time and space, of doing and being, into neat two-dimensional axes specifying static properties and numbers."[21] Population regulation and public health discourse, insofar as they share statistical methods with financial models of speculating on risk, could very well move toward three-dimensional models using differential geometry and statistical mechanics to predict volatility.[22] But no matter how nuanced and complex the models get, Paisley Currah and Susan Stryker's provocation to consider how trans disrupts configurations of "statistical citizenship" opens up a queering of speculation and perhaps even a queering of statistical data as numerical or categorical, discrete or continuous, nominal or ordinal.[23] By "queering speculation," I refer to a host of reconfigurations of our relationships to the "financialization of daily life" and the manifestation of a "risk society"—which is to say a normative investment in quantitative data to project futurity.[24]

When José Muñoz asserts that "the future is queerness's domain," he posits a horizon of potentiality. Though that horizon might invoke Martin Heidegger's *Being and Time* and therefore asks us to contend with Heidegger's Nazism, Muñoz's articulation of a not yet draws more compellingly not only on Giorgio Agamben's formulation but also on Ernst Bloch's theorization of indeterminacy. Muñoz's presentation of the not yet of queer futurity suggests a way to seize the not yet of European historicity as described in Chakrabarty's waiting-room scenario. In Muñoz's words, "we are left waiting but vigilant in our desire for another time that is not yet here." Queer futurity offers a model for transforming the waiting room into a horizon. As it moves through examples of queer art, performance, and other queer utopian expressions, Muñoz's *Cruising Utopia* looks to the realm of the open-ended gesture as an alternative to the way other forms of speculation attempt to pull that horizon of the future into the present for profit.[25]

By enjambing these two formulations of the not yet—one that seeks to illuminate histories of empire and exclusion, and another that insists on futurity as an opening up rather than a closing down—I want to consider the relationship between the waiting room and the horizon. For it is precisely in the exile's relation to time—the point at which one is pushed out of what could be called straight time, settler time, or the profitable time of compound interest—that one can glimpse the horizon of the not yet, where not yet manifests itself not as a decree of foreclosure but as an embrace of the unknown. Building on the work of C. L. R. James, Muñoz writes: "To call for this notion of the future in the present is to summon a refunctioned notion of utopia in the service of subaltern politics."[26]

If speculation is indeed our zeitgeist, how can we imagine the future otherwise? In the face of a seemingly monolithic financialized future, as conceived by investment banks and international development funds, this book looks to speculative fictions that highlight the displacements and violences of global finance capitalism. *Migrant Futures* sets out to think speculation from below and highlights alternative engagements with futurity emerging from the colonized, displaced, and disavowed. Through close analyses of speculative fiction, film, and graphic narrative, I examine how the genre's emergent cultural producers usurp conventional science fiction tropes of abduction, alienation, and teleportation and recast them against the backdrop of slavery, histories of forced migration, and deportation. By excavating forgotten histories of science and empire, revising conceptualizations of technological subjectivities, and seeking out queer affinities that belie privatized futures, these works demonstrate how speculation can take the shape of radical unfurling, rather than protectionist anticipation. Instead of using predictive calculations that perpetually attempt to pull the future into the present, these alternative speculative fictions, films, and other media forms work to release speculation from capitalism's persistent instrumentalization of futurity. I hold up these works of speculative fiction by people of color not as antidotes in and of themselves to racialized global capitalism but as affecting experiments that, in the process of imagining another way of being in time, point to the limitations of the new world order's ongoing drive toward modes of privatization and securitization.

I focus my analysis on close readings of cultural texts from the 1990s on, written from contexts that challenge categories of national literatures and yet coalesce around critiques of global capitalism. These texts play across various geographies of colonialism (Latin America, the Caribbean, South and Southeast Asia, East Asia and the Pacific, and Africa), and they share an impulse to complicate Eurocentric ideas about the universal subject, modernity, science, and history. Together, they facilitate temporal and spatial disorientations that intervene in a neoliberal fantasy of a seamless world unified under the sign of global capitalism for the global (financial) citizen.

More specifically, I look to the genre of speculative fiction, wherein cultural producers from the global financial undercommons have refused to relinquish the terrain of imagined futures.[27] These migrant futures serve as theoretical models through which to reconfigure speculation as a modality more fundamentally rooted in inconclusive reflection; tidy resolution is not its ultimate goal. Rather, the term "speculation" carries with it a sense of lingering conjecture and registers hypothesis as beyond so-called fact. Speculative fiction is a genre of inventing other possibilities (alternate realities, upside-down hierarchies, and supernatural interventions). Speculation is not exclusively interested in predicting the future but is equally compelled to explore different accounts of history. It calls for a disruption of teleological ordering of the past, present, and future and foregrounds the processes of narrating the past (history) and the future (science). While speculation embraces an ethic of meticulous inquiry, it shifts the emphasis of scientific pursuit from fact-chasing to experiment-reveling. Speculation calls into question the genre-making practices of science fiction and interrogates the hierarchical and gendered relationship between hard and soft science fiction. The term "speculation" has also been helpful in that it obliquely and bleakly resonates with the discourse of venture capitalism. It tethers financial speculation to other forms of capitalist expansion, including land acquisition and purchasing on the margin.

The works of literature, film, and graphic narrative collected herein could be called Afrofuturist, Chican@futurist, or Asian futurist, but as they all highlight modes of exchange that move beyond national cultural traditions, they might better be brought into a rubric of "migrant futures." Taken together, these migrant futures configure a transnational counterpoetics to the predatory speculations of global capitalism.[28] On the one hand, "migrant futures" refers in this case to the ways futures markets have moved from place to place and built on the momentum of earlier forms of capitalist incentivization, such as civilizing missions and the rhetorics of development. On the other hand, this book investigates narratives of futurity alternatively fabulated by transnational speculative fiction authors who challenge neoliberal ideas of freewheeling global entrepreneurialism. Projections of futurity abound, each preoccupied with fears of oncoming deterioration, disaster, or accident. Some invite us to buy into these futures markets, placing bets on which will return the best dividends; others imagine things differently.

Decolonizing Futurity

At the outset of the twenty-first century, two momentous collections of science fiction sought to illuminate and show evidence of a long-standing tradition of speculative writing by black writers. Edited by Sheree Thomas, *Dark Matter: A Century of Speculative Fiction from the African Diaspora* (2000) and *Dark Matter: Reading the Bones* (2004) establish a rich collection of black speculative writing, reaching back to W. E. B. Du Bois's 1929 short story "The Comet." Another anthology titled *So Long Been Dreaming: Postcolonial Science Fiction and Fantasy* (2004), edited by Nalo Hopkinson and Uppinder Mehan, similarly broadened notions of a genre often associated primarily with white male writers from the United States and Europe. Furthermore, the *Dark Matter* anthologies and *So Long Been Dreaming* engage in a theoretical discussion about race and science fiction. In addition to featuring various short stories and excerpts of fiction, Thomas's collections include several critical essays by esteemed writers such as Samuel R. Delany, Octavia E. Butler, and Walter Mosley, who seek to complicate and expand notions of what constitutes and defines the genre of science fiction. In the introduction to *So Long Been Dreaming*, Hopkinson describes postcolonial speculative fiction as "stories that take the meme of colonizing the natives and, from the experience of the colonizee, critique it, pervert it, fuck with it, with irony, with anger, with humour, and also, with love and respect for the genre of science fiction that makes it possible to think about new ways of doing things."[29] Mentored by Samuel Delany through the Clarion Writers Workshop, Hopkinson both carries on a tradition of black speculative writing and urges a more transnational consideration of science fiction writing among diasporic peoples. Hopkinson's powerful statement begins to lay out some of the stakes of postcolonial science fiction: How useful can the genre of science fiction be as a critical tool in the hands of authors for whom "Science" has not historically been particularly kind? How might science fiction writers use this genre as the very occasion for interrogating a history of scientific racism, the collaboration of scientific institutions and the building of empires, and the disciplining of aberrant bodies under the rubric of "progress"?

Progress narratives, conceptualizations of modernity, and empiricist imperatives break across varied histories of imperialism, slavery, settler colonialism, and scenes of forced displacement from military and neocolonial incursions. Afro futurism and Chican@ futurism might have some similar stakes in writing black and brown bodies into the future, but they do so against different forms of racist primitivism. Asian futurism can be trickier to fabulate, given science fiction's persistent fascination with techno-Orientalist themes and landscapes. When it comes to futurity, it's not so much that Asians have been written out of it. We've become the sign of it, the backdrop to it, and the style manual for it.[30] As some scholars of modernity and postmodernity have demonstrated, modernity and — we can extrapolate here — futurity get mobilized and experienced differently across global contexts, in part because of the varied ways racial difference gets mapped onto colonial projections of elsewhere as well as onto neoliberal fantasies of one world. What might a more comparativist approach to decolonizing futurity reveal about some of the consistencies across futurity's omissions? *Migrant Futures* takes up this minoritarian sector of a genre as a counterpoint to other forms of speculation — specifically, a financial speculation assumptive of a naturalized empiricism and universal financial subject, which may pretend not to care about race but that nonetheless traffics across histories of racialized capitalism.

The emergence of these anthologies at the outset of the twenty-first century provides an occasion for examining how science and the fictions of science participate in the construction of national and international ideas about modernity and futurity. How are these narratives about science, modernity, and futurity intertwined with how we think about race, gender, and sexuality? Given the long and complicated relationship between science and empire, what critical considerations and contributions does postcolonial speculation offer the genre of science fiction and scientific disciplines? The critique levied by these postcolonial speculative fiction writers examines some common science fiction tropes — an emphasis on exploration, the settlement of new lands, potential alien invasions, and technological advancement that emerges from and characterizes the First

World—and questions to what extent the genre itself reproduces the social and political ideologies of a system of science that has historically operated in close conjunction with imperialist and neocolonial enterprises.

One of the most prominent themes of postcolonial speculative fiction is the revision of Western origin myths of technoscience to encourage a radical shift in the epistemological assumptions of scientific endeavors. In other words, one of the fictions about science that these writers contest is that because of the Enlightenment, Europe has an exclusive claim to science's origins. At stake in this debate is that, as David Harvey has argued, "Enlightenment thought . . . embraced the idea of progress, and actively sought that break with history and tradition which modernity espouses."[31] Pursuing alternative technocultural origin myths also means rejecting the progress narratives that Enlightenment thought encourages. In my analysis of postcolonial speculative fiction, I foreground the critique of progress narratives that makes this emergent set of science fiction writing so vital a countersite for development models of capitalism.

The colonization of the future works to justify and rationalize imperialist expansionism by mobilizing ideological narratives that characterize its predation as a civilizing mission. In the case of finance capitalism, statistical projection transforms the untenable future into a futurescape—akin to the transformation of land into landscape—that materializes the abstract, rendering it available for possession, even as a sight to behold, or an imaginary to occupy. Art historians and indigenous studies scholars call such manifestations of the imaginary into the real the "visual regimes of colonization," with the idea that to aestheticize a landscape is to lay claim to it as if creating "portraits of property."[32]

Sixteenth-century cartographers drew dragons at the end of the known world on their maps. They used magic and the fantastic to mark where uncertainty lay in waiting.[33] Mary Louise Pratt demonstrated in *Imperial Eyes* how empire's "mapping of progress" manifested itself in European imperialist cartography and travel writing, alongside European economic and political expansion since 1700.[34] Pratt's work needs to be read in conjunction with Ian Hacking's history of probability theory in the largely overlapping period of the seventeenth to late-nineteenth centuries as part of the history of speculation. If the literary and cartographic speculations of *Imperial Eyes* emerge alongside Hacking's historical mapping of the probabilistic "taming of chance,"[35] these concomitant proliferations of speculative fictions and financial speculation suggest a prehistory for the contemporary convergence of speculative practices in world markets and global cultural imaginaries. I turn to the future as a temporal geography, as a contemporary extension of how temporality gets narrativized in the service of imperial conquest, from the fantastical maps that facilitated the settler colonial conquest of the Americas in the fifteenth through seventeenth centuries through eighteenth- and nineteenth-century EuroAmerican representations of a racialized and gendered evolutionary family Tree of Man.[36] Thriving on the calculation and redistribution of projected risk and volatility, the derivatives markets work "to colonize the future,"[37] wherein the future becomes *terra nullius*, emptied of its true uncertainty, filled with securitized risk, and sanctified by a positivist accounting of projection. Critical inquiry into speculation demands not only a study of genre but also a critique of an ideology. The gambit of *Migrant Futures* is to examine futurity from the perspective of the dragons at the edge of the map.

Toward an Antipositivist Science Fiction

The future is an always already occupied space. Though often idealized as blank and empty, primed for projection and population, the future is in practice never so fixed or consolidated, though financial instruments work precisely toward actualizing the future in order to monetize and profit from it. The future exists as absolute uncertainty, which capitalism attempts to contain through the calculation of risk, but ultimately cannot foreclose entirely. Indeed, with the faltering beginning in 2007–8 of an ever-flexible system of speculative capital, the bubble of the subprime mortgage crisis popping, and the failure to predict and protect against the 2011 Tōhoku earthquake and tsunami that caused the meltdown of three reactors at the Fukushima Daiichi Nuclear Power Plant, the early twenty-first century seems a particularly interesting time to be theorizing speculation. We have recently witnessed the ramifications of the betrayed promises of speculative capital in the form of empty returns on financial derivatives, the collapse of the hedge fund promise, and the disastrous impact on low-income homeowners of a credit bubble bursting.

Simultaneously filled with corporate fantasies of limitless profit and leftist antihierarchical possibilities, the future—or, rather, the endless multiplicity of futures—can never be fully colonized. Even as the speculative fictions highlighted in *Migrant Futures* fabulate anti-racist, queer critiques of global capitalism, financial speculation similarly invests in converting possible futures into calculated risk. When used to orient subjects toward normativity, the future offers seemingly flexible but always narrow projections of improvement. Capitalism, after all, is interested in normativity only to the extent that it produces insecurity and consumerist desire. Mark Fisher's *Capitalist Realism* conjures a spectacularly absorptive foe, a blob capitalism indiscriminately folding would-be outliers into its ever-expanding domain. If it is to remain a space of possibility, the future must always also be a multiply occupied space.

Migrant Futures concerns itself with speculative fiction. By using this term instead of the genre's more commonly used moniker of "science fiction," I invoke a decades-long debate about a literary genre's relationship to a form of knowledge production called science. For the science fiction theorist Darko Suvin, science fiction is a genre delimited by works "whose main formal device is an imaginative framework alternative to the author's empirical environment."[38] The genre produces, for Suvin, a useful tension between estrangement (a departure from realism) and cognition (the possibility that the world described could be real, as opposed to myth and fantasy). Suvin's theorization of cognitive estrangement has long served the field of science fiction studies as the definitive account of what distinguishes science fiction from other genres, and it operates firmly on the universalist assumptions of an "empirical environment" and the presumption of a universally agreed upon "estrangement" (or for that matter, "realism"). But strangeness and familiarity both remain inherently attached to situated, subjective experiences. Suvin's definition of science fiction through this formulation of cognitive estrangement has always sought to nail down, pinpoint, and close off the boundaries of a genre in ways I have always found rather limiting. For this reason, I have generally preferred more capacious terms that are less interested in literary taxonomies than in the various modalities of writing and reading that can alter relations between writer and reader, shift ways of thinking, and produce different kinds of subjects. I take up the term "speculative fiction" not to identify a genre wholly distinct from science fiction, but to use a more expansive term that might include related genres such as fantasy, horror, and historical fiction; and that highlights the speculative mode of the "What if?"

Some works of science fiction bear an aspirational fidelity to the trending ideals of scientists, but science, like futurity, is contested terrain, consisting of varying arenas of scientific production and publication situated in specific historical contexts and political economies. Nevertheless, many science fiction scholars have often adhered to a "one world" idealization of science that performs a degree of globalizing visioning itself. For example, in his discussion of "hard" science fiction, Gregory Benford works to align science fiction writers and scientists by pointing to a shared "internationalist idealism" and engagement in the "free trading of ideas."[39] Benford writes of a free trade idealism that could well describe global economic neoliberalism. Published in 1994 in an anthology titled *The Ascent of Wonder: The Evolution of Hard SF*, Benford's essay laments ("Alas!") the genre's yielding to "the old styles," in which "scientific accuracy and worldview are subordinate to conventional literary virtues of character or plot, style or setting." In his valuation of internationalist idealism and the scientific worldview, Benford reveals the global scale of his aspirations for the futures of both science and science fiction. His privileging of "hard SF" over "old," "soft" forms of science fiction—beyond invoking a rather gendered set of criteria—suits the narrative arc of a genre's "evolution" set forth by the anthology's subtitle.

In this matter of narrating the evolution of science fiction, though, Benford bumps up against the genre's own preoccupation with novelty. Benford's "old" forms actually refer to the "New Wave" of U.S. speculative fiction that emerges throughout the 1960s and 70s, a period when increasing numbers of women, queers, and people of color took to writing in and around the genre.[40] By calling the New Wave "old" and mapping a rubric of "evolution" onto his genealogy of the genre, Benford participates in the social reproduction of science fiction as the exclusive privilege of white men.[41]

Though Benford sets out to advocate for a vigorously collaborative approach to knowledge production that models itself on research published in scientific journals that might have fifty authors' names attached to the article, the model has some flaws, as the sciences continue to present a pool of thinkers with rather homogeneous profiles. In addition, Benford's language gives away some of his preconceived valuations of worth. In his praise of communally developed ideas, he lauds the "family" feeling of collaborative research and points to the "fidelity" of facts definitional to the "hardness" of fiction.[42] In repeatedly referring to "faithfulness to the physical facts of the universe," Benford conjures a heteronormative marriage between science and science fiction, and he mobilizes a decidedly patriarchal rhetoric, evoking not only gendered allocations of value ("hard" not "soft") but also eugenicist language (the "simon-pure breed" of "physical science" over the social sciences) to perform his generic gatekeeping.[43] This normative policing of what deserves the designation "science fiction" seems ill-conceived for a genre ostensibly interested in pushing the boundaries of the possible.

Understanding the production of scientific knowledge, as with other forms of knowledge production, requires critical attention to the conditions and contexts that shape these knowledges. Following the work of Donna Haraway, I approach the sciences as "specific historical and culture productions" and consider them "radically contingent" upon the situations that give rise to them.[44] Haraway's cyborg manifesto, for example, not only calls forth a feminist epistemology, but also situates the need for a radical revision of technoscientific origin myths in the political context of science-based industries that capitalize on the exploitation of a transnational female labor force.[45] Haraway also famously looks to feminist works of science fiction as cultural contestations of what she calls "the god trick."[46] Advocating for the production of "situated knowledges" and narratives with multiple meanings, Haraway sees in science fiction a site for unmooring scientific knowledge production from a pursuit of mastery or claims to perfect objectivity.[47]

In her investigation of the history of scientific autonomy, Nancy Leys Stepan questions how claims to scientific authority became, in the nineteenth century, "increasingly conceptualised as 'a sharply-edged, value-neutral, a-political, non-theological, empirical and objective form of knowledge unlike any other'" through a relentless process of "boundary-setting between science and non-science."[48] Stepan argues that science emerged from this proliferation of dichotomies as a distinct form of knowledge production that positioned itself as "pure," "rational," "objective," "hard," and "male." The writer and theorist Samuel Delany argues that a concomitant positivism during the "precritical period in SF when scientism dominates the field" imagines that "all the difficulties of the world are presented as amenable to scientific solution."[49]

Rather than policing genre borders of what counts and what does not count as science fiction, I attend to the imaginative work this speculative mode, which engages a specific relationship to futurity, does on what kinds of knowledges we produce. For Haraway, "SF" includes "Science Fiction, Speculative Fabulation, String Figures, So Far"—practices that model worldings that redo "what counts as—what is—real."[50] For Delany, speculative fiction exemplifies "paraliterature," which names those forms of writing—"comic books, mysteries, westerns, science fiction, pornography, greeting card verse, newspaper reports, academic criticism, advertising texts, movie and TV scripts, popular song lyrics"—deemed extrinsic to but therefore also dialectically constitutive of "literature."[51] As a paraliterary form, speculative fiction virally occupies the structural site of "proper" fiction. So, rather than a "genre," which Derrida understood as an announcement of normative delineations that does not "risk impurity, anomaly, or monstrosity,"[52] speculation harbors a promiscuous impulse.

Though this promiscuity and disregard for the proper may be what makes speculation such a formidable instrument of capitalist appetite—it is not unlike Fisher's blobular capitalism, after all—it is also what makes speculative fiction such a well-matched alternative to capitalist realism. For the future is on the move, and though finance capitalism attempts to monopolize it through speculative instruments that render it a profitable space, the future remains profoundly unknowable and unpredictable. If the financial, actuarial, and statistical seek to produce predictive models sold to economic markets as scientific, perhaps this is precisely the moment to reassert Delany's provocation that "fiction makes models of reality."[53] In one of his earliest essays on speculative fiction, co-written with Marilyn Hacker, Delany takes up mathematical modeling as a counterpoint to speculative fiction. He writes: "As soon as we want to look at 'the real world' with any greater accuracy and sophistication . . . other models than the arithmetically predictable are more useful to help us appreciate what we are looking at."[54] "On Speculative Fiction," by Delany and Hacker, appears as an introduction to the fourth volume of *Quark: A Quarterly Review of Science Fiction*, published in 1971, at the dawn of the global financial system—when capitalism in the United States and European contexts had to restructure itself vis-à-vis the emerging markets of the "Asian tigers." The result, of course, was the rise of the financial derivatives markets and the proliferation of futures contracts.[55] As LiPuma and Lee note, "in 1970 the yearly valuation of financial derivatives . . . was probably only a few million dollars. The sum swelled to about $100 million by 1980, to nearly $100 billion by 1990, and to nearly $100 trillion by 2000."[56] Writing at the onset of this rapid ascent of finance capitalism, Delany was already calling for an alternative approach to imagining futures. More specifically, he was calling for a mode of speculation that moved beyond the "incantatory function—a better word than 'predictive.'"[57] Delany was after an antipositivist science fiction. He was theorizing a speculative fiction wherein "the impossible relieves the probable, and the possible illuminates the improbable."[58] It is this striking move from the instrumentalization of probability to the unboundedness of possibility that this book posits as a response to the "corrosion of social imagination" that so preoccupied Fisher.[59]

Temporal Geographies of the Speculative Undercommons

The texts I examine herein posit critiques and alternatives to the speculations of globalization and interject radical revisions of progress narratives by attending to the markedly uneven accumulation of wealth of late capitalism. These counterspeculations tend to refuse strictly utopian or dystopian trajectories for technoculture, and they attempt to intervene in developmental teleologies by denaturalizing linear arrangements of time. These speculative fictions enact what Lisa Lowe and David Lloyd have called "the excavation and connection of alternative histories and their different temporalities that cannot be contained by the progressive narrative of Western developmentalism."[60] In the recent years of rampant speculation, late capitalism has insistently faced forward, driving Walter Benjamin's Angel of History along, if not attempting to push it aside. When speculative futures run wild, excavation, historicization, and haunting become increasingly important modes of contingency to slow the storm of progress.[61]

The speculative fictions that I discuss come from a wide range of geographical contexts, each the site of some form of U.S. imperialism. Under the rubric of speculative fiction, various historical networks of affiliations (among Asian immigrants to the Caribbean and Mexico, Malaysian workers in Singapore, and Asian Brazilians who migrate for a second time to Southern California) are evoked that decenter the United States in the narrative of immigration to the Americas. The authors I examine posit the geographical loci of the Brazilian Amazon, the U.S.-Mexico borderlands, and the Southeast Asian archipelago as speculative spaces, wherein histories of colonization and labor exploitation have produced markedly different relationships to Western science and technology. My project, therefore, suggests that these speculative fictions forge transnational affiliations by positing diasporic movement as a technology that works covalently with other intensified global flows. *Migrant Futures* considers speculative fictions that create transnational affiliations among communities of color that extend networks of care beyond national narratives of "risky subjects" and the calculations of global financialization.[62]

I write at a moment when Asian Americanists and queer theorists alike have witnessed neoliberalism's all-too-easy co-optation of rights-based advocacy work. Queer theorists have named a homonormativity, homonationalism, and queer liberalism that point to the limitations of social movements for legal recognition, one that ultimately locks the struggle into a juridical framework that demands the production of a fixed subject, tethered to the nation as its citizen.[63] A similar dissatisfaction has emerged among Asian Americanists who not only continue to grapple with the inadequacy of a term that attempts to span an unwieldy range of disparate economic living and working conditions as well as diverse histories of migration and cultural negotiations but also grow impatient with the false prophecies of multicultural triumphalism, model minority achievements and beneficent refuge.[64]

Given these frustrations with neoliberal pluralism, it is heartening that the search for sociopolitical alternatives, or the will to "imagine otherwise" is still on, especially via a "critique of subjectification rather than the desire for subjectivity."[65] In her formulation of "subjectlessness, as a conceptual tool, [which] points to the need to manufacture 'Asian American' situationally,"[66] Kandice Chuh discusses Lowe's demonstration in *Immigrant Acts* of how the nation-state advances Enlightenment liberalism's promises of citizenship as key to freedom even as capitalism requires differentiation and uneven distributions of power. Chuh indicates the limitations of rights-based advocacy that is already orienting the battle toward a notion of the liberal citizen-subject who might find herself knee-deep in multiculturalism but still without much in the way of justice or equity.[67] Chuh's call for a redefinition of the political involves a departure from a nation-framed politics of inclusion and the positivism of identity politics. Calling critical attention to the rights-bearing subject as one tethered to Enlightenment ideals of citizenship and notions of universal subjectivity that emerged from a historically specific moment when slavery and other institutions excluded many from the category of the human, practitioners of queer theory and ethnic studies have pointed to the limitations of a politics that seeks recognition from a system fundamentally bound to prerequisties of normative belonging.[68]

Queer critiques, in particular, offer alternatives to the developmental and aspirational drives ascribed to heteronormative life courses. "Queer subcultures," writes Jack Halberstam, "produce alternative temporalities by allowing their participants to believe that their futures can be imagined according to logics that lie outside of those paradigmatic markers of life experience—namely, birth, marriage, reproduction, and death."[69] One of the reasons Halberstam looks to Delany's *Times Square Red, Times Square Blue* is to illustrate how "queers use space and time in ways that challenge conventional logics of development, maturity, adulthood, and responsibility."[70] Rather than seeing "no future" in systems driven by the clock time of sexual and social reproduction,[71] Halberstam—along with Elizabeth Freeman, for starters—limns the political potentiality of queer failure, refusal, recalcitrance, withholding, and other techniques of disrupting what Benjamin calls "homogeneous empty time."[72] As "denizens of times out of joint," queers unsettle the temporal ordering practices of *"chrononormativity."*[73]

Freeman's attention to the ways laboring bodies in the industrial era are "bound into socially meaningful embodiment through temporal regulation" and tempered into normative rhythms of work and productivity directs us to consider the pivotal role temporality plays in producing modern subjectivities and marching out the tempo of modernity itself. The aspirational "chronobiopolitics" (to borrow Dana Luciano's term)[74] of neoliberal futurity capitalizes on subjective orientations toward flexible temporalities (such as the use of "flex time" to obscure the increased number of overtime hours) and perpetual self-improvement (with achievement badges for every stage of endlessly upgradeable life). Lauren Berlant's notion of the impasse seems particularly apt as a refusal of this relentlessly anticipatory trajectory of time.[75]

In the chapters that follow, I emphasize the continuity across finance speculation's harnessing of futurity and an older imperialist practice of leveraging white supremacist notions of modernity toward the same end of extracting profit. I draw on the work of historians of science and technology who trace how technoscience—from its material inventions to its ideological disseminations—has aided and abetted (and sought to rationalize) colonizing forces in the conquest, subjugation, and/or exploitation of other peoples.[76] At the same time, rather than approaching science as a hegemonic force, my readings of speculative fictions emphasize the reciprocal, dialectical relationships in technocultural formation. I investigate how speculative fiction helps shift the conventional framework of "technology" to consider other types of knowledge-networks that cut across center-periphery models of scientific production. My attention to a more inclusive account of scientific practice is motivated by an effort to recognize the often invisible labor that supports scientific enterprises and discovery claims. From the explorer's indigenous translator to the factory worker who assembles laboratory instruments, the production of scientific knowledge has been contingent upon a labor force that takes a much more central role in the speculative fictions I analyze in this project. Labor becomes more visible in these narratives as part of more cooperative models of intellectual, and material, production that emphasize cross-class, interethnic collaborations and transnational circulations of knowledge. I argue that speculative fiction can foster alternative forms of connectivity that exceed and defy the privatizing logics of nation, corporation, and nuclear family. The fictions I examine formulate innovative structures of belonging and possible coalition building across conventional differences that emerge from alternative genealogies of speculative fiction, including 1960s Latin American magical realism, Caribbean carnival, Afro futurism, manga, anime, Chinese folklore, and *rasquachismo*. These paraliterary genealogies call our attention to the significance of imaginative literary forms that arise out of paracapitalist contexts and therefore might provide even more grounds for imagining the world beyond capitalist realism.

In the first chapter of this book, "Imperial Rubber: The Speculative Arcs of Karen Tei Yamashita's Rainforest Futures," I examine the work of Yamashita, a Japanese American writer whose speculative fiction *Through the Arc of the Rain Forest* (1990) exhumes the traces of multiple empires that have shaped contemporary transpacific circulations of labor and culture. Set in the Amazon jungle, the novel unearths U.S. neocolonial enterprises in Brazil by excavating the ruins of Fordlándia, a Ford rubber plantation cultivated in the 1920s and abandoned in the 1930s. By analyzing archival material on Fordlándia alongside Yamashita's text, I situate the civilizing mission Henry Ford used to rationalize his plantation building within the longer history of nineteenth-century European imperialist discourses on tropical nature, health, and race, which sustained ethnographic and scientific expeditions to the Amazon. If both financial speculation and speculative fiction draw on at least the recent past, what are their extrapolation points? If those points of departure shift, or if authors of the future look to alternative historical flash points, how might their projections change? Chapter 1 extrapolates from the historical narrative of Fordist ruin and failure rather than Fordist triumphalism to inquire what might have happened if the fortune of global capitalism had foretold ecological disaster rather than only spectacular profit. By understanding Yamashita's *Through the Arc of the Rain Forest* as a dystopian tale of flexible citizenship and neoliberal economic policy, I foreground how global finance capitalism provides only a partial utopian perspective of what such globalizing moves will unleash.

The second chapter, "Homeland Futurity: Speculations at the Border," examines the U.S.-Mexico border as a site of historical and ongoing speculation. Frontiers and borders—whether imagined by Frederick Jackson Turner in the late nineteenth century as unruly wilderness demanding containment and civilization or reimagined a century later by Gloria Anzaldúa as spaces of mythical transformation—have perpetually been called into being through fantastic speculation. As decades of scholarship in Latin American and Latinx literary studies show, the production of borders involves a practice of worlding, of fabulations of time and space.[77] Amid discussions of surveillance technologies, the War on Drugs, the War on Terror, and anti-immigration campaigns, I analyze late twentieth- and early twenty-first-century examples of critical speculations that renegotiate border futures by contesting the strategies of risk management and containment that fill the Homeland Security imaginary. Yamashita's novel *Tropic of Orange* and Alex Rivera's independent film *Sleep Dealer* provide helpful counternarratives to more predatory forms of speculation by producing the possibilities of cross-border coalitions that disrupt the corporatization and militarization of the Southland, a region that always also shares a border with the Pacific Ocean.

Carrying through the project's critique of speculation in the service of securitization and surveillance states, chapter 3, "Speculation and the Speculum: Surrogations of Futurity" turns to another important field of imagining futurity: reproduction. In my consideration of Alfonso Cuarón's film *Children of Men* and Nalo Hopkinson's science fiction *Midnight Robber*, I examine two speculative narratives that foreground black pregnant women as bearers of a new tomorrow while overturning techno-utopian visions of progress. Though a radical revision of P. D. James's 1992 nationalist novel of the same name, Cuarón's *Children of Men* ultimately disappoints because it imposes a gendered and racialized reproductive imperative onto the pregnant body of Kee, the "fugee" woman who must navigate her way through the heavily surveilled police state of near-future England, with limited awareness of how this reproduces the kind of necropolitical violence the film sets out to expose. While the protagonist Theo tries to get Kee to a boat called *The Tomorrow*, the film reinstates the promise of the white savior, even as they pass through a dystopian futurescape through which Cuarón launches an unequivocal critique of the War on Terror, carceral states, and securitization measures. *Midnight Robber* articulates the conditions of survival in end-of-the-world scenarios quite differently. Hopkinson emphasizes cross-species alliances and gender-queer family formations that dislodge futurity from models of heteropatriarchal reproduction.

The fourth chapter, "The Cruel Optimism of the Asian Century," leaps across oceans to focus on Singapore and its self-conscious marketing as a place of optimism about the future. The chapter questions Singapore's optimism by examining Sonny Liew's *Malinky Robot*, a graphic story collection by a Malaysian-born Singaporean writer-artist, in which the protagonists eke out an existence in a dystopic, near-future, pan-Asian city where the future's promises have clearly passed them over and instead left them with ramshackle shelters to inhabit and mutant life forms with which to commiserate. These graphic narratives about street urchins trying to survive in a foreboding landscape interrogate what it is like to live amid the towering edifices of futurity without the means to make a home. *Malinky Robot* also opens onto questions about life in the Capitalocene, where humanistic aspirational subjectivity has only sustained what Berlant calls a "cruel optimism."[78] Finally, as two of the main characters are nonhumans, surrounded by humans who inexplicably accept the dehumanizing conditions to which they are subjected in their everyday lives, *Malinky Robot* provides an occasion to think futurity beyond the human. This query about multi-species futures is a thread that continues more intentionally in chapter 5, in which a feminist-queer commons emerges as one response to the individualist structures of capitalist subjectivity.

That final chapter, "Salt Fish Futures: The Irradiated Transpacific and the Financialization of the Human Genome Project," turns to Larissa Lai's *Salt Fish Girl*, an Asian-Canadian speculative fiction set in a near-future where corporate enclosures have replaced international cities, genetically modified organisms proliferate both within and beyond zones of regulation, and the Island of Mist and Forgetfulness enlists immigrants in telemarketing schemes securing investors in offshore business ventures. Living in this world shaped by predatory speculation, Lai's protagonists nevertheless experiment with unpredictable ways to foment collective dissent across species, spaces, and temporalities. I read *Salt Fish Girl* as one example of radical speculation that explores histories of transnational migration and nuclear holocaust, transgenic mutations and transcultural memory, as well as queer sex and anticapitalist forms of exchange to articulate a strange futurity that disrupts the smooth surfaces of techno-Orientalism.

Speculating from the margins, the migrant futures explored herein offer alternative approaches to futurity. Yamashita's exhumations of failed plantation futures in the Brazilian Amazon stage the disintegration of capitalism's gleaming promises in the form of a new resource with seemingly limitless potential that ultimately proves to be structurally flawed. In *Tropic of Orange* and *Sleep Dealer*, the elusiveness of the horizon and the cross-ethnic solidarity across fugitive networks sustain a mode of looking to the future without hoping to contain it. In *Malinky Robot*, the children of the future take truant paths through makeshift geographies to eke out a life in the shadow of an Asian Century. Finally, *Salt Fish Girl* formulates a transgenic commons that intervenes in the privatization of the future. Taken together, these speculative acts model a cultural politics of decolonizing futurity, of occupying the not yet, to hold it open for the yet to come.

1

IMPERIAL RUBBER *The Speculative Arcs of Karen Tei Yamashita's Rainforest Futures*

I will outnumber you.
I will outbillion you.
I am the spectacle in the forest.
I am the inventor of rubber.
I will outrubber you.
Sir, the reality of your world is nothing more
than a rotten caricature of great opera.
—WERNER HERZOG, *Fitzcarraldo*

In Werner Herzog's 1982 film, *Fitzcarraldo*, the eponymous protagonist dreams of building an opera house in the middle of the Amazon rainforest. His impossible dream is realized by staging an opera aboard the steamship he originally commissioned for the purpose of securing a fortune in rubber. Fitzcarraldo, using the suspiciously volunteered labor of hundreds of Indians, succeeds in dragging his ship over a mountain to gain access to untapped rubber trees, only to have his boat cut loose and set adrift into perilous rapids by the same indigenous workers on the other side.[1]

The "discovery" of rubber proclaimed by French geographer Charles-Marie de La Condamine in the mid-eighteenth century occasions one early manifestation of what could be called science fiction, in the sense that his expedition journal—later published as a scientific treatise—reads as a rather fantastical travel narrative. As elucidated in Mary Louise Pratt's *Imperial Eyes*, La Condamine's report on his expedition to the Amazon is strikingly speculative in nature, "written mainly not as a scientific report, but in the popular genre of survival literature."[2] Rubber is just one spectacular character among many in La Condamine's narrative, which describes the strangeness of a tropical "new world"[3] and even attempts to verify the existence of the mythic Amazon women warriors. As it narrates an encounter with an otherworldly landscape, populated with alien (to the French scientist) flora, fauna, and other entities, La Condamine's account of his scientific expedition reads like speculative fiction, particularly because it is produced in the service of empire both to sensationalize and rationalize—or to rationalize through sensational fantasy—the possible wealth to be controlled and wildness to be domesticated in the Brazilian jungle.

The history of the rubber industry necessarily stretches across multiple geographies and temporalities. It links the tropical forests of the Amazon and Southeast Asia, highlighting the competing imperial holdings of England, the Netherlands, and the United States. This history also connects La Condamine's 1744 expedition with that of Carl LaRue, a Ford Motor Company geographer, in 1927—the year Henry Ford bought approximately 2.5 million acres of Amazon rainforest in the northern state of Pará, Brazil, and established a sizable rubber plantation.[4] "Fordlândia" was designed to be an all-inclusive neocolonial system, extending the plantation infrastructure beyond sawmills and processing plants to include U.S.-style hospitals, schools, white clapboard houses, and even recreational facilities such as a motion-picture theater and an eighteen-hole golf course. As documented in the company's archives, the Ford rubber plantations in Brazil worked to fulfill a Fordist fantasy of bringing "modernity" and "progress" to the "almost impenetrable tropical jungle."[5] Ford's ventures in Brazil attempted to impose a vision of the future, as conjured up by commerce, profit making, and Western modernity, upon a geography he imagined to be stuck in prehistoric time. In this way, this U.S. captain of industry extends the imperialist logics of Victorian England, for example, by figuring "geographical difference across *space* [. . .] as a historical difference across *time*."[6] Furthermore, these land speculations—brokered through a collusion between scientific and economic interests—relied on the production of several fictions about the working habits of indigenous peoples, the rainforest's resilience, and capitalism's deliverables to succeed.

Roughly twenty years before Greg Grandin's 2009 history of Fordlándia brought renewed attention to Ford's Amazonian exploits, the Japanese American writer Karen Tei Yamashita excavated this largely forgotten scene of U.S. imperialism in Brazil when she set her 1990 speculative fiction, *Through the Arc of the Rain Forest*, largely at the scene of rubber extraction in the Brazilian rainforest. *Through the Arc* extrapolates from Ford's imperialist legacies to project into the near future what might happen to the Amazon when a valuable, rubber-like resource is unearthed during an age of global capitalist restructuring.

By calling attention to the buried histories to which Yamashita playfully alludes, I place *Through the Arc*'s historical speculations in critical dialogue with other kinds of scientific fictions that have worked on behalf of European and U.S. empire building to render the resource-rich jungle available for imperial conquest and expansion. To do this work, Yamashita's speculative fiction itself suggests a methodology of excavation, both archaeological and genealogical in the Foucauldian sense. Because *Through the Arc* presents itself as a form of speculation in conversation with other forms, including land and financial speculation, this methodological experiment—of extrapolation via excavation—highlights how modernity and indeed futurity traffic in racisms that emerge from a discursive relation to older discourses of race that are, in Ann Laura Stoler's words, "'recovered,' modified, 'encased,' and 'encrusted' in new forms."[7] Excavation, as Lisa Lowe and David Lloyd formulate it in their introduction to *The Politics of Culture in the Shadow of Capital*, enacts a practice of "looking to the shadows" for "alternative histories and their different temporalities that cannot be contained by the progressive narrative of Western developmentalism."[8] Along these lines, Yamashita's *Through the Arc* looks to the shadows of capital in the Amazon rainforest to offer an alternative to developmental historiography, to teleological narration, to a profit-driven futurity.

This chapter considers a history of imperial and neocolonial structures in Brazil, the overlapping nature of various empires in South America, and the technoracialization of the global Asian subject.[9] In *Through the Arc*, Yamashita focuses on the presence of U.S. multinational corporations in Latin America as a manifestation of a longer history of empire in Brazil. The narrative suggests that earlier empire-builders shrewdly cultivated a racialized understanding of the tropics and established the beginnings of a history of imperial efforts in the guise of benevolent enterprises, including tropical medicine, technological development, and philanthropic foundations that supported scientific and medical research.

Despite bearing many of the characteristics of science fiction and fantasy, Yamashita's oeuvre rarely gets categorized as speculative fiction. Various literary critics and book reviewers call *Through the Arc* a "fine, satirical piece of writing," a "freewheeling black comedy," "a burlesque of comic strip adventures and apocalyptic portents,"[10] and "an exuberant melodrama."[11]

What I am calling the speculative arcs of Yamashita's works refers to arcs across both space and time. Yamashita's speculative fictions operate as technologies of memory that revisit historical narratives even as they are drawn into the transtemporal fabric of futuristic and alternative worlds. If, as Marita Sturken has argued, a "culture of amnesia" in the United States not only does not remember war and trauma but also generates "memory in new forms,"[12] the process constitutes a form of temporal colonization, violent in its displacement of subjects and events that expose contradictions between capitalist expansionism and the neoliberal rhetoric of "free" trade. The Eurocentric narration of the discovery of rubber by La Condamine, for example, displaces indigenous memories of foreign incursion. It is at that scene of temporal colonization that Yamashita revisits to recalibrate a skewed extrapolation point. In the context of speculative fiction, which posits space-time as a four-dimensional continuum of time and space, speculation serves as a useful tactic for those who would travel through time to revisit obfuscated historical moments that nevertheless continue to inform narratives of the present and extrapolations of the future.

In the speculative landscape of *Through the Arc*, it is not only a legacy of globalization but also a history of science that Yamashita excavates in the Amazon rainforest. Through subtle yet striking allusions to Fordlândia and to nearly obsessive European ethnographic forays to Brazil during the same time period, Yamashita's *Through the Arc* implicates Western science's collusion with European and U.S. imperialist enterprises. In my analysis of Fordlândia, I examine the larger project of Fordist social reform, which extended its reach beyond the United States under the banners of benevolent science and technological progress. Because the plantation met with consistent financial difficulties, Fordlândia's justification for renewed funding and support relied heavily on its self-promotion as a civilizing mission. The rubber plantation unrelentingly disciplined its primarily indigenous laboring subjects through the imposition of U.S. social institutions (schools, churches, and hospitals), cultural practices (the prohibition of drinking and smoking and viewings of Hollywood films), and labor administration (the insistence that workers punch in and out at a central mechanical timeclock, abide a nine-to-five workday despite prohibitive midday heat, and wear identification badges). By foregrounding this Fordist experiment in her decolonial speculative fiction, Yamashita provides the occasion for readers to understand the continuity across La Condamine's expedition and Ford's enterprises in the Amazon rainforest. If Charles de La Condamine saw a profit to be made from sensationalizing his account of the tropical jungle, Henry Ford recognized an opportunity to string investors along by promising to bring assembly-line, plantation-style order to it. EuroAmerican notions of technoscientific modernity prepare the ideological groundwork for neocolonial capitalist enterprises that exploit already racialized and gendered ideas of the tropics to subject workers at the equator to labor practices imported from Michigan. The unexpected and thrilling maneuver that Yamashita plots is for *Through the Arc* to meet Fordist ideologies of development at the level of representation, critiquing imperialist fantasies of the tropics by staging an oversaturated, fantastical spectacularization of the rainforest itself, allowing those deeply embedded, earlier colonial fantasies to surface and be examined.

Spectacular undertakings in the Amazon rainforest hardly begin or end with Fordlândia, and Yamashita references several more notable examples in *Through the Arc*. When the CEO of a multinational corporation decides to transport its twenty-three-story headquarters in its entirety from Manhattan to the dense tropical rainforest, Yamashita cites two "historic precedents for such a grandiose move" (76).[13] The first is the Teatro Amazonas opera house in Manaus, Brazil, built in 1896 with the desire to bring the material signifiers of European civilization to the heart of the jungle, achieved by incorporating imported French tiles, Italian marble, and Murano glass chandeliers. Similarly, the opera house in the novel has "imported . . . every detail from the iron fixtures to the parquet floors from England" (76). The novel also references U.S. billionaire Daniel Ludwig's far-fetched plan to float a fully constructed pulp mill and factory on two giant pontoons from Japan to the Brazilian city of Munguba in 1978 "for the purpose of churning everything into tons of useful paper" (76). Ludwig's almost science-fictional proposal perhaps also inspires Fitzcarraldo's hoisting of a steamship across a mountain in Herzog's film.

I pull these spectacular shenanigans from the Brazilian Amazon to demonstrate how empire in its various permutations—from Ford to Herzog, and from opera houses to floating factories—has historically rendered the Amazon a speculative space in at least two ways. First, these commercial and cultural incursions point to European and U.S. capitalist speculations, which have attempted to lay claim to tropical resources in the rainforest since the early colonial period. Second, these enterprises work in conjunction with a system of fantastical speculations that constructs a tropicalist imaginary sustained through colonialist visual and literary representations of the jungle.[14] The cultural production of the jungle as feral and overgrown sets up the narrative occasion for staging a neocolonial intervention. Yamashita's alternative fabulation shifts the site of agency to an always already willful rainforest, where the seemingly indefatigable capitalist appetite for more consumption of human and natural resources must be kept in check.

Extrapolation through Excavation:
Through the Arc of the (Haunted) Rainforest

Narrated by a sentient alien sphere orbiting around the head of a Japanese Brazilian migrant, *Through the Arc* revisits the speculative space of the Amazon and summons several extraordinary, if not extraterrestrial, subjects to the site, including Kazumasa Ishimaru, the former Japanese railroad inspector from whose cranial orbit the gyrating, rubberized sphere narrates the novel; Batista and Tania Aparecida Djapan, who manage a worldwide, fortune-telling, courier pigeon service; Mané Pena, a healer indigenous to the Amazon Valley who cures people of their afflictions using a magical feather; Chico Paco, a religious pilgrim turned radio evangelist whose love for his disabled neighbor, Gilberto, motivates his faith; and J. B. Tweep, a three-armed entrepreneur from the United States who becomes enamored not only with corporate expansion in Brazil but also with a triple-breasted French ornithologist named Michelle Mabelle. Through these characterizations, Yamashita presents an Amazon populated not only by indigenous inhabitants but also by local and global travelers who arrive at the rainforest via circuits of migration, capital expansion, and religious journeys.

Manifestations of the alien in this Asian American speculative fiction take the shape not of racially marked invader-others but of Northern and Western mutant agents of empire (such as the aforementioned triple-breasted European scientist and three-armed U.S. businessman). Mabelle and Tweep embody the overindulgent desires of colonial and neocolonial enterprises in the Amazon. Their marriage—a union between science and capitalism—unlocks a "capacity for insatiable lust" and "the possibilities of unmitigated pleasure" (123). Mabelle, who "came from a long line of bird lovers," including a great-grandfather who "met Paul Gauguin in Tahiti" (122), studies exotic birds of the Amazon through the cultivated, colonial gaze of the tropics, exemplified in Gauguin's fetishization of Tahitian women in his paintings and writings.[15] Mabelle pursues her research in the vein of the scientific expeditions that occasioned many of the first European ventures to South America. For example, the French anthropologist Claude Lévi-Strauss conducted some of his earliest ethnographic fieldwork in Brazil between 1935 and 1939. The resulting *Tristes Tropiques*—a combination of memoir, field journal, and social science manifesto—begins with the paradoxical declaration: "Je hais les voyages et les explorateurs" (I hate traveling and explorers).[16] The volume, which Yamashita references in her "Author's Note" to *Through the Arc* and which reveals Lévi-Strauss's constant wrestling with the ethics of ethnographic fieldwork and professed disgust with scientific adventure writing, has become a staple in anthropological debate. While describing the "basic elements" of the Brazilian soap opera, or *novela*, form that inspired *Through the Arc*, Yamashita writes: "Claude Levi-Strauss described it all so well so many years ago: *Tristes Tropiques*—an idyll of striking innocence, boundless nostalgia and terrible ruthlessness" (Author's Note). By juxtaposing a foundational text of Western social science with Brazilian popular culture, Yamashita asserts that *Tristes Tropiques* and the Brazilian *novela* share a penchant for melodrama and sensation that render them both speculative texts, participating in the perpetual reconstitution of a national and international understanding of Brazilian culture.

Tweep's enterprising efforts in the Amazon point to the commercial involvement of the United States in Brazil during the early twentieth century and its efforts to incorporate Latin America into its manifest destiny. With three arms, he is the figuration of relentlessly reaching, U.S.-based, multinational corporations with interests overseas. Through Tweep's story, Yamashita complicates the alien encounter. His experience of his alien body asserts a level of acceptance not usually associated with mutation and difference: he thinks of his physical difference as an asset. "As far as J.B. was concerned," writes Yamashita, "he had entered a new genetic plane in the species.... He was a better model, the wave of the future" (30). In his eyes, his third arm renders him so exceptional that he exceeds the normative bounds of the world around him. He finds that the assembly line, musical compositions, and conventional sporting rules cannot adjust their logics for his extraordinary abilities. He throws off the rhythm of production by working too efficiently, gets bored with Beethoven and Chopin because "there was nothing written for his particular expertise," and gets kicked off his baseball team "because there were no rules for a two-mitt player" (31). In Tweep's case, difference may lead to unemployment and ostracism, but it is quickly converted to a position of exceptionalism. His extraordinary abilities find their ultimate fulfillment in the service of the ever-insatiable appetite and ever-expanding domain of capitalism. On the one hand, Yamashita's critique of a bilaterally biased world interrogates the systemic scope of normativity. On the other hand, her depiction of the multinational corporation leader is one of excess and mutation.

The terrain *Through the Arc* examines is itself a mutant space. Described as "an enormous impenetrable field of some unknown solid substance, stretching for millions of acres in all directions" along the floor of the rainforest, the Matacão attracts the attention of "scientists, supernaturalists and ET enthusiasts, sporting the old Spielberg rubber masks" (16). Though early conjectures characterize the Matacão as alien, this miraculously pliable and tensile material turns out not to be otherworldly but very much a product of earth's own making:

> The Matacão, scientists asserted, had been formed for the most part within the last century, paralleling the development of the more common forms of plastic, polyurethane and Styrofoam. Enormous landfills of non-biodegradable material buried under virtually every populated part of the Earth had undergone tremendous pressure, pushed ever farther into the lower layers of the Earth's mantle. The liquid deposits of the molten mass had been squeezed through underground veins to virgin areas of the Earth. The Amazon Forest, being one of the last virgin areas on Earth, got plenty. (202)

Rather than animating the Matacão plastic as an invasive foreigner, Yamashita insists that it is the disavowed slag of capitalist overaccumulation and hubris. As the text unfolds against the backdrop of the Matacão, Yamashita denudes the mystique constructed around it, revealing the black plastic to be the compressed regurgitation of First World waste—the by-product of the most powerful and productive economies, surfacing in the Third World. The rubbery and plastic properties of the Matacão allude to the resilence and flexibility of empire, which continues to resurface in mutated form in Yamashita's extrapolation of this near future that emerges from an excavated history of U.S. and European empire in the South American tropics. *Through the Arc*'s rainforest is a speculative space in which all sorts of discarded, forgotten, and disavowed histories bubble to the surface. Henri Bergson might consider it a symbol of duration: "Duration is the continuous progress of the past which gnaws into the future and which swells as it advances."[17] Just adjacent to the Matacão rests a graveyard of military vehicles, war planes, and Ford Model Ts. Amid the gray, sticky goop of napalm, this rainforest "parking lot" gives rise to a strange new species of mouse and spectacular new colorations for butterflies, birds, and amphibians (99). Yamashita writes: "The entomologists were shocked to discover that their rare butterfly only nested in the vinyl seats of Fords and Chevrolets and that their exquisite reddish coloring was actually due to a steady diet of hydrated ferric oxide, or rusty water from the oxidation of abandoned US military vehicles" (100).

In this example, Yamashita upsets the teleological narrative of scientific discovery. The most exotic looking tropical species of the Amazon are already biologically entangled with clandestine neocolonial projects in Brazil. The spectacular colorations of these jungle organisms come from their nibbling on the rusty skeletons of U.S. industrial and military vehicles. This surprising diet serves as a piquant reminder of the U.S. military presence in Latin America throughout the twentieth century. In another example of resurfacing discarded histories, Yamashita continues to interrogate Western interpretations of the Amazon through the questionable lens of early ethnographic research. She writes: "Some anthropologist ran about frantically re-editing and annotating a soon-to-be-published article about the primitive use of mirrors in ancient religious rites" after encountering the shiny bumpers and rearview mirrors stripped from the cars in the rainforest parking lot (100). Yamashita's construction of the Amazon forces a revision of romanticized and overdetermined views of the tropics held over from nineteenth-century European representations of the jungle as a space of unspoiled, unfettered nature, in need of discovery and discipline through interpretation, conquest, and/or exploitation. This anthropologist's forced reevaluation of the tropics also points to productions of scientific knowledge in the Amazon that changed medical history in Europe. In her history of "tropical empiricism," Brazilian scholar Júnia Ferreira Furtado writes: "Knowledge gleaned from new elements found in these exotic environments ... would later transform medicinal practice in Portugal, the East, and in South America, and would force authors to adopt new classification schemes, which in turn stimulated the extensive production of literature mixing medicine and natural history."[18] In this way, the multidirectional flow of scientific knowledge production depicted in *Through the Arc* upsets the colonial construction of center and periphery.

The historian of science Nancy Leys Stepan situates the enduring tropicalist representations of the rainforest in the context of European empire building, the emergence of racist pseudoscience, and ethnographic travel and tourism to Latin America.[19] Yamashita revises the jungle narrative of tropical danger and contagion by tracing the perception of a wild, unbridled, mutant landscape back to not only imperial fantasies but also the material operations of empire in the Amazon. By embedding the rainforest floor with a mantle of manmade, first-world solidified sludge, Yamashita suggests that the jungle, when excavated, reveals a cavernous system of Northern or European appetite for mining resources and disavowal through a projection of exoticism. This disavowal takes material form in the pollution, waste, and overaccumulation of capitalist imperialism.

While the novel tropes mutated bodies as indicators of U.S. and European imperialist developments in the Amazon, it also—through Ishimaru's intricate and profound attachment to his satellite orb—raises questions about Japan's sometimes contradictory connections to the expansive logics of late capitalism. As Rachel Lee has deftly argued, Yamashita's characterization of Ishimaru gestures not only to the familiar archetype in Asian American literature of the Chinese American railroad worker, but also to "an elite transnational" in "a world where Asian immigrants to the Americas are just as likely to be the owners of capital and the exploiters of labor as to be the persecuted migrant worker."[20] Because it detects new sources of Matacão plastic, the orbiting sphere and Kazumasa Ishimaru become "the key to this incredible source of wealth" (144). As Ishimaru's monetary and spinning peripheral assets become increasingly embroiled in the expansionist project of Tweep's multinational corporation, the ball remarks: "Greed was a horrible thing. Kazumasa could, if necessary, divest himself of his monetary fortune, but he could not rid himself of me" (145). The ball, a gravitational force with its own narrative voice, attaches to Ishimaru, pulling him toward the epicenter of neocolonial transformation of the Amazon. What exactly can Kazumasa divest himself of and what can he not? Wealth. Monetary fortune. But not this constant relationship to the buried past, to history, to the seething substrate of the planet's materials and the human and nonhuman entanglements therein. The ball's attraction to the Matacão points not only to Japan's history as an empire hungry for resource-rich territories (resulting in increased military expansionism during the 1930s in Manchuria, Micronesia, and Southeast Asia), but also to more contemporary investments of Japanese global capital in Latin America, which, according to recent studies of Japanese-owned maquiladoras, are responsible for the generation of an egregious amount of hazardous waste.[21] The orbital adjustments that Ishimaru and the orb make in conjunction with one another's trajectories enact precisely the nature-cultural entanglements feminist science studies scholars such as Donna Haraway and Karen Barad have theorized through other examples.[22] At the end of the novel, Ishimaru suffers and mourns the loss of his attachment to that which marked him as alien. While still tenuously connected to Western capitalist enterprises, he negotiates multiple transnational affiliations, which remain visible in "the tropical tilt of his head" (211).

Ishimaru's sphere is comprised of the same magnetized and extremely durable plastic material as the Matacão, and, despite its crash landing into the text (and Ishimaru's orbit) from outer space in chapter 1, its path of migration reveals it to be not an alien but an indigenous body, returning to its point of origin. This revelation raises the question: What is alien? If even the most alien-looking entity in this work of speculative fiction turns out to be of the earth, then can one extrapolate that migrant subjects are not so easily defined as alien or native either? If the Amazon rainforest yields a seemingly new raw material that turns out to be the recycled detritus of the so-called civilized world, then what is excavated in the Third World is already tangled in the machinations of the First World. The story of the alien thus always returns the reader to a layered history of imperialist ventures into the Amazon that mine the rainforest for its resources. The irony of this connection between the alien and the imperialist invader is the history of jungle narratives that imagine the jungle from the perspective of the colonizer or the neocolonial entrepreneur as an alien space of extraordinary flora and fauna and primitive peoples. To this extent, *Through the Arc*'s rainforest becomes a site of excavating imperial legacies rather than a site that empire relentlessly mines.

The text works structurally to emphasize this theme of returns and disrupt the developmental narrative that has often accompanied the relating of Asian American history and the story of developing nations. While

Through the Arc is an Asian American immigrant narrative, it belies one kind of very limited immigrant narrative that constructs the trajectory of immigration as one that involves leaving a homeland to arrive in a new world where assimilation is upheld as the path to success. Structurally, *Through the Arc* rejects such a teleological organization, moving through parts titled "The Beginning," "The Developing World," and "More Development" but then to "Loss of Innocence," "More Loss," and "Return." It is a structure that refuses the developmental narrative that often accompanies the discourses around both immigration and developing countries. In Ishimaru's name and in the title of a related Yamashita work, *Brazil-Maru*, Yamashita riffs on the Japanese suffix "maru," which means cycle or circle. The suffix also significantly gestures toward the names of the transpacific ships that facilitated Japanese immigration to South America. In 1908, the *Kasato-Maru* brought the first 781 Japanese immigrants to the port of Santos in São Paulo, Brazil, and the *Brazil-Maru* was the name of the vessel that shuttled tens of thousands of Japanese settlers to Brazil, Argentina, and Peru for two decades following World War II.[23] From its title and epigraph, *Through the Arc* emphasizes the cyclical processes that reflect Yamashita's fascination with these transpacific migrations, which reveal dynamic and diverse circulations of people rather than unidirectional movements from one place to another. The epigraph reads: "I have heard Brazilian children say that whatever passes through the arc of a rainbow becomes its opposite. But what is the opposite of a bird? Or for that matter, a human being? And what then, is the great rain forest, where, in its season, the rain never ceases and the rainbows are myriad?" Yamashita's ruminations here—on arcs of migration, myriad passages across ephemeral boundaries, and the complex unfolding of transformation—characterize the central themes of her work and attest to her refusal of an uncomplicated narrative. The passage presents the rainforest as an already speculative space, where constant precipitation yields a propensity for messy mutation, not neatly packaged transformation.

Through the Arc's account of movement proves too dynamic, varied, and unpredictable to abide the artificial parameters of an immigrant narrative uncomplicatedly plotted along the Old World to New World telos. Published in 1990, Yamashita's text pays attention to the profound shifts in the conditions of Japanese-Brazilian immigration to Brazil that occurred during the 1980s. Migration from Japan to Brazil had begun shortly after the abolition of slavery in Brazil in 1888, but Japan had long since outpaced Brazil in economic development, recovering from World War II as "an industrial power of the first rank."[24] In 1990, Japan, in an effort to fill a deficit of unskilled industrial labor, issued an invitation to overseas Japanese and their descendants, including about 200,000 in Brazil, to "return" to Japan, though for most, the return actually constituted immigration. Though Japan had initially turned to workers from Pakistan, Iran, and Bangladesh, Japanese Brazilians were considered more assimilatable subjects who could fill the same labor niche without presenting Japan with an overtly visible (and racialized) face of migrant labor.[25] In Yamashita's *Through the Arc*, movements of peoples are understood to be incredibly complex, in that multiple systems of racialization and shifting centers of global capital inform and shape the patterns of migration. The substantial migration of Japanese Brazilians to Japan in the late 1980s and 1990s renders the telling of Asian American history as having only one trajectory an impossibility and inaccuracy. The alien invader, in Yamashita's revision of a well-rehearsed science fiction trope, turns out to be a return of the repressed and literally attaches itself to the story of Japanese Brazilian immigration.

Through the Arc is a haunted text occupied by a repressed history of Fordist tropicalism. In *Ghostly Matters: Haunting and the Sociological Imagination*, Avery Gordon asks us to approach haunted texts and the ghosts they produce as an opening to remember the disappeared, the dispossessed, and the disavowed by threading "the ghost story" through materialist historiography.[26] Yamashita's *Through the Arc* similarly combines fantastical genre with feminist, indigenous, decolonial critique of European imperialist and U.S. neocolonial enterprises in the Amazon. While the fabulist tale strikes a degree of levity in tone, *Through the Arc* issues a critique of ecological nonchalance, the avaricious tenacity of multinational corporations, a history of racist science in a racially mixed and idealized country, and U.S. neocolonial presence in Brazil under the guise of scientific improvement and benevolent medical care. Through a blend of magical realist and science fictional conventions, Yamashita explores the troubling collusion between science and neocolonial enterprises in developing countries, the layered and intertwined legacies of empire in the Americas and Asia, and the relationship between nationalism and narratives of progress. These are the various ghosts that haunt *Through the Arc*, and the ectoplasm that bubbles up from the floor of the Amazon jungle is the "seething presence" of the Matacão.[27]

*Imperial Rubber: Residues of U.S. Empire
in the Brazilian Rainforest*

Take away from us the motor vehicle, and I do not know what would happen. The damage would be more serious and lasting than if our land were laid waste by an invader. We could recover from the blowing up of New York City and all the big cities on the Atlantic seaboard more quickly than we could recover from the loss of our rubber.
—HARVEY FIRESTONE, *Men and Rubber*

"History is more or less bunk."
—HENRY FORD, *The Chicago Tribune*

"The ghostly matter will not go away. It is waiting for you and it will shadow you and it will outwit all your smart moves as that jungle grows thicker and deeper."
—AVERY GORDON, *Ghostly Matters*

The rubbery resource excavated at the Matacão can be molded into any shape and has the structural integrity of steel. One of the most fantastical manifestations of the malleable material's architectural possibilities is an amusement park. "Chicolándia," named after the local entrepreneurial character Chico Paco, who conceived of and constructed it for his gay lover, also constitutes *Through the Arc*'s most concrete allusion to the U.S. neocolonial presence in the Amazon. Ford's plantation project instantiates an extension of U.S. cultural and economic imperialism in Brazil, and *Through the Arc* revisits the Amazon as a speculative space haunted by this history of neocolonial enterprise, known more generally as the Amazon rubber boom. In this section, I consider the conditions already in place that enabled the Ford Motor Company to establish itself so readily in the Amazon rainforest. Through an examination of company-archived pamphlets and photographs, newspaper articles, and plantation managers' journals of the 1920s through the 1940s, I show how Ford's civilizing mission borrowed from preexisting discourses on tropical nature, race, and sexuality promulgated by nineteenth-century French and British scientific expeditions into the Amazon.

Since the 1870s, Dutch and British entrepreneurs had established an expansive and successful rubber tree empire in Asia. In 1922, the British Rubber Restoration Act (also known as the Stevenson Plan) sought to double the price of rubber, which would exert pressure on the growing U.S. automobile empire. British domination of the world rubber market threatened Ford's vision of complete vertical integration of his automotive industry (from rubber tree plantations to tires on Model Ts). In retaliation, Ford and Harvey Firestone mobilized a campaign to break the emerging rubber cartel. Because rubber tree cultivation is restricted to tropical climates, the resulting competition among British, Dutch, and U.S. rubber industries in Malaysia, Indonesia, and Brazil, respectively, creates an interesting connection between British and Dutch imperialism in Asia and U.S. neocolonial investments in Latin America.[28] Two decades later, between 1942 and 1945, British Malaya and Singapore came under Japanese imperial rule. Japan's interest in these regions was arguably due in large part to the rubber resources it would gain access to and control over during World War II. These connections suggest the multiple, interconnected, and various machinations of empire.

Organized and run as a U.S. plantation, Fordlândia implemented a series of social ordering structures that helped sustain the racialized aspect of benevolent supremacy rationalizing the U.S. neocolonial presence in Brazil. To conform to U.S. work practices, local laborers were required to work during the most exhausting midday hours, wear identification badges, and eat hamburgers and hot dogs in a cafeteria. In December 1930, when the workers at Fordlândia revolted, they targeted all things emblematic of Fordist ideologies and practices. The workers made a point of overturning automobiles and smashing the time clocks (see figure 1.1). In the Amazon, so close to the equator, it would seem sensible that rhythms of work abide by the sun. At high noon, workers would do well to find a cool spot and rest, saving their energy to labor under the less punishing temperatures of the early morning and post-sundown hours. Not so at Fordlândia, where—as noted above—the managers enforced a nine-to-five workday, requiring workers to punch in and out as they would on the factory floor in Detroit. In fact, watches and clocks in Fordlândia were set to Detroit time, an hour earlier than the rest of the state of Pará.

Although Fordlândia sought to deliver the "homogeneous, empty time" that, as Walter Benjamin argues, forms the cornerstone of the concept of progress, time instantiates the Fordist fantasy of exercising social and economic controls over labor and leisure in the Amazon.[29] By dismantling fixtures of Fordist ideas of modernity and developmental notions of progress, the workers demonstrated their profound objection to the temporal and gustatory imperialism that arrived with Ford's neocolonial plantation settlement.

Workers also directed their frustrations at other invasive cultural systems that sought to force a certain digestive and temporal regimenta-

FIGURE 1.1. Fordlándia time clock, destroyed in the riot of December 1930. From the Collections of The Henry Ford. Gift of Ford Motor Company. Object ID: 64.167.74.5

tion onto their everyday lives. Images of Fordlândia resemble a suburban grid, complete with stucco dwellings, power lines, (segregated) swimming pools, and a hospital. Inhabitants of Fordlândia were forbidden from drinking and smoking; the children wore school uniforms; and in their leisure time, employees could attend the company-run churches and motion picture theaters or even play golf on the eighteen-hole course "700 miles from civilization"—"everything necessary for the health, happiness and wellbeing of Ford employees."[30] A company brochure emphasizes the plantation's role in "modernizing" the tropics, calling attention repeatedly to the "modern hospital" and describing Fordlândia as "a modern city" that took the place of "the trackless green waste" of "the almost impenetrable tropical jungle." Targeting current and potential investors, the promotional pamphlet blames the Brazilian plantation's shortcomings on increased demand for rubber and the more rigorous scientific development of rubber cultivation technologies in Asia. It suggests that in "the early days of automobiles, before the need was so great, the unskilled methods of natives produced most of the world's supply of rubber from the jungles of Brazil." The company characterizes preplantation rubber cultivation as the rudimentary and primitive production of "jungle natives." With increased demand, though, the brochure explains: "Brazil lost its preeminent place to the Far East, which developed scientific methods of tree culture that resulted in greater yield and higher quality of crude rubber." In this way, the brochure renders a history of the Amazon that narrates the need for technoscientific intervention to restore Brazil's preeminence in the rubber industry. Many pages of the brochure comment on the transformative power of industry, comparing Fordlândia's residences to "any midwestern [sic] town" or "a winter home in Florida" and taking great pains to amplify the remarkable nature of such a feat "in the heart of Brazil": "Shades of Tarzan! You'd never guess these bright, happy, healthy school children lived in a jungle city that didn't even exist a few years ago." News media coverage of Ford's developments in the Amazon rainforest highlighted the plantation's school system and included several photographs of Indian children in clean white uniforms standing and saluting the motto on the Brazilian flag: *Ordem e Progresso* (order and progress). Through the company brochure and other media engagements, the Ford Motor Company and Ford himself produced "*consumer spectacles*" for the general public and potential investors.[31] Set in the Amazon rainforest, these spectacles capitalized on an already existing imperialist imaginary of the tropical New World passed on from EuroAmerican artifacts of knowledge such as the fantastical accounts of the La Condamine expedition. Ford's speculative productions, in which he promises a civilizing mission that could tame not only the unruly jungle but also the denizens of the Amazon Valley, had a prequel in the form of eighteenth-century travel writing that passed as scientific knowledge production. But these Fordist fictions also drew on other sources of inspiration, including early twentieth-century ideas about race and evolution, emerging alongside a contemporaneous eugenics movement and U.S.-led sterilization campaigns in the Global South. Because much of the scientific world, as it lived in both individual scientists and institutions backing scientific research in Europe and North America, was arranging racial difference along a hierarchy, Ford's global capitalist ventures, which benefited from such stratifications in producing cheap labor, took up these notions readily, while also combining them with Brazilian ideas of race mixing from thinkers such as Gilberto Freyre, who wanted to move Brazil toward a "racial democracy," to more overtly white supremacist notions of racial whitening.[32]

In a document titled "Living Conditions in the Amazon Valley," written on May 6, 1927, Carl D. LaRue depicts first and foremost a destitute Pará state: "In the smaller villages and along the rivers, the people are everywhere poor and forlorn. Most of them are penniless and without hope for the future" (box 1, "History and Cost," accession #74, 1). In this scouting report, LaRue sets the stage for Fordist reform by describing the need for a civilizing mission, a need for a restoration of "hope for the future" through financial, international speculation. LaRue's sympathetic attention to the poor living conditions of the local peoples, though, quickly reveals itself to have more than one motivation. His concern for the health and happiness of these people stems from his estimation of them as potential laboring bodies in Fordlándia's future workforce: "These people are usually called lazy, improvident, thriftless, etc., and it is true that they are not energetic, but when we consider that they are racked with disease, and have never been properly nourished in their lives, one wonders at their powers of endurance" (1). LaRue's characterization of these potential laborers as disease-ridden and poorly nourished establishes an occasion for a medical intervention as a means of bolstering the labor supply while assuming a position of humanitarian aid, benevolent force, and civilizing mission. Indeed, historian Elizabeth Esch notes that it was precisely "the people of the region and their capacity for the modernizing the company intended" that became a prime factor in deciding whether Sumatra or the Amazon would serve Ford's needs best.[33] In his exploratory report of the area, LaRue reports that in 1927: "No attention is paid to housing such people or looking after their health." His subsequent call for medical aid that a Ford-run operation could deliver is tied to a racialized concept of health and hygiene prevalent among eugenicists of the time. Referring to the potential plantation workers as "magnificent specimens," LaRue writes: "The dwellers of the Amazon Valley are of three main stocks: Indian, Portuguese and Negro." LaRue's taxonomic approach to race continues as he explains how "admixture has gone on so long that it is difficult to distinguish the different types. The mixture is not a particularly good one from a racial standpoint, but it is by no means a bad one."

What "racial standpoint" does LaRue take for granted here? In the United States around 1927, the wide acceptance of scientific racism and eugenicist thought led to compulsory sterilization practices and immigration restriction legislation. However, 1927 also marks the height of Brazil's own debates around race that emerged in relation but also in contradistinction to European and U.S. racial ideologies. Prior to the publication of Freyre's work on racial democracy, this period witnessed efforts among Brazilian authorities and landed gentry, informed by European racial pseudoscience, to push for a "whitening" of the Brazilian population in the decades following the abolition of slavery in 1888.[34] As a natural scientist and as a Ford employee, LaRue likely brought to his scouting report on the Amazon his own version of white supremacy, bolstered by the prevailing racial ideologies of U.S. science and industry. Concurrently, the converging discourses of Brazilian racial improvement and Ford's civilizing mission are rather suggestive.

LaRue's conclusion to his report reinforces this connection between the two discourses of improvement: "The salvation of these people lies in some development which will give them employment at reasonable wages and with decent living conditions. . . . This is an opportunity to do a great service to hundreds of deserving folk" (5). For LaRue, capitalist development leads to "salvation," and he thus reveals himself to be a devout believer in Fordist reform as a universal imperative.

LaRue's final rallying call reveals the racial typologies of this period, largely built around now-discredited areas of pseudoscientific research such as craniometry and phrenology. "The fate of these people," he reports, "is the more tragic because they are not possessed of the stolidity of many of the orientals, but have enough of the white race in them to suffer keenly and long intensely for better things. As it is, their condition is worse than that of any of the coolies in the East; far worse even than that of the average slave in the old days" (4). In this astonishing quotation, LaRue's preoccupation with the competing rubber industry in Southeast Asia manifests itself in this racialized comparison between Asian and Brazilian mixed-race labor. Conscious of the fact that local Indian labor "is somewhat more expensive than in the East," LaRue argues that this cost differential is offset by the fact that Brazilian "labor is also more intelligent than the average labor in the East" ("A Report on the Exploration of the Tapajos Valley"; April 19, 1927, box 1, "History and Cost," accession #74, 5). He also explains that "the use of machines on the modern plantation should offset this advantage in the East" (5). In his entreaty to Ford to create his rubber empire in Brazil rather than in Sumatra, LaRue mobilizes two contradictory Orientalist formulations of Asia as, on the one hand, hopelessly unmodern and less intelligent, and on the other hand, at an advantage and in less need of being saved by Fordist progress.

The passage also reveals LaRue's efforts to distance his and Ford's mission in the Amazon from the systems of oppression at work in European colonization of Southeast Asia, the United States' own slave past, as well as other rubber operations in Brazil. In one of the more remarkable passages of his report, LaRue encounters and disparages another rubber plant run by a Syrian named Michel. "In common with the other Syrians," reports LaRue, "he grinds down his men and gives them less than enough to buy an adequate supply of even the simplest food" (3).[35] LaRue sets up Ford's vision as a liberatory intervention: "One of the great things which the development of this country will bring is the relief of these unfortunate people" (3). To position U.S. capitalist expansion as humanitarian relief, LaRue intertwines his roles as a geographer, anthropologist, and corporate scout. He becomes a speculator of potential natural and human resources, projecting narrative and fantasy across those geographies in order to attract the venture capital needed to sustain the plantation. In this way, LaRue's report does the promissory work of speculative writing. It, along with the promotional brochure aimed at potential investors, not only reflects but also produces the fantasies of rendering laborers docile, delivering modernity to the jungle, and accumulating high-density wealth that were all part of Ford's material and ideological speculations in the Brazilian Amazon.[36]

Contrary to the Fordist fantasy of modernizing and regulating the tropics, Fordlândia ultimately and utterly failed. The workers rebelled, as did the rainforest, and the Fordist project in Brazil settled into relative obscurity. Therefore, Yamashita's late twentieth-century excavation of this largely forgotten Amazonian rubber plantation helps situate her extrapolative imagining of twenty-first century capitalization on rainforest resources in a longer history of trans-imperial endeavors in Brazil. Linking European ethnographic and scientific expeditions of the nineteenth century to the Fordist project of plantation building in the early twentieth century, Yamashita also connects these imperial traces to the more contemporary moment of post-Fordist global capitalism in Latin America. In this way, Yamashita's transformation of the Amazon rainforest into a speculative space unearths the historical layers of European and U.S. claims to Brazilian natural resources. More generally, Yamashita takes issue with the historical and continued scientific exploration of the Amazon under banners of benevolent research but through the perpetuation of tropicalist stereotypes of "jungle nations."

Yamashita's description of the inevitable collapse of the industries that profited off the Matacão mimics the historical decline and ultimate failure of Fordlândia and, indeed, most U.S. and British endeavors to cultivate rubber on a large scale in the Amazon. In his history of U.S. ecological degradation of the tropics, Richard Tucker explains that capitalist greed spawned growth of rubber trees in overly concentrated plantations, which ultimately resulted in massive leaf blight.[37] Unable to control the spread of the fungus, the corporate rubber plantations stubbornly held to densely populated planting techniques because "intensification of production . . . became a hallmark of the industry and one of the most dramatic triumphs of tropical agronomy."[38] In this sense, the failure of Fordlândia precisely demonstrated the deleterious effects of intensified accumulation of global capitalism. The rubber cultivation process could have been, and had already been for many years, a renewable resource extraction. The more ecologically respectful methods were primarily used by local Brazilian *seringueiros*. Global capitalism not only severely altered the ecology of Amazonia, but it also in effect displaced Brazilian workers who had been supporting their own lives by cultivating rubber in a more sustainable way.

What the Fordlândia propaganda erases in the process of disseminating narratives of improvement, progress, and development are the stories of displacement, loss, imposed capitalist greed, and ecological devastation that Yamashita's tale so cleverly resuscitates. Yamashita excavates not only histories of empire in the rainforest but also unofficial stories that emerge from the perspective of the displaced and disremembered, such as her character Mané Pena, who spent his days "wandering the forest like the others—fishing, tapping rubber and collecting Brazil nuts" before a "government sort" informed him that his land had been cleared but that they would send an agronomist to "show [him] how to plant" if he signed a contract (16). Before "the fires, the chain saws and the government bulldozers," Pena worked as a *seringuero* and thus depended on the rainforest for his livelihood until U.S. entrepreneurial interests and European scientific endeavors laid claim to his property, even as they congratulated him, offered him a contract to sign, and suggested that he "get some barbed wire, fence [his land] in properly" (16). Yamashita describes one of the central contradictions of global development policy, which seems to transform land into designated property only to dispossess its denizens of it, bestowing rights on Pena only to then impose capitalism's right to reap the benefits of property once it is deemed as such. From Pena's perspective, the government seized and destroyed his land even as they pretended to extend the rights of ownership and the sense that they were doing him a favor.

Pena's story serves as a cautionary counterpoint to the maverick economic theories of Hernando de Soto, who believes that lack of formal property rights is the source of poverty in the Global South. Named by *Forbes* magazine as "one of 15 innovators who will re-invent your future,"[39] de Soto has called the extralegal shacks, stalls, and plots of the poor "dead capital," existing beyond the rule of law.[40] In his 1986 book *The Other Path*, de Soto explains: "They have houses but not titles; crops but not deeds; businesses but not statutes of incorporation."[41] De Soto advocates a development model that Third World economies can follow to turn a profit on a new accounting of territorial assets that have heretofore gone unrecognized as sites of potential, "enabling tens of millions of poor entrepreneurs across the third world to become part of the system rather than excluded by bureaucracy and red tape."[42] By identifying untapped sites of growth, de Soto's model pulls the poor and stateless into the fold of capitalism, magically infusing their land with new titles. By apparently adding $9.2 billion worth of new assets to the system, de Soto's plan writes the dispossessed into a global capitalist future. Yamashita's tale quickly points to the devastating effects of Pena's property being "liberated" from obscurity: "The agronomist never did come, but the rains did and the wind and the harsh uncompromising tropical sun. Even Mané's mud-and-thatch house was eventually washed away" (16). The rainforest forcefully rejects the development model. As the failure of Ford's rubber plantation demonstrated historically, the dense planting of rubber trees on such a clearing is a terrible idea—one that the agronomist's analysis would only have reinforced. Ford would replace the local mud-and-thatch houses of the rainforest denizens, but Yamashita clearly suggests that such domiciles could withstand all but the most uncompromising conditions of rainforest climate.

The story of Pena illuminates how development and discovery are both embedded in settler colonialist logics of laying claim to land through capitalist constructs of property deeds, proofs of ownership, and legal contracts. In Yamashita's revisionist tale, it is Pena who discovered and even named the subterranean resource of the Matacão long before any scientists when, years earlier, he told TV reporters who had come to film a documentary on poverty in the Amazon "about the underground matacão, or solid plate of rock that always blocked well-diggers" (17). However, because the reporters "were used to interviewing illiterate, backward and superstitious people," the record of Pena's discovery was filed away as "fantastico" and "collect[ed] dust until the late 1990s" (17). The documentary film, a genre that continues to mediate the First World's view of the rainforest, foreshadows the mercenary interest in the Amazon. The Matacão fails to make the news as an odd substrate that prevents indigenous farmers from digging wells and producing enough manioc crops for survival and only makes headlines when it becomes identified as a potential resource to exploit. The documentation of truths is a process limited by the producers' primitivist outlook on the Amazon and their understanding of indigenous stories as disposable footage. When it is eventually "discovered" that the Matacão is manmade and not natural, almost everyone is surprised; however, "that the primeval forest was not primeval was hardly news to old Mané" (17). What's old and what's news, what's artificial and what's of the earth, Yamashita seems to suggest, is a matter of perspective.

Considering the disastrous history of Ford's rubber plantation in the Amazon, the post-Fordist capers of *Through the Arc*'s Matacão are hardly surprising. Chicolándia's demise is foreshadowed by Fordlándia's overly zealous attempts at extracting the Amazon's resources. Yet Chicolándia also serves as a referent for another compulsion of empire: to preserve its version of history by fixing that narrative in time. Described as a "paradise of plastic delights" (168), Chicolándia's main attractions are the lifelike replicas of Gilberto's favorite Hollywood film sets and of famous cityscapes of the world. At any given moment Gilberto "could suddenly be somewhere else in time and space" (168). It is a theme park, not unlike Disneyland or Universal Studios, that seeks to replicate Hollywood. It is also a bit like Greenfield Village, a historic theme park located in a Detroit suburb called Dearborn, Michigan, that is dedicated to the preservation of pre-Fordist modes of production (which Ford was convinced would disappear once his assembly line and new technologies of industrial production proliferated). Greenfield Village's buildings are either transplantations of original homes and structures or they are exact replicas. The freed slave farmhouses and artisanal glass-blowing workshops mark a change in modes of production and participate in a historical narrative that distinguishes Fordism from an earlier capitalist system that relied on chattel slavery and plantation labor, even as it stages its reproduction. Much of the official, company-recorded history of Fordlándia resides in the Benson Ford Research Center, part of the sprawling complex of Ford-related attractions in Dearborn. Yamashita's excavation of Fordlándia suggests a continuity between Ford's twentieth-century automobile assembly lines and forms of exploitation and indentured servitude physically occurring outside of, but nevertheless closely tied to, U.S. industry. Even as the Ford Motor Company sought to separate itself from the plantation, it was actively establishing itself as an "empire-building corporation" with colonial holdings in both Brazil and South Africa.[43] As LaRue's scouting report reveals, Ford's speculations in Brazil relied on European colonial formulations held over from the eighteenth and nineteenth centuries.

Through the Arc intervenes in and disrupts such imperialist fantasies of a jungle perpetually uninhabited and virginal, unruly and in need of outside regulation, and ripe and available for development. It was never primeval, nor was capitalism's various intrusions into it ever really new. Both the fantasy of the rainforest as untapped and the promise of new capitalist technologies to bring it under the yoke of order get recycled at the colonial moment of encounter, the Fordist neoplantation, and Tweep's global entrepreneurialism. One way *Through the Arc* undermines settler colonial fantasies of a primordial rainforest of primitive peoples is to undercut Tweep's speculative projections on the Amazon with a Native perspective. Yamashita asks us to compare Tweep's view of the Matacão with that of Pena. Despite being mocked and dismissed as a dreamer, Pena understands a lived experience of the Amazon's magic that turns out to be quite real. In contrast, Tweep, despite exerting dominion over that speculative space, sees only his own fixed imaginary of the Amazon as an endlessly exploitable resource. As a consummate proponent of globalization, Tweep depends on the abstraction of the jungle to make it available for resource extraction. By including the story of an indigenous inhabitant of the Matacão, Yamashita allows Pena's memories of that place to serve as a counter-cartography of the Amazon.[44] Similarly, *Through the Arc* does not aspire to realism—or even scientific fiction—but prefers to revel in the disjuncture between the fantasies of global capitalism that imagine the jungle as primitive and the magical healing powers of Pena's feathers. This playful juxtaposition of fictitious capital and mystical commodities suggests that capitalism's reliance on fantastical representations of space and time is itself a kind of science fiction.

Yamashita's excavation and fabulation of the Matacão demonstrates how a place can be both real and imagined at the same time. The rainforest is a space that is produced through the ways in which it is perceived, conceived, and lived. At once a cautionary tale of deforestation, exploitative labor practices, and abusive extraction of natural resources on the part of an avaricious First World capitalist machine, *Through the Arc* interrogates the narratives spawned from empire's deployment of scientific discourses about progress and development. By rearticulating the science fiction trope of alien invasion as a resurfacing of disavowed, domestic detritus, and by excavating the histories of exploitation buried under tropicalist constructions of untamed jungles and primitive geographies, Yamashita's speculations provide an alternative to the practices of forgetting that help perpetuate imperialist endeavors. She interrupts the ongoing project of transforming Latin America by suggesting that the so-called developing world has always already been in a state of transformation.

Conclusion

Researching this chapter involved spending some time in and around Detroit, where one does not have to look hard for evidence of the history of the auto industry and its participation in a racial capitalism. While I was digging up files about Fordlándia, I could not help thinking about Vincent Chin and his violent murder in 1982 at the hands of disgruntled auto workers who arguably targeted the twenty-seven-year-old Chinese American engineer as a racialized sign of the threat of the competing Japanese auto industry, which was perceived as the cause of pervasive layoffs and increased pressures at work. Insofar as Chin's murder is a story about racial violence in the moment of global restructuring of the auto industry, the event is worth revisiting in the additional contexts of the financialization of the Japanese economy in the 1980s as well as Detroit's earlier connections to global movements of capital, people, and goods. Chin's murder occupies a place in a broader history of racial capitalism that violently destroys that which stands in its way. In my analysis of *Through the Arc*, I have examined how European colonial science provided a racialized discourse of tropicalization that facilitated U.S. neocolonial plantation-building in Brazil. I have argued that the Fordist rhetoric of improving and civilizing the Amazon built on earlier established colonial discourses. Furthermore, I have demonstrated how Ford's ideas on race drew on eugenicist hierarchies that compared Brazilian, mixed-race laborers with Asian workers to the extent that those ideas informed his decision to establish his rubber empire in South America rather than in Southeast Asia. Finally, I have asserted Yamashita's work as a counter-speculation that uses the genre of science fiction to excavate these layered legacies of imperial projects in the Amazon. To conclude this chapter, I would like to return to the broader questions of financial speculation and speculative fiction as competing narratives of futurity.

Yamashita's novel addresses the spaces of both the Global North and the Global South, with particular attention to those parts of the Global North embedded in the Global South. *Through the Arc* represents both transnational business elites who move between the United States and Europe and the dispossessed undercommons who occupy the spaces of the rainforest and the favela. By returning to the imbricated labor histories of Asian Americans and Latinos as well as the displacement of indigenous peoples from the Amazon, Yamashita's speculative fiction also performs a more transnational set of futures. Adopting a Latin American framework to consider North-South dynamics that move beyond narratives that position the East only in relationship to the West, *Through the Arc* sets up some of the transpacific migrations that challenge the United States as the central vantage point from which to form speculative globalities. In the next chapter, I examine Yamashita's third novel, *Tropic of Orange*, which turns its attention to the U.S.-Mexico borderlands as another space where migrant futures might form a horizon that experiments with the flexibility of global capitalism.

HOMELAND FUTURITY
Speculations at the Border

I've got the future in my throat.
—GUILLERMO GÓMEZ-PEÑA, "Border Brujo"

Capitalism, having already found a way to turn a profit on disaster, also attempts to harness the energy of forecasting and preempting it. In 2007, the year in which Naomi Klein's book on disaster capitalism was published, a group called SIGMA—comprised of science fiction writers Arlan Andrews, Greg Bear, Larry Niven, Jerry Pournelle, and Sage Walker—traveled to a Department of Homeland Security conference at the government's invitation. Formed in the late 1990s, SIGMA organized itself around the motto "Science Fiction in the National Interest." When asked why the Department of Defense had included a group of science fiction writers in its military strategy planning meeting, a spokesperson explained: "We need to look everywhere for ideas, and science fiction writers clearly inform the debate."[1] By including SIGMA in policy-building conversations about border security, airport screenings, and antiterrorist strategies, the U.S. government actively recruited science fiction writers to help produce a near-future national imaginary. Speculating on potential threats at the U.S.-Mexico border or in cyberspace on behalf of the Department of Homeland Security, these fictional world-smiths collaborated with policy makers in producing border futurities that, when operationalized, cohere not only in the rhetoric of regulation and securitization but also the military and economic structures that actualize fantasies of nation, homeland, and threat. This chapter examines such speculations at the border, where science fictional narratives proliferate from within a military-industrial complex to form a security-defense imaginary constructed through scenario-based exercises, video games, and surveillance scan projections.

SIGMA's collaboration with the Department of Homeland Security follows a more general turn in military strategy toward preemptive thinking that manifests first as scenario thinking during the atomic era of the mid-twentieth century and later, in the post-9/11 moment, as full-blown "scenario-based exercises," with Hollywood-scale budgets.[2] In his analysis of scenario-based exercises, Andrew Lakoff characterizes this new phase of defense strategy as "imaginative enactment,"[3] stopping just short of connecting these scenarios and the work of science fiction more forcefully. In his account of the affective qualities evoked by Dark Winter—the smallpox attack simulation staged at Andrews Air Force Base in 2001—Lakoff emphasizes the feeling that viewers needed to be forewarned of its similitude to reality, lest they be accidentally tricked into believing the training exercise was an actual emergency. He quotes the director of the Center for Strategic and International Studies telling Representative Christopher Shays: "Let me also emphasize, sir, this is a simulation. This had frightening qualities of being real, as a matter of fact too real. And because we have television cameras here broadcasting, we want to tell everyone, this did not happen, it was a simulation. But, it had such realism, and we are going to try to show you the sense of realism that came from that today."[4]

As with Orson Welles's powerfully convincing dramatic radio performance of *War of the Worlds* in 1938, the recounting of a possible threat—the imaginative enactment of an emergency—provoked disquieting states of uncertainty.[5] Dark Winter made congressional leaders feel as though they'd been "in the middle of a movie."[6] Lakoff makes the case that Dark Winter was "successful in that it convinced participants—and later briefing audiences—of the urgent need to plan for a bioattack."[7] The fiction of disaster became pivotal in catalyzing a system of emergency management. Preemption, as Patricia Dunmire has argued, moves rhetorical and ideological futurity into policy during George W. Bush's presidency in part by "reifying the 'threat.'"[8]

The emergency simulation, according to Jean Baudrillard, constitutes science fiction that has "lost its charm" because it has lost its ability to play on the doubling of real and unreal.[9] In these forms of speculative narration yoked to the military-industrial complex and the policy-producing bodies of the state ("science fiction in the national interest"), the play of potentiality caves to the predictive pressures of securitization. In the case of Dark Winter, the "broader lesson was the need to imaginatively enact the event in order to adequately plan for it."[10] Witness here the quick conversion of imagination into management. The plan is not only inadequate, it is tautological—producing the very crisis it seeks to contain. Crisis simulation is self-fulfilling because it inevitably calls for increased securitization, anticipating and fomenting uncertainty all at once.[11] Imagination for the sake of planning, rather than the sake of open-ended potentiality, skips the initial question of whether increased militarization and capitalization should be the primary approach to the border or whether there is an alternative understanding of how (and on behalf of whom) the border might be configured. Such speculative narratives inform, produce, and sustain the security state precisely through states of insecurity.[12] The methodology of the speculative security state is one of anticipation and prediction. It gambles.

As the Department of Homeland Security looks to science fiction authors and their speculations on alien invasion, apocalyptic scenarios, and uncertain futures, the future emerges as a speculative space where various narratives compete for influence not only in the allocation of resources but also in the ideological configuration around homeland defense. SIGMA and Dark Winter are just two examples of a fairly pervasive merger between science fiction and the logics of preemption that have proliferated under the rising aegis of the security state. There are also science-fiction-themed video games that are designed and sold to train military forces; Hollywood blockbuster films about alien invasion that glorify war practices, while shoring up rationales for more robust homeland defense; and military tech chat rooms that compare unmanned aerial vehicles to cylons from the science fiction television series *Battlestar Galactica*. When these cultural imaginaries conceptualize risk at the border, they project into that space forms of securitization that manifest themselves as armed checkpoints fortified by surveillance technologies. The task of this chapter is to look to alternative models for speculating the border.

The U.S.-Mexico borderlands offer a particularly rich site to investigate narratives of futurity, precisely because border regions have been the testing grounds for so many surveillance and military technologies as well as rhetorical technologies of U.S. exceptionalism before and after 9/11.[13] Risk and threat are long-term denizens of the borderlands, where nuclear disaster, terrorism-linked drug wars, and even nefarious strains of influenza seem constantly to press their urgency in the form of crisis.

Sergio Arau and Yareli Arizmendi's 2004 film, *A Day without a Mexican*, is one example of a speculative fiction that provides an ironic engagement with the rhetoric of emergency and apocalypse. Imagining the systemic breakdown of the U.S. capitalist engine in the face of the disappearance of its immigrant workforce, *A Day without a Mexican* shifts the site of emergency from the xenophobic imaginary of barbarians at the gate to the negligence of immigrant laborers' rights. Arizmendi calls her project "emergency filmmaking" in that it responds to a series of legislative moves in California such as Proposition 187 and the Sensenbrenner Bill that were designed to place harsher restrictions on immigration and migrant laborers' rights to health care, social services, and public education.[14] The film's tagline—"On May 14, there will be no Mexicans in California"—provided inspiration for the student and worker walkouts in the spring of 2006 to protest anti-immigration legislation in the United States. May 1st Movement organizers adopted the science fiction premise of Arau and Arizmendi's film by naming the day of the walkouts "A Day without Immigrants." Both the science fiction film and the grassroots movement featured the sudden disappearance of large groups of U.S. workers—disappearances that held an especially chilling resonance with the ongoing disappearances of women working in the maquiladora system and the daily disappearances of migrant laborers who attempt the perilous crossing of an increasingly militarized border.

A Day without a Mexican joins other speculative fictions that use the conventional science fiction trope of alien abduction to highlight capitalism's reliance on racialized labor. In Derrick Bell's "The Space Traders" (1992), aliens come to earth seeking to trade enough gold to end all international debt and enough technology to end global warming—in exchange for all the people of African descent on the planet.[15] The abduction of low-wage and slave laborers also has catastrophic consequences in a 1965 play by Douglas Turner Ward titled *Day of Absence*, which speculates on what would happen if people of color spontaneously disappeared from the workforce.

These revisions of end-of-the-world narratives by African American and Chicano cultural producers creatively retool science fictions of emergency and disaster to protest anti-immigration legislation and unfair labor practices.[16] Such speculative responses to other fictions of crisis make important interventions into the ways in which national and international emergencies animate these discursive and ideological cultural contestations.

Several more recent science fictions reconfigure how we imagine the U.S.-Mexico borderlands, including Rosaura Sanchez and Beatrice Pita's novel, *Lunar Braceros*, and ongoing media projects such as the Transborder Immigrant Tool of the Electronic Disturbance Theater group.[17] Both look to the repurposing of technological tools to cultivate transnational coalitions rather than militarized securitization.

The two speculative texts I use to reimagine border futures in this chapter are Karen Tei Yamashita's novel *Tropic of Orange* (1997) and Alex Rivera's film *Sleep Dealer* (2008). These works experiment with the horizon and the network as two relational structures that reconfigure migrant futurity around a transnational commons rather than a securitized homeland. Both texts also maintain a critical distance from techno-utopianism, wary of its already having been incorporated into a development discourse.[18]

Yamashita's and Rivera's considerations of border technologies include not only neoliberal technologies such as free-trade policies and anti-immigration legislation, but also the mechanisms of the surveillance state and newly mobilized discourses of preemption, threat, and risk. This pairing of texts illuminates the eternal flexibility of the border in its ability to maintain a stark unevenness between flows of *bios* and capital. Rather than depicting the borderlands as a site in need of increased regulation and containment through restrictive technologies, *Tropic of Orange* carefully revamps the borderlands as a geography already populated with techno-cultural agents working across diasporic networks. The transborder and cross-ethnic collaborations among characters in both works facilitate the undoing of global capital's border speculations. Multinational corporations suffer backlash from mutant environmental agents, corrupt governmental institutions collapse under the pressure of their own contradictory logics, and grassroots transnational futurities emerge. Ultimately, both narratives work to dismantle what Donald Pease has called the "symbolic drama" of the homeland, through which promises of protection and warnings of imminent threat reconstitute the political body of "the people" into a biopoliticized population.[19] By shifting the site of emergency, *Tropic of Orange* and *Sleep Dealer* invite us to interrogate for whom the future is secured, and the answer resounds in these dystopian landscapes wherein human well-being has been superseded by capitalist interest.

Migrant Oranges: The Fruits, Labors, and Technologies of the Borderlands

In the introduction to *The Anarchy of Empire in the Making of U.S. Culture*, Amy Kaplan writes: "The idea of the nation as home . . . is inextricable from the political, economic and cultural movements of empire, movements that both erect and unsettle the ever-shifting boundaries between the domestic and the foreign, between 'at home' and 'abroad.'"[20] Kaplan opens her analysis of U.S. imperialism with an examination of the *Downes v. Bidwell* case of 1901, highlighting the discursive acrobatics involved in determining whether shipping oranges from Puerto Rico to the United States mainland should be taxed as a foreign or domestic exchange of goods. To support its ruling that Puerto Rican exports to the United States should indeed be subject to overseas taxation, the Supreme Court characterized Puerto Rico's relationship to the United States as "'foreign' in the 'domestic sense.'"[21] This flexible and slippery status points to a long and ongoing history of elaborate equivocations around the rhetoric of U.S. neocolonial projects in Latin America and Asia, regions connected not only by economic systems, migration patterns, and military interests, but also by submarine and outer-space superstructures of communication technologies. Even as it seeks to deny sovereignty to Puerto Rico as a separate, distinct state, the United States simultaneously must produce differences between home and abroad through flexible rhetorical strategies such as those exercised in *Downes v. Bidwell*.

Written in the context of the War on Drugs, first declared by President Ronald Reagan in 1984, *Tropic of Orange* traces the connections among the culture wars, narratives of race conflict surrounding the Los Angeles riots of 1992, and the national acceleration toward neoliberalism, culminating in the implementation of the North American Free Trade Agreement (NAFTA) in 1994. Beginning in Mazatlán, México, Yamashita's *Tropic of Orange* tracks the northward migration of the Tropic of Cancer. A geographical marking rendered more legible in Yamashita's speculative fiction. As the Tropic of Cancer takes on material form as a translucent and resilient filament running through an orange growing around it, the movement of that orange causes a physical disruption of space that intensifies the ramifications of both natural and manufactured borders on peoples and nations. As the "Tropic of Orange" moves north toward Los Angeles, it compresses longitudinal space, pressing otherwise disparate groups and events into closer proximity. Seven fragmented yet coalescing points of view narrate the effects of this time-space compression and, interwoven throughout the text, provide multiple, imbricated accounts of flexible accumulation that relies on flexible borders.[22] Over the course of the story, other oranges (such as Agent Orange, O. J. Simpson, and narcocitrus) also come to light, allowing Yamashita to revisit particularly dramatic examples of neoliberal practices that demonstrate how discourses of liberal multiculturalism collide with nativist rhetoric invoked to maintain inconsistent regulation of traffics across borders.

In *Tropic of Orange* the movement that Kaplan describes of "the evershifting boundaries between the domestic and the foreign" takes shape quite literally in the journey of the migrant orange. As the novel's geographical setting shifts northward to the U.S.-Mexico borderlands, its temporal location of the early 1990s urges the reader to connect *Tropic of Orange*'s spectacular events with anti-immigration legislation, pluralistic multiculturalism, U.S. neoliberalism in the form of NAFTA, and the militarization of the border, all of which function as technologies of the border. *Tropic of Orange* explores several alternative, strategic appropriations of technologies to reconfigure border operations to quite different ends. Yamashita uses speculative fiction to draw connections between and comment on the histories of empire and technology that continue to shape the material reality of the border.

Beyond the coincidence of oranges playing such pivotal roles in both Yamashita's and Kaplan's texts, reading *Tropic of Orange* and *Anarchy of Empire* alongside one another provides a helpful framework for discussing the trafficking of goods and laborers across borders and noting the flexible ways in which the border incorporates some things as domestic and renders others alien. In the construction, regulation, negotiation, and renegotiation of the border, multiple technologies come into play. While devices and machinery used for U.S. military and police regulation of the border may be the most apparent and well-funded technological manifestations at the U.S.-Mexico border, their implementation is clearly linked to other border technologies. For example, many border technologies are tested first in Iraq and Afghanistan under wartime conditions, a relationship indicative of the militarization of the border zone. Infrared, night vision, and x-ray scanning comprise a visual culture of surveillance managed by the military-(techno)industrial complex. In addition, legal infrastructure and carceral systems work in conjunction with this arsenal of equipment and become part of the border regulation machine. Beyond these more overt forms of border technologies, the social and economic policies and legislative acts that fund and support these technological apparatuses provoke mass migrations to border cities, foster the proliferation of maquiladora plants along the border, and capitalize on anti-immigration movements and xenophobic sentiments. As in Kaplan's example of the *Downes v. Bidwell* case, legislative acts, rhetorical strategies, and economic policies participate in the conceptualization and reconceptualization of the border. By calling attention to the concentration of regulatory, managerial, and biopolitical forces at work, *Tropic of Orange* underlines the ways in which disciplinary models have not given way to regulatory ones but in fact find ways to co-occupy the border.

Quarantine, Paranoia, and Militarization

We are in the habit of discarding those, and that's what should be done.
—FRANK YOUNG, U.S. Food and Drug Administration Commissioner

In March 1989, suspicion over two discolored grapes from Chile caused the U.S. government to order the destruction and/or quarantine of tens of thousands of crates of Chilean fruit. The incident arose during a time when xenophobic reactions to global terrorism had recently been stirred up in the United States. The bombing of PanAm flight 103 had occurred in the previous December, and the news media focused their coverage on emerging concerns in both public and official discourse about security during uncertain times in the Middle East.[23] The declaration by the Food and Drug Administration (FDA) that the grapes were contaminated and dangerous brought Chilean fruit exports—not only to the United States, but also to Japan and Canada—to a standstill for about a week, causing thousands of Chilean agricultural workers to lose their jobs and costing the Chilean economy millions of dollars in revenue for its second-largest export. The grape scare, now generally perceived as an overreaction on the part of the FDA, nevertheless resulted in "more stringent inspections" at shipping ports and became the occasion for Commissioner Young to urge consumers to do their part in the detection of suspicious-looking fruit.[24]

Yamashita's *Tropic of Orange* centers its border queries on a similarly impounded fruit. "It's like the Chilean grape thing but bigger," declares one character about the government's rapid crackdown on oranges suspected in the narrative to have been injected with narcotics.[25] Picked up by the media, the *"illegal alien* orange scare" (141) starts a panic, resulting in a nationwide hoarding of oranges. Both the Chilean grape scare of 1989 and the War on Oranges in Yamashita's speculative fiction propagate a risk discourse that leads to widespread paranoia, calls for more radical screening methods, and search-and-destroy practices at the border. Unlike the allegedly cyanide-filled grapes from Chile, Yamashita's oranges arrive by truck, and the government is far less successful at containing this particular kind of threat. Yamashita's narcotic-filled oranges allude to the failed War on Drugs of President George H. W. Bush's administration and its connection to another pivotal event of 1989: the U.S. invasion of Panama. "Thus, while official sources often represent the drug problem as a menace that the state is dedicated to eradicating," writes Curtis Marez in *Drug Wars*, "in recent history drug traffic has just as often served to sustain and reproduce state power."[26] Marez also offers compelling evidence of the science and technology industries' investment in sustaining the war on drugs: "The aerospace industry (which supplies drug enforcement planes, helicopters, and other technology), chemical companies (which produce the poisons that are dropped on drug fields), and the prison industry directly benefit from the drug war and hence actively lobby for its continued expansion."[27] Furthermore, drug cartels "are often equipped with extremely high-tech armaments and other technologies, sometimes more advanced than those possessed by the police forces working against them."[28]

Tropic of Orange is as much a tale about a fruit scare as it is about the paranoia cultivated around undocumented labor. Written in the wake not only of NAFTA but also of the passage of California Proposition 187 in 1994, *Tropic of Orange* conjures up tales of border-crossing fruits to interrogate the nativist sentiment and anti-immigration legislation that were redeployed in the 1990s. Yamashita's allusions to the Chilean grape scare of 1989 point to the culture of privatization, manifested in economic policy and anchored in notions of one's private responsibility to detect interlopers. After all, Proposition 187, as George Lipsitz explains, "required private citizens to become government informants, ordering doctors, nurses, teachers, social workers, and other state employees to report to immigration authorities all persons 'suspected' of living in the United States without proper documentation."[29] Citizens were no longer being asked to discard suspicious-looking, mushy grapes but to deport and "deliver excruciating pain and punishment to undocumented workers and their families."[30] The 1990s witnessed a particularly powerful wave of anti-immigrant sentiment and legislation, especially in California. Two years after Proposition 187, California Proposition 209 passed, setting the pace elsewhere for similar efforts to eradicate affirmative action at the state level. This period also gave rise to a noticeable militarization of the U.S.-Mexico border.[31] Operation Blockade/Hold the Line in El Paso, Texas, in 1993 and Operation Gatekeeper in San Diego, California, in 1994 became models for intensification of border regulation and policing that gained even more momentum after the events of 9/11.

Propositions 187 and 209 built on an already well-established base of nativist rhetoric. The two-headed beast of anti-immigration legislation and neoliberal trade agreements yields a contradiction in border fictions. Anti-immigration sentiment works in conjunction with NAFTA's effects on Mexican agriculture: workers are displaced by rapid importation of goods from the United States because local farmers cannot compete with post-NAFTA prices. María Josefina Saldaña-Portillo calls this NAFTA's "fictions of development."[32] "NAFTA," she writes, "was promulgated under the operative fiction that territorial borders could be porous to goods and capital but closed to those laborers whose impoverishment is often the result of NAFTA-style development."[33]

By investigating the multiple oranges of the novel, I suggest that Yamashita links U.S. imperialist projects in Asia and the Middle East with U.S. neocolonial enterprises in Mexico by connecting the military technologies deployed during U.S. wars abroad to surveillance technologies in place at the U.S.-Mexico border. I argue that Yamashita's dramatic remapping of the borderlands occasions a spectacular collision of transpacific and transcontinental routes in the form of the traffic jam and the stalled semi, and that each character seizes on everyday media technologies to document the suddenly visible threads of global capitalism. In defiance of the invisibility of the women of color who form the majority of the techno-labor force in Asian and Mexican manufacturing plants, Yamashita offers alternative narratives about transgressed boundaries, grids of cross-ethnic affiliation, and technologies of memory that exceed the scope of the nation.

Writing during an onslaught of simultaneous media representations of racial conflict and liberal multiculturalism in Los Angeles, Yamashita connects events such as the O. J. Simpson trial, the Rodney King verdict, and the Los Angeles riots of 1992 with debates about border regulation, immigration, and NAFTA. *Tropic of Orange* uses a rubric of transnationalism to question the formulation of multiculturalism and race relations in the national framework. The mechanism that brings all these interventions into play is that of speculation. Through fantastic revisionist cartographies, *Tropic of Orange* dramatically remaps *la frontera*. By highlighting transborder technologies such as activist radio channels and online chat rooms repurposed to conduct *sous*veillance, or surveillance from below, Yamashita's novel also offers productive ways of rethinking speculations at the border, remapping the uneven terrain of the U.S.-Mexico borderlands, and rearticulating the homeland through the intertwined labor histories of Asian and Latino migrant workers in the American Southwest.

The Orange and the Truck

Tropic of Orange deploys two border crossers—the orange and the truck—that help us examine how these interlinked technologies work to shape the border. Characterizing the orange as "an immigrant, through and through,"[34] the *Nation*'s Molly Rauch opens her review of *Tropic of Orange* with a condensed history of the orange as a migrant subject, whose transplantation roughly followed the path of empire. Columbus first transported the citrus fruit to the New World in an effort to stave off scurvy among his sailors. In an elegant mapping of the orange's transnational and transoceanic migrations, Rauch explains that oranges once grew in greatest numbers and varieties in China, and that Columbus's oranges arrived in Spain by way of India, along with the spread of Islam. Today, the United States has become the world's largest producer of oranges, and the marketing of domestic Californian navel oranges and Floridian Valencias elides the orange's longer history and attachment to the movements of empire. Yamashita's depiction of the orange as a migrant directs attention to its global peregrinations, including its navigation of U.S. imperialism in Latin America as perpetrated by the United Fruit Company and the proliferation of "banana republics" and plantation systems in Guatemala, Honduras, and Colombia in the mid-twentieth century, for example. To invoke the border crossing of fruit is to reference a century of U.S. multinational corporations wreaking economic, environmental, geographical, and political havoc in Latin America.[35] While literary attention to the United States' tropical empire often gets told through the banana (as in Gabriel García Márquez's *One Hundred Years of Solitude*), the orange works to tie the history of U.S. neocolonialism in Latin America to a more global history of migration that includes routes originating in Asia.

Due in large part to the facile relationship between the federal government and private military contractors, George W. Bush's administration put into action a high-tech Secure Border Initiative, entailing a "virtual fence" comprised of interconnected surveillance technologies such as ground sensors, live-feed cameras, unmanned aerial surveillance drones, and a series of 90-foot-tall towers to relay images to Immigration and Naturalization Service (INS) trucks and command centers. The initiative to build a 700-mile-long wall along the U.S.-Mexico border, passed by Congress in October 2006, is one recent implementation of the most literal of border technologies.

Whereas much of the rhetoric surrounding the border wall discussion revolves around national security, threat of terrorist attack, and "alien invasion," Yamashita's *Tropic of Orange* returns focus to the issue of labor—most notably: the labor that goes into building walls and other technologies that regulate border permeability; the labor rendered invisible by neoliberal discussions of free trade and unencumbered movement across borders; and the laborers who must cross the border "illegally" in order to sustain the contradictory demands for cheap labor on the one hand, and a racially consolidated national identity on the other. In *Tropic of Orange*, those who first perceive the dramatic spatial warping caused by the orange's migration north recognize the shift because they are so close to the labor of constructing such walls. In this way, global shifts register most palpably for those employed on the production side of the fence.

When the character Arcangel stops near Mazatlán to help build the wall demarcating an estate's property line, he "wondered if it wasn't a wall that could conceivably continue east and west forever. Labor for a lifetime" (149). While an exploitative capitalism might fantasize about an endless supply of cheap labor that extends east and west forever, dividing the world into owners from the Global North and workers from the Global South, Yamashita's depiction of an endless wall is one of horror from the perspective of the laborer, to whom that prospect would mean a lifetime of work. Arcangel's interface with the ever-extending wall foregrounds a laborer's concerns. From this perspective, such an elastic wall represents an eternity—a future of never-ending backbreak in the flexible future rather than a comforting sign of security.

For Rafaela Cortes, a Mexican woman in the domestic employ of a Chicano journalist's second home in Mazatlán, moving north and crossing the border constitutes a formidable struggle that seemingly defies even basic laws of physics. Her destination seems perpetually out of reach, and her burden of heavy, modern bathroom faucets picked up from the post office further encumbers her. The bathroom fixtures may be aesthetically pleasing to their owner, Gabriel, but they remind Rafaela primarily of the labor required of her: "They were modern-looking things with a sort of industrial look, the sort that Gabriel seemed to like. Rafaela was indifferent to its style. It still had a surface like any other that had to be cleaned" (68). Purchased in and mailed from the United States but "Hecho en México" (made in Mexico), the faucets serve as a reminder of how commodities flow freely across the border, manufactured by underpaid workers in Mexico who can later neither afford to buy the very products they have created nor travel with such abandon across security checkpoints. Whereas the faucets flow freely from their site of production in Mexico to their destination in the United States and then back again to Mexico for installation in a luxury home, Rafaela's movement north is contrastingly encumbered by the threat of rape and the abduction of her child.

Rafaela's precarious journey crosses the same terrain as female maquiladora workers, whose perpetual and unaccounted for disappearances since the 1980s indicate the ways in which border surveillance technologies, despite ostensibly being designed to render bodies visible, fail to trace certain subjects. The notorious conditions for female workers in border cities such as Juárez, Mexico, provide one egregious example of how surveillance technologies at the border support a system of rendering labor invisible even as they perpetuate a myth of barbarians at the gate. For the people (primarily women) whose work involves the production and manufacturing of the electronic and computer technologies installed at the border, it is unlikely that these systems of surveillance will in turn work to protect them. The promises of a better tomorrow or a secure future overlook these women whose daily lives consist of a series of dangerous presents that constantly threaten to foreclose the possibilities of futurity.

Yamashita's speculative fiction critiques these uneven relations to the future by dismantling the temporal architecture of a progressive narrative. Instead of advancing relentlessly toward a culminating moment, the plot of *Tropic of Orange* dramatically stalls out in the middle of the book; the culmination of the orange's journey is the action of coming to a screeching halt:

"A truck with a load of oranges was stalled in the street just at its narrowest place. Behind it was a line of cars and trucks and carts filled with produce, meats — dead and alive — grains, and kitchen utensils, all temporarily stalled in their progress toward the marketplace" (72).

This bottleneck of transborder flow becomes an opportunity to focus on the laboring bodies often excised from narratives of free trade. The traffic jam sets the conditions out of which emerge the impossible heroics of Arcangel, a character of epic proportions: "In each hand flashed a large metal hook. . . . When the cable was in place, Arcangel secured both ends to the two hooks and drew the hooks through the very skin of his body, through the strangely scarred lobes at the sides of his torso. He moved slowly forward until the entire contraption was taut, until he was harnessed securely as an ox to its plough" (73–74).

Arcangel's pulling the truck to free up traffic and the pulling of the Tropic of Cancer across the border are speculative acts threaded together with the enchanted orange. As if inspired by the performance artist Guillermo Gómez-Peña, Arcangel hooks his body into the body of the eighteen-wheeler, where the body of the worker is no longer stowed away in the cargo of the truck but out in the open, making border crossing visible through cyborg performance.[36] At the very moment when one type of transborder technology has broken down, Yamashita presents her audience with this fantastic deconstruction of the other laboring bodies whose travel across and existence at the border can be much more perilous.

When Yamashita describes in spectacular and visceral terms the labor of Arcangel pulling the semi across the border, she reinserts the physicality of laboring bodies back into the U.S.-Mexico border. Arcangel's spectacular labor evokes a feeling of inescapable immanence, enchainment to the materiality of the body and to the historical past as bound to his experience. Tethering the human and the truck performs the agential entanglements of alienated labor and calls forth the question of what it means to matter. Arcangel's performance suggests a formulation of labor as it exceeds the human (he is also an ox, angel, and engine). He is what Gómez-Peña might call a "border brujo," a supernatural figuration that invokes the possibility of a politics that crosses biopolitical and national fields.

Tropic of Orange is more generally a story of entanglements. As Arcangel, Bobby, Rafaela, Gabriel, and the novel's other protagonists discover how their movements are inextricable from those of the border itself, the novel renders the space at once palpable and elastic. The human characters' cross-border movements become enfolded with not only the border itself, but also the various national economies and cultural exchanges they must negotiate to subsist. These entangled movements of peoples, goods, oranges, trucks, money, and other materials may well be theorized by feminist physicist Karen Barad's description of quantum dis/continuity and diffraction: "There is no overarching sense of temporality, of continuity, in place. Each scene diffracts various temporalities within and across the field of spacetimemattering. Scenes never rest, but are reconfigured within, dispersed across, and threaded through one another. The hope is that what comes across in this dis/jointed movement is a felt sense of différance, of *intra-activity*, of agential separability—differentiatings that cut together/apart—that is the hauntological nature of quantum entanglements."[37]

Barad theorizes entanglement at the quantum scale of the electron as a "way of thinking with and through dis/continuity."[38] Threading Barad's description of quantum entanglement through Yamashita's figuration of a border-crossing orange provides a provocative reimagining of transborder movement as a quantum leap: "A cut that is itself cross-cut. . . . A passable impassability . . . an im-passe (from the Latin *a-poria*), but one that can't contain that which it would hold back . . . a means of getting through, without getting over, without burrowing through. . . . Identity undone by a discontinuity at the heart of matter itself."[39] The aesthetics of diffraction in Yamashita's novel—the bullets that bend in space, the fence that seems to extend to the never-ending horizon, the kidnappers who never quite reach Rafaela in the car, the laboriousness of crossing a street that seems to distend in the middle—substantiate a reading of the borderlands that renders discrete notions of homeland and nation impossible. The analogy has its limits, though, for when one scales up the quantum to the scale of human organ trafficking, of semis stuck in traffic, the obstinate impermeability of the border pushes the quantum back into the distant horizon as sheer potentiality.

To examine the inconsistency of border regulation more closely, Yamashita tugs at the geographical fabric of the U.S.-Mexico borderlands. She begins this speculative work with the Tropic of Cancer, "a border made plain by the sun itself, a border one can easily recognize" rather than a border drawn by "plotting men" (71). Yamashita's quick pun on "plotting men" refers to the scheming of imperialist cartographers who, as Mary Louise Pratt astutely observed, feminized depictions of the New World as a land that empire had not yet penetrated.[40] Rafaela, who is able to perceive the dramatic shifts that the Tropic of Orange sets in motion, positions herself as an interpreter of geographies rather than an object of them. Yamashita rejects the practice of mapping the world onto a sexualized representation of a woman of color's body. Instead, *Tropic of Orange* is a story whose geography remains in constant motion, evading the fixating and fetishizing of the imperialist cartographer. Yamashita also puns on the narrative "plot" lines that follow unidirectional, linear trajectories to suggest progress and development. To emphasize the intersectionality and overlapping narratives at work in her novel, she offers alongside a more conventional table of contents a matrix of "HyperContexts," in which a list of characters forms one axis and a set of weekdays forms the other. On this graph, a reader could plot her own course through the novel, choosing to jump from chapter 4 to chapter 13 to stay with a certain character for a while, or to plot the points when or where the characters' movements intersect. The move from a table of contents to this matrix reconfigures a reader's relation to the space-time of the novel. Whereas one might be trained to read from front to back, the HyperContexts page invites other reading practices and understandings of movement.

Above all, though, Yamashita's imagining of these cartographical filaments suggests an elasticity of borders that responds to the constantly shifting and contested dynamics of social power. In the midst of Arcangel's revelatory dream, in which he comes to understand the connection between the orange and the Tropic of Cancer, he perceives the orange as "rolling away to a space between ownership and the highway" (71). The orange, taken from private land in Mexico to the public thoroughfare of a highway that continues across national borders, provides Yamashita with the primary plot device through which to explore an imperfect system of transnational trafficking, where products and labor slip between owners on conduits that cannot be wholly governed, controlled, or policed, no matter the lengths state, national, and international regulations go to do so.

In the chapter "The Hour of the Trucks," these slippery shipments of commerce and labor are carefully followed and interpreted through Manzanar Murakami, a Japanese American who orchestrates and conducts fantastical symphonies from the rumblings of traffic coursing through the concrete spaghetti below his perch on a Los Angeles freeway overpass. It is through Manzanar's perspective that "the beastly size of semis, garbage trucks, moving vans, and concrete mixers" takes on the characteristics of "the largest monsters of the animal kingdom" whose "purpose was to transport the great products of civilization: home and office appliances, steel beams and turbines, fruits, vegetables, meats, and grain, Coca-Cola and Sparkletts, Hollywood sets, this fall's fashions, military hardware, gasoline, concrete, and garbage. Nothing was more or less important. And it was all moving here and there, back and forth, from the harbor to the train station to the highway to the warehouse to the airport to the docking station to the factory to the dump site" (119–20). *Tropic of Orange* locates the confluence of these commercial traffics at a freeway interchange in Los Angeles, where the scene of trucks in gridlock provides the occasion for Yamashita's critique of neoliberal globalization and "free trade" on the freeways.

Early versions of border patrol in Texas first targeted Chinese migrants hoping to cross the border from Mexico to the U.S. in search of work after the Chinese Exclusion Act of 1882 came into effect.[41] As Claudia Sadowski-Smith documents, the passing of this anti-Asian legislation first institutionalized the category of the illegal immigrant in U.S. border discourse.[42] The process of rendering migrants as alien subjects emerged as part of a matrix of U.S. racializations that sought to manage the variable flows of Asian and Latino migration at the U.S.-Mexico border during the early twentieth century.

Asian American scholars, by reinvigorating attention to Asian migrations to Latin America, have intervened in the understanding of the region as a historical site of only European colonial encounters. More specifically, historians such as Julia Camacho, Jason Oliver Chang, Konrad Chang, Evelyn Hu-Dehart, Erika Lee, and Eleanor Ty, all work on reformulating the transpacific borderlands. This legacy of Asian immigration to the United States by way of Latin America is a history that Yamashita addresses in both *Through the Arc of the Rain Forest* and *Tropic of Orange*. In the latter, she narrates this set of migrations primarily through the character of Bobby Ngu, whom she introduces through the voice of a Chicano in Koreatown: "If you know your Asians, you look at Bobby. You say, that's Vietnamese. . . . If you know your Asians. Turns out you'll be wrong. And you gonna be confused. Dude speaks Spanish. Comprende? So you figure it's one of those Japanese from Peru. Or maybe Korean from Brazil. Or Chinamex. . . . Bobby's Chinese. Chinese from Singapore with a Vietnam name speaking like a Mexican living in Koreatown" (15).

In her description of all the kinds of Asian-Latino migrant that Bobby is not, Yamashita provides a brief litany of multiple histories of Asian migration to Latin America. Bobby's experience of crossing many borders also shows up in Yamashita's depiction of his being perpetually in motion: "He don't have time to tell stories. Too busy. Never stops. Got only a little time to sleep even. Always working. Hustling. Moving. . . . Sorts mail nonstop. Tons of it. Never stops" (16). For his day job, Bobby sorts mail at a large newspaper. A deft sorter, Bobby navigated his way to the United States through the cracks of such institutional sorting. In 1975, he and his brother slipped into a refugee camp in Singapore, where U.S. soldiers presumed them to be Vietnamese orphans, rendered mute by the war. Interpellated into a U.S. narrative about Vietnamese refugees, the two boys obtain U.S. passports and gain overseas passage under the name Ngu (significant because Bobby's father sends them off to "start a future all new" [15] when a U.S.-owned multinational corporation puts their family out of business in Singapore). Already marked by U.S. empire at multiple points in his migration to the Americas, Bobby repeatedly encounters the divisions of U.S. policy: first, when he and his wife, Rafaela Cortes, must negotiate the border between them; and second, when Bobby must help his cousin cross the border after being smuggled by boat to Mexico. The story of Bobby, with its connections to Mexico (by his marriage to Rafaela), the border (through his task of smuggling his cousin across it), and Asia (in his childhood of shifting national affiliations), reminds us that the border has always been shaped by the negotiations of power on multiple fronts.

The filaments that run through the various story lines of *Tropic of Orange* constitute a much more intricate account of how the U.S.-Mexico border comes into being through transnational and multiple border histories. Yamashita connects these narrative strands through technologies of memory. In one sense, characters communicate with each other across space, using recording devices, broadcast media, and online community uplinks. They share experiences of negotiating U.S. empire and racializations at work both abroad and domestically. In other words, these seven interwoven narratives connect via material technologies that circumvent the divisive strategies of the border and by collectively producing a cultural memory of the borderlands that defies the divisive strategies of U.S. racial discourse.

The Vietnam War, for example, shapes the conditions of Bobby's childhood and migration to the Americas, and it also looms over the past of Buzzworm, an African American Vietnam veteran and self-described "Angel of Mercy" to his community. Geographically, Bobby and Buzzworm navigate downtown Los Angeles, Buzzworm beginning his narrative at Jefferson and

Normandie and Bobby starting out from Pico and Union, just on the other side of the freeway. Also, in a novel about oranges, Vietnam and South Central Los Angeles intersect in the shadow of the use of Agent Orange and the car chase and subsequent trial of O. J. Simpson (highly mediated events about race and technologies of visibility).[43] The specter of war also looms over the character of Manzanar, whose memory of internment as a Japanese American during World War II is triggered when the Tropic of Orange crosses his path.

Another cross-racial, technological link Yamashita makes is between Gabriel Balboa, a newspaper reporter stylized after Chicano activist Rubén Salazar, and Emi, a Japanese American TV news reporter. When Gabriel ends up in El Zócalo, Mexico, he uploads genealogies of revolutionaries for the Zapatista movement, streaming data to Emi in Los Angeles. While investigating the black-market traders in infant organs threatening Rafaela and her son Sol, he creates and monitors online newsgroups, which he calls a "net of loose threads" in which he might catch a bit of information (246). In his research on drug-infused oranges that incite a panic about fruit and borders in the United States, Gabriel follows a paper trail of shipments that do not follow "the normal route" but instead move from Brazil to Honduras, Guatemala, and Mexico and then to the United States. He discovers "a bunch of bureaucratic papers to make transactions look legal, to make the connections fuzzy." We find ourselves tracing the hidden routes not just of global oranges but also of hidden labor. "The invisibility of those who fingered the threads mocked my every move," Gabriel notes: "I wasn't going to get this story right away, but I'd get it eventually. After all, it was my story." At first pursuing the story of smuggled produce, he follows the hidden labor behind the free flow of capital in an era when documentation for illicit commodities can be easier to manufacture than paperwork for migrant workers:

> International crime cartels with access to satellite tracking devices. Tracking illegal merchandise in dozens of cities. . . . Conceivably, there was a villain at the beginning and end of every signal. Multiple uplinks and downlinks to a constellation of satellites. But who was tracking all this? The commerce was on the ground; the threads pulling them around were in the air. . . . The cartel, if that was what it was, was a big invisible net. If I had a strategy, it would be to get in there and snarl the net without entangling myself. (247)

Characterized as "truly noir, a neuromancer in dark space," Gabriel becomes a technojournalist, himself linked into networks on the ground and in the air (245). Like Bobby (mail envoy and Singaporean coyote), Buzzworm (radio savant and community organizer), Rafaela (domestic worker and border crosser), Emi (television news anchor and renegade broadcaster), and Manzanar (freeway conductor and homeless internment survivor), Gabriel reports not only on the visible but also the invisible filaments that connect the Americas and the Pacific Rim.

Tropic of Orange offers a counternarrative to the liberal vision of a multicultural Los Angeles that works through rendering labor invisible or at least abstract and "forgetting" histories of exclusion and racialization.[44] Yamashita's retelling of these histories of migration brings together Los Angeles's Asian American, African American, and Mexican American populations around shared experiences of being crossed by border technologies and suggests that these populations also have connected histories of citizenship curtailed by a state that reaps the benefits of cheap labor and an uneven international trade system. In *Tropic of Orange*, Yamashita connects the primarily lateral transatlantic and transpacific routes of ships to the transamerican, North-South routes of trucks. Her cartographic reconfiguration situates the history of the U.S.-Mexico border within a more transnational framework of imperial dynamics, including the traces of U.S. empire-building in Asia, which occasioned an influx of Chinese, Japanese, and Korean immigrants to both Southern California and Northern Mexico. Yamashita structures her speculative fiction under this rubric of intersectionality through her HyperContexts matrix, which makes visible the conjunctural relations between the geographical locations of Koreatown, Tijuana, and Singapore and also between the temporal beats of news reporting, performance art, and palm reading. In Yamashita's revisionist cartographies, the borderlands constitute a matrix of hypertextual associations informed by imbricated histories of alien exclusion acts, internment and deportation, 1990s anti-immigration policies, and the use of black and Latino military labor during U.S. wars in Asia, for example. In its fantastic literalization of a flexible border, its consideration of border politics and discourse as magically real, and its positing of strategies of remembering that exceed official narratives of the border, *Tropic of Orange* deploys speculative fiction itself as a technology.

Dealing in Sleep, Trading in Futures

In "A Visible Border," the third part of his 2002 series of film shorts titled the *Borders Trilogy*, filmmaker and new media artist Alex Rivera investigates surveillance technologies at work at the border, developed by American Science & Engineering, Inc. The entire length of the film is preoccupied with one image, which is at first unintelligible but is eventually revealed to be the x-ray image of a semi containing a shipment of bananas and a concealed container of human laborers on their way to the United States. It is important to note that the opening orientation of the image is upside-down, purposefully defamiliarizing what viewers will eventually come to identify as a human head. The eerie, filmy outlines generated by the x-ray impart a certain ghostly appearance on the image, and the human bodies pictured are rendered alien and spectral by the transparency of their bodies. As the camera spirals and simultaneously zooms out from the image, a voice-over of a market analyst explains the x-ray technologies that produced it and the occasion for its application. For over a decade, the company called American Science & Engineering has provided the U.S. government with the technology to x-ray trucks crossing the border between Mexico and the United States with the explicit purpose of separating desirable and undesirable subjects. Rivera's filming of this still image directs our attention to the ways this policing technology renders certain bodies alien. Yet his insistence on using new media and film technologies to issue these critiques is significant. He is unwilling to capitulate the terrain of technocultural production as something that only serves state or capitalist enterprises. The spectator must question the mechanisms through which we come to assimilate subjects into our visual understanding.

Sleep Dealer could be considered the outgrowth of Rivera's 1997 science fiction film short *Why Cybraceros?*, in which the multimedia artist first plays with the idea of cyborg labor: "all the labor without the worker."[45] Taking up the *cybracero* (cyber migrant worker) figure, who can "jack in" and operate machines remotely from *el otro lado* (the other side), Rivera's feature-length film *Sleep Dealer* intervenes at a later moment in the neoliberalization of the border, when the maquila industry, a decade or so later, has firmly implemented NAFTA in the economic and ecological systems of the borderlands. By 2008, when the film was released, the INS had been absorbed into the larger entity of the Department of Homeland Security, and SIGMA had already pulled up a chair to its table.

While there are continuities across the border discourses in the late 1980s and early 1990s of risk, terror, and insecurity exemplified by the War on Drugs and the rhetorical flash points of the War on Terror and post-9/11 anxieties about the border, one significant difference between the two moments resides in the role of spectacle in producing the conditions of exception. Spectacle and speculation share etymological derivations from the Latin *spectare*, meaning to see or behold. Given the pivotal role that spectacle plays in the formation of a homeland security state, it is perhaps fitting that a post-9/11 critical border speculation such as Rivera's *Sleep Dealer* speaks back to its historical moment through visual culture.

New biometric technologies along the border facilitate the proliferation of identificatory systems, including passports with radio-frequency identification tags and facial recognition software at border checkpoints. The implementation of such technologies in the U.S. risk society accelerates alongside vigilante border militias such as the Minutemen, as well as myriad police dramas like CSI, 24, *Person of Interest*, and *Hawaii Five-O*, which conscript audience members (already conveniently primed by the "scopic drive" of televisual engagement)[46] to become citizen-detectives taking part in an ongoing battle to secure the homeland through surveillance systems tailored to the amateur user.

Sleep Dealer introduces us to a near-future borderlands, in which the border itself has been officially closed because technology has supplied the means to effect a neoliberal fantasy of extracting cheap and disposable labor from the Global South without those bodies ever crossing the border physically. Maquiladoras still exist but in the form of "sleep dealers"—vast factories where workers "jack in" virtually via data port implants called "nodes" to remote-controlled jobs in the North. The protagonist Memo Cruz makes his way from his "dry, dusty, disconnected" town in the southern state of Oaxaca, Mexico to Tijuana where he hopes to find work remotely driving a cab in London or a high-rise construction robot in San Diego. Though off-site, this work remains precarious in that electrical surges can leave plugged-in laborers blind, disabled, or dead. Working hours are not regulated. "Sometimes," Memo's opening voice-over discloses, "during long shifts, we'd hallucinate . . . [and] if you work long enough, you collapse."

Though node technology has significantly changed the realms of labor and leisure (nodes also facilitate more direct access to pleasure receptors), the near-future landscapes of everyday San Diego, Tijuana, and Oaxaca depicted in the film reflect modest yet notably uneven degrees and areas of technological change. The shiniest new tech radiates around corporate interests and military defense—two arenas that find themselves increasingly enmeshed in this future because privatization and remote securitization feed one another's needs. Remote-controlled automatic weapons guard local water sources, and biometric scanners monitor and control people's access to work and home. Meanwhile, Tijuana's infrastructure remains ramshackle: factory workers still occupy makeshift shelters on the hills surrounding the city, but door latches have given way to biometric scanning devices. While an army of surveillance cameras and automated weapons guard the local water supply, Memo gets jumped and robbed when he goes to an unmonitored back alley to find a *coyotek* to implant his black-market nodes.

In these ways, *Sleep Dealer* demonstrates its preoccupations with the politics of futurity. The film offers bookend pieces of dialogue to signal this self-conscious problematic of narrating the future. At the beginning of the film, Memo helps his father bring water to the family *milpa*, that ancient technology of Mayan agriculture where cultivating the right mix of maize, beans, and squash produces a mostly self-sustaining plot of land. Though Memo, who is an amateur hacker enthusiast, criticizes his father for not knowing "the world is bigger than this milpa," his father explains that the milpa is an investment in the future. "Is our future a thing of the past?" he asks Memo. "No. We had a future. You're standing on it. When they dammed up the river . . . they cut off our future. You weren't even born yet. You don't know how that felt." Linking the corporate privatization of Mexico's water supply to a colonization of the future, Memo's Papa hopes to secure a future by clinging to an agrarian past. The film, though, is careful not to over-romanticize this past, posing instead a critique to organizing a politics around mythical homelands that get taken up by primitivist racializations of brown people as naturally closer to an agrarian past. The film ends with Memo's concluding voice-over: "But maybe there's a future for me here. On the edge of everything. A future with a past. If I connect. And fight." The film refuses to relinquish the realm of technology and the worlding of futurity to corporate discourses of innovation and science fiction writers working on behalf of the Department of Defense. Instead, *Sleep Dealer* argues for and instantiates the production of alternative futures that fight against not only obsolescence but also obfuscations of the past that pave the way for the colonization of the future.

Sleep Dealer brings to bear one pivotal component of critical speculation: transnational collaboration. It is the transborder coalition of Memo the *cybracero*, Rudy the Chicano drone pilot, and Luz the online storyteller that facilitates the eventual takedown of the dam that stole Memo's father's dreams of a future. This team of activists connects through the shared means of their labor. While working for a sleep dealer requires the physical transformation of laboring bodies through nodal implants into tissue, blood, and nervous systems, remote-controlled work also exists north of the border. Drone pilot Rudy Ramirez, whom we first encounter at the Del Rio Security Headquarters in San Diego, "works at protecting the assets of Del Rio Water." Piloting a drone plane also requires Rudy to obtain nodes, and in this way, the film marks his labor. Rudy's first mission sends him to eliminate a "terrorist target," which turns out to be Memo's hacker listening device in Santa Ana del Río. Facial recognition technology and profiling systems overseeing Rudy's mission identify Memo's father as a suspect terrorist. Rudy obeys his order to kill Memo's father, and the ensuing compunction he feels for his actions sends him searching online for traces of what he obliterated. The search brings Rudy to Luz, who is a writer selling her memories of Memo to TRUNODE, "the world's number 1 memory market." Luz's creative process also requires her to have nodes, as TRUNODE invests only in true stories, monitored and regulated through nodes by a "bio-thentication" process akin to an extreme lie detector test. Rudy explains his interest in Luz's stories about Memo by expressing their connection to remote labor. "It's interesting to know that he's a node worker. I'm a node worker, too," Rudy says, linking the three protagonists via these connective biotechnologies.

The conditions that bring Memo, Rudy, and Luz to their work also inform their future collaboration. Rudy understands his work at the Del Rio Security Headquarters to be a form of military service. He explains: "My mom and dad went military, so I'm following in their footsteps." A Mexican American born to parents who both served in the U.S. military, Rudy becomes part of a longer history of Chicano soldiers who fought in Vietnam and Korea as one way to secure an education, work, and/or citizenship in a country that perpetually seeks to evict, deport, or incarcerate Chicanos. Despite his pride in his family's military service, it is this state-level contradictory logic of recruiting some while executing others that cannot sustain itself after Rudy sees someone like his own father in his face-to-face encounter with Memo's father, who has been misidentified as an enemy of the state.

We also understand that Luz sells her memories to TRUNODE to pay down her student loans, which, she is notified, are in severe default. Student loans constitute a capitalist infrastructure for financing education; they instantiate financial speculation in that loans are issued with the expectation that the student has a lucrative future. The moral bankruptcy of lending institutions that bank on students not being able to repay their loans except at exorbitant interest rates shadows Luz's venture into writing for TRUNODE. She calls her collection of stories "El Otro Lado del Mundo" (The other side of the world), a title that announces not only a Third World perspective but also resonates with the science fiction genre of the film in which her character appears. Amid this coagulation of various forms of speculation, Luz's labor of compiling and curating her memories must also be understood as speculative in nature. The visualizations of her creative process reappear across Rivera's film as well, as if *Sleep Dealer* itself works like a TRUNODE story. *Sleep Dealer* asserts this continuity across Luz's TRUNODE memory collection and the film's aesthetic choices to enact the practice of producing futures with pasts.

Sleep Dealer capitalizes on the speculative genre by blurring the distinction between realism and fantasy, taking on the dreamlike qualities of the state between waking and sleeping. The dissolves bleed like watercolors, a seemingly impossible medium for telling the story of the parched, drought-enforced landscape Mexico has become in this future where multinational corporations based in the United States have privatized and militarized the regulation of water through a system of dams and aqueducts.

The hacker sensibility that emerges from the cross-border cooperation works against state uses of technology, and the cinematography articulates this contrast between on-the-ground, pedestrian tactics and the more surveillant modality of looking from the top down. In his essay "Walking in the City," Michel de Certeau theorizes the difference between, on the one hand, the vantage point from the top of the World Trade Center, which offers a god's-eye view of the city's ordered grid, and, on the other hand, the pedestrian acts of the passer-by whose movements position the walker in constantly changing relation to the surrounding city.[47] In *Sleep Dealer*, the drone that pursues supposed terrorists and enemies of the state is equipped with "Fly-Eye Cameras," and a reality TV show uses these images to articulate a narrative about "blowing the hell out of the bad guys." Rudy, who flies on behalf of the U.S. military in the service of the Del Rio Water Corporation, has the ability to "see every angle of the action" through these cameras, which are enlisted to deliver this flying superhero perspective—what de Certeau calls a "voyeur-god" perspective[48]—to viewers of the show DRONES!

The scene cycles rapidly among several cameras at play. We cut from the DRONES! footage to a shot of Memo and his brother watching the show on their television set in Mexico, to the pilot's-eye view of the ground from the drone, to Rudy's targeting system screen, to a shot of the live audience silhouetted against a large screen playing the show. The reality TV show invites its at-home audience, including Memo and his brother, to participate in the spectacle of pursuing and eradicating supposed bad guys. Through these practices of looking, the DRONES! audience members occupy a policing gaze. Even Memo and his brother join Rudy in the cockpit, right up to the moment when they themselves become part of the show, running toward their home, which is about to be mistaken as a terrorist threat and destroyed. As the two brothers race home, they move from the space of the spectator to the space of the spectacle. At this point, it becomes clear that Rudy and the television audience cannot possibly see every angle of the action; theirs is not a perfect or all-seeing vision. The only camera that follows the brothers on foot as they sprint and stumble across the desert is Rivera's camera, which reorients our gaze from that of the voyeur-god-drone to that which hovers at foot level, where we witness urgency and helpless haste. From this vantage point—the viewing position of Rivera's film—so-called reality has suffered a glaring case of misperception. Memo may be a hacker to the extent that he has retooled a radio to eavesdrop on other people's conversations, but he is an innocuous listener, not a terrorist threat.

In an earlier scene, we see that Rivera's cameras follow Memo and his father as they wind their way through the dried riverbed canyon to get to the Del Rio dam. To walk with Memo through the river canyon evacuated of its water, its local livelihood, and its past is to maintain a stubborn resistance to the Del Rio vision of consolidated water and power, guarded by guns and security cameras that see in Santa Ana only a blur of desert to be exploited. As *Sleep Dealer* bounces between drone cameras and more pedestrian perspectives, we in turn must come to terms with the ironic fantasy of reality TV and the gritty realism of science fiction film. In DRONES! reality helps fabricate the state's fantasy of risk and terror at the border, while *Sleep Dealer* uses science fiction to interrogate the mediated production of terror and imminent threat.

Through its cinematographic and narrative interventions, *Sleep Dealer* highlights the need for on-the-ground hacker coalitions in lieu of technology imposed from above. By playing with the dynamics of spectatorship throughout the film, Rivera critiques the state's use of technology, even as the film itself remains invested in technology as a tool that can be creatively repurposed. The film disrupts narratives of progress and U.S. exceptionalism by laying bare the fabricated tensions between reality and fantasy in the state's efforts to heighten securitization and the proliferation of military technologies at the border.

Refusing to relinquish technology as a site under the purview of the state, science fictions such as Rivera's *Sleep Dealer* work to reclaim the ever important imaginative terrain of speculation, of futurity, so as to contest the ways in which capitalism has already bought, sold, and parceled the future into portions of risk to be managed, waves of fear to be stemmed, and threats of terror to be contained. The notion of "homeland security" pivots on an imagining of the future that demands the assessment of risk and projections of threat. Rivera's science fiction, employing a kind of critical speculation, provides a useful way to reimagine both homeland and futurity.

This chapter has focused on the California borderlands by dint of the two cultural texts that anchor the conversation. However, I want to conclude it with the broader space-time configuration of the borderlands that includes Arizona and New Mexico as two more places where science and fiction collide. Proximate to the U.S.-Mexico border as well as the Isleta, Laguna, and Sandia Pueblos, U.S. Southwest locations like Albuquerque, New Mexico constitute what Alex Lubin has called a "transnational crossroads," entangled in "multiple legacies of colonialism."[49] One of these crossroads is that of military science and science fiction at sites like Los Alamos and Area 51, as well as all the nuclear testing sites and waste repositories in between—which Joseph Masco has named the "nuclear borderlands."[50] Like the Los Angeles basin, the U.S. Southwest also harbors an intense conjuncture of science, industry, and military interests that generates speculative fictions of the multiple kinds this project engages.

One of the most chillingly iconic sites of science's collusion with U.S. military aggression, Los Alamos is a national laboratory installed on behalf of national security. Operated either entirely or in part by the University of California since its establishment in 1942, the laboratory represents how scientific research affiliated with institutions of higher education bumps up against state and military interests.⁵¹ In addition to Los Alamos, New Mexico—called the Land of Enchantment on its license plates—is also home to the White Sands Missile Range, where the first testing of the atomic bomb occurred and when Robert Oppenheimer invoked the Bhagavad Gita in saying: "Now I am become Death, the destroyer of worlds." This meeting of science and myth is amplified at another site in the U.S. Southwest: Area 51, a tightly guarded, secretive military base in southern Nevada around which rumors of UFO sightings and conspiracy theories accumulate with ongoing zeal, fascination, and horror. Protected by one of the last remnants of the Internal Security Act of 1950 (also known as the McCarran Act), officials at Area 51, along with those at Guantánamo Bay, retain the authority to detain and use deadly force on suspicious subjects crossing its borders. Though much of this McCarthy-era legislation has been repealed, its legacy of emergency detention clauses was recently resuscitated during President George W. Bush's War on Terror.

I began this chapter with a discussion of SIGMA and homeland security, and I now conclude by connecting Area 51, the science fictions that surround it, and the McCarren Act's capitalization on discourses of emergency. These conjunctures of science fiction and national security rely on discourses of emergency as part of a risk management program designed to extract profit from projections of an ever-susceptible border. In her analysis of "shock doctrines" and "disaster capitalism," Klein provides a close reading of the document that originally called the Department of Homeland Security into being. This alarmist text declares: "Today's terrorists can strike at any place, at any time, and with virtually any weapon."⁵² Designed to incite fear and panic that would provide the occasion to securitize against looming uncertainties—or, as Klein puts it, to protect against "every imaginable risk in every conceivable place at every possible time"⁵³—the document invokes a homeland against which it plots a simultaneously abstracted and racialized terrorist threat. These border speculations seek to turn a profit on imaginable risks and yoke military mobilization and financial speculation in the way the Bush administration "played the part of the free-spending venture capitalist" in the wake of 9/11 as it encouraged the proliferation of security-oriented lobbying firms—whose numbers grew from 2 in 2001 to 543 in 2006.⁵⁴ The preemptive logics that undergird financial derivatives markets also sustain the profitable growth of the military-tech industry in the name of homeland futurity.

3

SPECULATION AND THE SPECULUM
Surrogations of Futurity

An image from the cover story of a November 2008 issue of the *New York Times Magazine* instigated a series of debates on the assisted fertility blogosphere.¹ The original article about surrogacy, titled "Her Body, My Baby: My Adventures with a Surrogate Mom," was written by Alex Kuczynski and has been characterized as an "unapologetic" and "honest" narrative of an upper-class white woman's hiring of a financially struggling surrogate mother from Harleysville, Pennsylvania.² The story and accompanying image, which features a well-manicured Kuczynski standing in front of her well-manicured summer home and lawn in the Hamptons, received more than four hundred comments online before the *New York Times* shut down the conversation. Kuczynski's story garnered attention not only because of her confessional style—she admits that she was "happy to exploit [her] last few months of nonmotherhood by white-water rafting down Level 10 rapids on the Colorado River, racing down a mountain at 60 miles per hour at ski-racing camp, drinking bourbon and going to the Super Bowl"— but also because of the double page spread title and image, which positions Kuczynski holding her blue-eyed son, while the baby's nurse, Margo Clements (a woman of color), stands to the side, in a white uniform, eyes on the child rather than engaging the camera. While clearly not meant to be the focus of the image, Clements nevertheless remains an important part of the story of reproductive labor.³ Though Clements was not the surrogate mother in this arrangement, she, as the baby's nurse, enables Kuczynski's ability to participate in a privileged lifestyle of leisure activities and social events. While Kuczynski describes how hiring a surrogate felt "liberating" from "the burdens of pregnancy," even after the baby was born, the political economy that underpinned the surrogacy continues to run through Kuczynski's relationship to Clements as nanny.

While the term "reproductive labor," as formulated by Karl Marx and Friedrich Engels, and given nuance by feminist scholars like Arlie Hochschild, sets out to name the often overlooked, gendered division of labor in the domestic sphere, the case of surrogacy as well as other assisted reproductive technologies that often travel across class and racial differences, sheds light on reproductive labor in its biopoliticized form. In its twenty-first-century iteration, reproductive labor must also include new world orders of fertilization, gestation, and birth. Under the aegis of ART, reproductive labor has come to fall on the bodies of poor women from the Global South in even more biologically entangled ways.

International surrogacy agencies, specializing in connecting affluent parents on the assisted fertility market with so-called wombs for rent, have come to roost in Anand, a town in the state of Gujarat, India. The Akanksha Infertility Clinic in Anand cares for a booming population of local women pregnant with the children of couples from the United States, Britain, Taiwan, and Japan. Commercial surrogacy, made legal in India in 2002, remains largely unregulated, though in 2015 the Assisted Reproductive Technology Bill proposed banning foreign intending parents and restricting surrogacy services to Indian couples, or foreigners married to Indian citizens. Renamed the Surrogacy (Regulation) Bill in 2016, this debated piece of legislation will be heading before Indian Parliament as this book goes to press. If passed, it will ban commercial surrogacy in India and set a precedent for other countries like Cambodia, where the transnational surrogacy industry has yielded a high potential for both fast-growing profit and rampant exploitation.⁴

The promise of transnational surrogacy—the futures that industry holds up—must be understood as projections that concatenate from a biopolitical field already made uneven by histories of empire and exploitation of laboring brown bodies. Given that one of the promises of cross-racial surrogacy is that a surrogate, no matter what her phenotypical presentation, will not affect the racial profile of the infant to be delivered, an understanding of the racial dynamics of transracial surrogacy needs to consider the history of antimiscegenation laws and beliefs that racialized imperialist architectures so often put into place at moments of contact or conquest. Understanding this history might prove useful in understanding how transnational surrogacy arrangements profit from not only a racialized past but also the potentiality of a racist future.

This chapter focuses its inquiry around the migrant futures that emerge from the conjuncture of speculative economics and reproductive technologies—of speculation and the speculum—where the futures markets and narratives emerging around reproductive technologies exploit the lives of women of color who have very little recourse to earnings comparable to what the global fertility market offers them for the renting of their wombs. Interrogating the connections among personhood, reproduction, labor, and futurity, I examine the discourses as well as the material transactions of economic futures as they inform a racialized reproductive futurity.

In addition to the Kuczynski story, other popular media narratives about transnational surrogacy and assisted reproductive technologies have surfaced in the early twenty-first century. Putting the transnational surrogacy industry in conversation with more domestic discussions about race and ARTs, I unpack the popular mediatization of Nadya Suleman's pregnancy and birth of octuplets. Referred to in the headlines as "Octomom," Nadya Suleman stood at the center of a highly racialized set of public debates about labor, risk, care, contracts, ownership, and insurance. The racial production of Octomom points to a larger story about the racialization of reproductive futurities, particularly as those narrative futures get delivered alongside the material asymmetries of the global ART market.

These contemporary conditions emerge from a longer history of racialized reproduction under slavery and empire, when the presupposition of a universal human subject was built around the exclusion and exploitation of people of color who were denied the rights of liberal humanism. One cultural text that picks up on this history is the high-profile, Hollywood film *Children of Men* (2006). Directed by the Mexican filmmaker Alfonso Cuarón, *Children of Men* projects onto the silver screen a dystopian future in which eighteen years of unexplained infertility has led to a reproduction crisis. Set in near-future England, the storyline places the burden of reproduction on the body of a black female refugee named Kee, who is discovered to be pregnant and therefore carrying the future of humankind. I investigate what histories haunt this film to unpack the complicated and sometimes contradictory meanings elicited from Cuarón's casting of a black woman in this role—a choice made all the more noticeable because, in P. D. James's novel on which the film is based, the main black female character is the midwife, not the child-bearer herself. I again draw on Avery Gordon's formulation of haunting as a "transformative recognition" to read the "ghostly matters" conjured both purposively and unwittingly in Cuarón's film.[5] I argue that by forcing our attention on certain background scenes and emphasizing moments of interruption and disorientation in the hero's journey, Cuarón opens a space for critically encountering the apparitions of torture, state-sponsored violence, and surveillance that inhabit and puncture our experience of the central plot. I also argue, though, that the film asks us to feel this haunting primarily through the experiences of a character who, though affected and depressed by the repressive systems around him, is not directly targeted by them.

Like the Octomom story, *Children of Men* is a racialized narrative about reproduction and technology that comes into popular circulation at the beginning of the twenty-first century. While Octomom takes shape as a cultural text through press coverage, tabloid speculations, and online posts of people's opinions and comments, *Children of Men* is a big-budget film adaptation of James's dystopian novel, perhaps more overtly connected to science fiction. The public narrative constructed around Suleman's birth of octuplets borrows many of its vocabularies and ideological trappings from welfare discourses that emerged in the late 1980s and early 1990s. Meanwhile, because Cuarón's *Children of Men* is based on a novel that was published in 1992, it indirectly engages the same set of discourses about reproduction and amplifies the stakes by casting Kee as a woman of color. In both speculative texts, critical questions about reproductive futurity work across the bodies of women of color whose narratives seem simultaneously distinct from, supplemental to, and emblematic of a story about reproduction in a globalizing world extrapolated from the unborn child.

That feels all the more alarming when couched in the terms of speculative futures markets, wherein the mother's labor would be considered supplemental to the promise of the child's potential in the economy of human capital. Nalo Hopkinson's science fiction novel *Midnight Robber* (2000) explores alternative possibilities at the intersection of technology and reproduction by imagining cross-species partnering and queer family formations. The ex-slave, postapocalyptic societies Hopkinson depicts survive not through a return to heterosexual reproduction and vigilant adherence to "family values," but through the emergence of migrant communities in which reproductive bodies are queered and dislodged from heteronormative domesticity. I argue that Hopkinson looks to the future not only with a wariness about mythologies of technological advancement but also with a keen attention to how oppressive systems of power reproduce themselves—even in processes of decolonization—through social systems that are shaped by gender hierarchies.

Hopkinson's revisionist speculations on technocultural origin myths manifest in *Midnight Robber*'s efforts to disentangle technology from its Western cultural codes, offering an alternative future that emerges from technologies that owe their names and architectures to African folklore and diasporic histories. By calling into question the narrative of technology's origins and even how and what we call "technology," Hopkinson challenges Western associations of technology with notions of progress, modernity, and freedom, which have historically served an ulterior purpose of rationalizing the exploitation of marginalized peoples in the name of development. In Hopkinson's words, the paradigms and stories about technology "shape not only the names for the technology we create, but the type of technology we create."[6] Hopkinson's worldings include alternative networks that emerge from the interlinked labor histories of black and Asian people in the Caribbean. An Afro-Caribbean-Canadian writer, Hopkinson calls for the forging of transnational—or, in this case, intergalactic and cross-species—coalitions in times of emergency. My analysis of queer kinship models and diaspora-inspired technologies in *Midnight Robber* also attends to the linkages between queer and diasporic networks as alternative formulations of belonging and community that extend beyond the reproduction of family and nation.

Both Cuarón and Hopkinson produce science fiction technofutures that critique the technological utopianism and neoliberalism avidly espoused at the turn of the twenty-first century just as tech companies first falter in the global economy. In *Children of Men*, technology does not deliver the future from poverty, state oppression, discrimination, illness, or death. Rather, the world suffers from near-total infertility, rampant pollution, and an abusive police state. Cuarón critiques neoliberalism as a contradiction of ideology and policy by portraying a near-future in which the gap between the First and Third Worlds widens when militarized border technologies work in conjunction with cultures of individualism to bolster isolationist state power.

The politics of reproduction and speculations on futures shift significantly from *Children of Men*'s masculinist and nationalist perspectives to *Midnight Robber*'s queer, feminist epistemologies. Taking into account theories of spectatorship and practices of looking, my analysis of *Children of Men* explores ways that Cuarón sets out to unravel the suturing of viewer to protagonist but ultimately cannot sufficiently de-center Theo as the white, male hero of the film. The film remains fixated on London as the epicenter of this future world in *Children of Men*; whereas in *Midnight Robber*, the cultural legacies that inform the otherworldly settings we encounter stem from the multiple and syncretic traditions most often found in the Caribbean. Hopkinson's tale provides a decolonial, feminist argument, warning against non-intersectional revolutions. The space community of exilic Trinidadians come to settle on the planet Toussaint, where they largely reproduce the structures of inequality and subjugation from which they fled. For the inhabitants of Toussaint, the Afro futurist promise of space travel does not deliver utopian finitude. What the reader learns from Hopkinson's rerouting of information-age technologies through Afro-Caribbean lore is that there is no postcolonial future as a destination. The analytics of diaspora studies help reveal that this speculative novel refuses the teleological ordering of departure and arrival in immigrant narrative conventions. Rather than arrange her vision of futurity around the promises of a new world, Hopkinson formulates postcolonial futurity as a continual and multidimensional mode of becoming.

If citizenship has often been tied to birthplace, it has also persistently been alienated through processes of racialization. Even in a postgenomic age, when trafficking in gametes, embryos, and wombs across state lines might force a reconfiguration or at least a reconsideration of nation-based citizenship, some might turn to a positivist embrace of technology and a promissory liberation narrative attached to its fictions. In contrast, science fictions that imagine technofutures as already mired in and tethered to a long history of racialized reproduction extend Ruth Wilson Gilmore's definition of racism as "the state-sanctioned or extralegal production and exploitation of group-differentiated vulnerability to premature death" to the temporality and scale of the "politics of life itself."[7]

The Speculative Futures of Race, Reproduction, and Citizenship

Deriving from the Latin subrogare, meaning "to appoint to act in the place of," surrogacy names an appointment that must at some point articulate itself in the form of a speculative claim—an enunciation of a future acting in place of. Surrogation, as Joseph Roach theorizes the concept in relation to cultural memory, functions as a projective substitution.[8] In this sense, it operates similarly to speculation. Commercial surrogacy has at times been called colloquially "wombs for rent," "outsourced pregnancies," or "baby farms," and agencies often orchestrate the legal, financial, and medical arrangements between potential surrogates and intended parents.

The speculative rhetoric of the transnational surrogacy industry, including insurance companies and medical tourism agencies, relies on preexisting narratives of race and modernity as well as historical practices of medical experimentation on slave women, incarcerated subjects, and other subjects rendered invisible to the state.

Genomic databanks and pharmaceutical trials require increasingly larger pools of people-made-data in order to be profitable. To ensure a steady and unregulated stream of research subjects, companies in the business of trading in biological materials encourage organ, tissue, and blood donors, including egg donors and surrogate mothers, to "gift" their biomatter out of "the goodness" of their hearts, "for the sake of public health," "to do their part for the fight against x/y/z disease." Expectant parents are advised to bank their newborn's cord blood as a resource for potential future health problems.[9]

In the global surrogacy market, clients from the Global North seek out surrogate mothers primarily from India and elsewhere in the Global South, where disparate valuations of life are leveraged to fund the reproductive ambitions of women of the Global North—whose labors are beholden to global capitalism differently. One story of transnational surrogacy that made international headlines in 2008 is that of Manji Yamada, whose "intended parents," Yuki Yamada and R. Ikufumi Yamada, sought out a surrogate mother in Anand who would serve as a gestational carrier for an implanted embryo comprised of genetic material from an Indian or Nepali donor's egg and Ikufumi Yamada's sperm. After Manji's conception and implantation, the Japanese couple got divorced, and Yuki no longer wished to participate in Manji's life. Ikufumi now faces the complication of trying to adopt Manji as a single man—a practice forbidden by Indian law.

In this moment of outsourced reproduction, when wealthy couples "rent" the wombs of less privileged women; when surrogacy costs about $12,000 in India versus upwards of $70,000 in the United States, with surrogate mothers earning perhaps only around $5,000 in India versus $20,000 in the United States;[10] and when contract reproduction remains illegal in many countries, we might ask what cultural discourses, norms, and contestations emerge at the conjuncture of reproductive technologies and reproductive labor? As Kalindi Vora has urged, "since it caters to clients from wealthier nations, transnational Indian surrogacy requires us to attend to the political-economics of the global division of reproductive labor" and reconceptualize surrogate bodies and their relationship to birth.[11]

The anxieties and assurances produced around transnational gestational surrogacy tend to be managed at least in part through the perception of racial difference. One surrogate mother at the Akanksha clinic explains: "It won't even have the same skin color as me, so it won't be hard to think of it as Jessica's."[12] A frequently asked question on multiple in/fertility blogs registers how intended parents wonder to what extent the baby will be genetically related to the gestational carrier. As more research points to possible migrations of fetal and maternal cells across the placental wall ("fetomaternal microchimerism") during pregnancy, the promise of absolute genetic separation seems untenable. And yet that uncertainty only generates more instruments for hedging against legal or medical complication. Fertility financing firms such as CapexMD, New Life Agency, and Prosper Healthcare Lending not only offer fertility loans but also assisted reproduction insurance. Whose futures are being secured in these transactions? What are the preexisting circumstances that inform how these transnational exchanges get brokered?

One online publication tells the story of a couple from Atlanta. Drew Miller and his (unnamed) wife published a forty-page booklet available online for $20 via PayPal, "to help us cover the cost of our own IVF costs."[13] Titled *IVF and Surrogacy in India*, the booklet serves as a guidebook for the burgeoning reproductive tourism industry. It provides a slew of information—from the drug protocols the Millers followed at the Akanksha clinic to the best hotels to stay in while in Anand—and the Millers market their booklet as part personal memoir, part medical documentation, and part tour book. "We've also included a map of Anand that includes points of interest," the Millers write. "There is a section on things to do in Anand where we also discuss the different hotel options, restaurants, shopping and getting around in Anand." Transnational surrogacy and international travel seem entirely enmeshed in the Miller booklet. Furthermore, the financial arrangements that facilitate the Millers' mobility build on credit they accrue from their status as documented and banked U.S. citizens with enough liquid capital to make an overseas trip.

Where do we begin to articulate a critical framework for addressing these circulations of racial ideologies in popular culture alongside the material exchanges of actual biomatter across an uneven global economic terrain? What historical contexts help us situate the emergence of racialized representations of reproductive bodies? How might a comparative ethnic studies approach help us unpack popular discourses around race and reproduction? And how can we put feminist science and technology studies frameworks in conversation with important questions arising in critical globalization studies about women's labor beyond EuroAmerican contexts? As the Global South develops new dependencies on U.S. pharmaceutical companies and medical aid organizations and as reproductive tourism and other forms of bio-trafficking suggest other manifestations of globalization on the move, how does a neoliberal model of global restructuring collide with transnational circulations of commodified bodies?

Nadya Suleman, sometimes referred to as Octomom, gave birth to octuplets on January 26, 2009. When the news first broke, before any details about Suleman and the conditions surrounding this reproductive event were publicized, the blogging and mediated public rehashed a familiar performance of exuberant congratulations, deploying the language of "miracles" and "blessings." As conjectures from the medical community that the octuplets must be a product of assisted reproductive technologies (ART) emerged, though, the narrative shifted in tone, hedging away from the story of medical triumph and moving toward one of serious complication and questionable ethics. Simultaneously, questions arose about Suleman's identity and her intentions. Once the press learned that Suleman was a single mother with six children at home already, the conversation turned ugly quickly, borrowing from late twentieth-century reproductive discourses about welfare, overpopulation, and immigration (often imbricated with xenophobic anxieties and racism) to alienate Octomom from the camp of heteronormative reproduction. As Dana Ain Davis argues, the uncertainty of Suleman's class and race frustrated attempts to fit her narrative into a preset social script about reproduction. Rather quickly, Davis remarks, "'the miracle' turned to disgust, which seemed to be fueled in part by an inability to 'profile' the woman who gave birth."[14] In the absence of these details, a predictably racist set of speculations arose about this single mother. According to Davis's research, bloggers associated Suleman's fecundity first with her being an "illegal alien mom" and later as an African American "welfare baby momma." Suleman's story puts pressure on the disjuncture between public assistance and assisted reproductive technologies. "Assistance," it would seem, bears wildly different connotations depending on its issuance as public versus privatized forms of care. That discussions about reproductive technologies so often get caught up in discourses about race, class, gender, and sexuality exemplifies how cultural discourses use medical discourses—which so often naturalize differences based on ethnicity and gender—to manage these discrepancies.

In the words of the NBC reporter Gordon Tokumatsu, "most of what's out there [about Suleman's octuplets' birth] is just creative speculation."[15] The celebrity news media, members of the medical community, and at-home online commentators crafted and circulated fictions about the occasion for, circumstances surrounding, and details of this octuplet birth. These speculative fictions, in turn, play out anxieties about how biological technologies should be regulated and to whom they should be made available. The quick turn from miraculous exception to distasteful excess not only signals the tenacious racialization of reproductive futurity but also throws into relief the different valences of public and private assistance.

The creative speculations generated around Octomom produced vituperative, venomous threats as well as calls for sometimes violent regulation and policing of reproduction, recalling the kind of eugenicist thinking from early twentieth-century reform movements. Critics, who included self-avowed psychologists, questioned Suleman's mental "fitness," asking whether she had been counseled regarding so-called selective reduction. Arguments about women not being mentally fit enough to reproduce worked to sustain sterilization laws in the infamous Supreme Court case *Buck v. Bell* in 1927, at the peak of the eugenics movement in the United States. Whereas Carrie Buck was deemed "feebleminded"[16] and thus characterized as a threat to the gene pool and therefore to the health of the state, discussions about Suleman's mental fitness more closely resemble the more "punitive" and more racialized rhetoric used in U.S.-backed sterilization campaigns in Puerto Rico, which combined eugenicist precedents with xenophobic anxieties about overpopulation.[17]

As the dramatized narrative about Suleman and her children continued to play out on irreverent celebrity news blogs and in tabloid newspapers and magazines of the same ilk, the story took on increasingly overt elements of science fiction. Unsettling images eventually emerged that frame Suleman's pregnant body as either freakishly alien or as hyperalienated, in the sense that Octomom became a racialized figure of biological and financial excesses. The text that accompanied one widely circulated image of Suleman eight days before her scheduled C-section reads: "Octopussy may not have to pimp out her wombmates for dollars on her website anymore, as this 'Alien' photo has just landed her a new gig—the poster mom for anti-in-vitro fertilization."[18] By calling Suleman an "alien," the staff writer for TMZ cast her story even more concretely into the genre of science fiction, aligning Octomom with the *Alien* movies, a series that is intensely riddled with anxieties about maternity in an age of assisted reproductive technologies and genetic cloning.

Suleman's very "public pregnancy" instantiates what Anne Balsamo recognizes as a troubling convergence of reproductive technologies and a desire to discipline the pregnant body through modes of heightened surveillance.[19] Suleman's case also brings into focus the ways in which media become reproductive technologies, producing again and again visual and textual narratives about race and class as they collide with the politics of reproduction. Some of the most helpful critical frameworks have looked beyond textual narratives to consider the significant role visual culture has played in the popular understanding of reproductive technologies. The Octomom story demonstrates how narratives about race, reproduction, and technology are speculatively formulated, rewritten, and variously deployed in the news media and blogosphere.

Calling Suleman "alien" also registers another, simultaneous anxiety, directly related to the spurious claims that she is undocumented. Stamped as the property of the celebrity and entertainment website tmz.com, the image consists of two side-by-side photographs—one frontal and one profile view—of Suleman's very large pregnant belly. This pairing of one front-view and one side-view photo seems designed to evoke the conventions of prison mug shots. Marked as "alien" and prisoner in this one image, Suleman inhabits the visual space of an alienated citizen. With her shirt pulled up to reveal her belly, Suleman poses in front of not the blank wall of a prison booking room but what looks to be a curtain of another institution: the clinic. In this image, the disciplinary settings of the prison and the hospital are drawn together, and the public discourse about Suleman's right to have octuplets becomes inextricably linked to questions about her right to U.S. citizenship and her implied criminality. Joann Killeen, Suleman's first public relations representative, distanced herself from the case once death threats were issued to both women. Killeen reported to Larry King in an interview: "They've said to me that I should be put down like an old dog, I should be paralyzed, my client's uterus should be ripped out, she should be put on an island . . ."[20] The eugenicist impulse to call for Suleman's compulsory sterilization bears a century-old legacy in the United States of cutting off certain members of the population deemed unfit to reproduce from the opportunity to do so. The intertwined histories of racism and forced sterilization in the United States reveal how women of color were often told that their status in relation to immigration, benefits, or housing, might be compromised if they did not agree to biomedical interventions into their fertility.[21]

If homeland futurity, as chapter 2 argues, projects a racialized threat of alien invasion to bolster arguments for increased militarization of the border, reproductive futurity not only orients subjects toward a reproductive imperative, but it also extrapolates from eugenicist rhetoric to ascribe a genetically selective future. These securitizing logics work across the scales of nation and genetic population in interconnected ways. In the context of the United States, at least, that connection presents itself most clearly when the state attempts to regulate racialized populations by controlling the reproduction of people of color.

Developing a biopolitical theory without decolonial analytics would be to miss many of the vicissitudes that constitute the contemporary global market in biomatter. Whereas biopolitics takes up questions of "the sovereign" and "the citizen" via a universal category of the human, the minor fields of critical ethnic studies, feminist and queer theory, and decolonial thought foreground histories of slavery, indenture, and empire, wherein citizenship itself is propped up by systems that produce categories of disavowed nonbeings through which citizenship emerges in contradistinction. Is it not possible that the politics of life might mean something very different for populations whose histories include the rendering of life into nonbeing?

With these questions in mind, I turn next to two speculative fictions — one film and one novel — that use the premise of species-scale reproductive imperatives to interrogate the racialization of reproductive futurity. Insofar as reproduction and labor are interlinked processes, these cultural texts help illuminate the necessity for an intersectional, and indeed interspecies approach to the concept of survival. Interrogating the histories of slavery and eugenics that underpin contemporary racially asymmetrical distributions of life-chances, these cinematic and literary hauntologies situate how we tell stories about the future, what role reproduction plays in those stories, and how one might begin to dislodge reproductive futurity from an equivalence with white heteropatriarchy, or even with the category of the human.

Whose Future? Technologies of Reproduction and Representation in Children of Men

Look, I'm absolutely pessimistic about the present. But I'm very optimistic about the future. I'm a pessimist about the present because I know my generation. But every time I see younger generations, I'm hopeful. That's the word. Hope. There you go.
—ALFONSO CUARÓN

Cuarón's film *Children of Men* depicts a near-future dystopia in which humans have been infertile for eighteen years, during which time state practices of regulating bodies have become increasingly insidious, totalitarian, and violent. Set in the United Kingdom of 2027, the film depicts a world that has witnessed societal collapse, rampant violence, and ecological devastation, in which national governments have crumbled with the exception of an increasingly authoritarian British state. Propagandist videos on the subway declare: "Only Britain soldiers on." Migrants, people of color, the poor, and the sick are, as always, hardest hit by this nationalist shift as anti-immigration legislation, military-backed deportation practices, and state-mandated fertility screening tests create a heavily policed, xenophobic, and paranoid environment—an environment so rife with pollution and toxic waste as to seem at the end of its life-sustaining capacity. Against a bleak landscape of religious fanaticism and violent struggles between ideologically and politically desperate groups, Cuarón's film remains invested in the figure of hope embodied by the pregnant African "fugee" (refugee) named Kee, played by Claire Hope Ashitey, a British actress of Ghanaian descent. Much of the film's central action revolves around Kee's struggle to reach a group called "the Human Project," a group of scientists who presumably will not take Kee's baby to co-opt it for political use and their own selfish gain. While the film is set in and around London, the

United States looms large in Cuarón's work. Released in 2006, Cuarón's primary narrative unfolds against the haunting backdrop of Abu Ghraib and other U.S.-backed torture camps, which take the form of refugee detention centers in the film.[22] These detention centers invoke not only the specter of Nazi concentration camps but also the militarization of the U.S.-Mexico border. Set to Krzystof Penderecki's "Threnody for the Victims of Hiroshima," these scenes are also haunted by another example of U.S. military aggression in the form of the nuclear attacks on Japan during World War II.

Children of Men levies a critique against techno-utopianism using similar strategies as Yamashita's speculative fictions, which I explored in the previous chapter. Cuarón presents a future in which technology has not delivered freedom, equality, and an open society, but rather, quite the opposite. Furthermore, his vision of the future also investigates various histories of human rights violations of the past century, including the Holocaust, Japanese internment during World War II, and the proliferation of offshore military detention facilities under the auspices of a global War on Terror.

Although it seems that from the opening scene, the viewer is sutured to the main character, Theo (Clive Owen), Cuarón does not always privilege Theo's perspective, which cannot always compete with the disturbing images of police violence and social unrest that occupy the unmistakably dynamic backdrop of the film. To an extent, the camera constantly asks the viewer to look beyond the plot's white male protagonist; however, the only alternative point of view Cuarón offers is perhaps his own, in the form of a disembodied, wide-shot perspective. But in a film that places the hope of the world's future on an expected child, where is the expectant mother? It is around Kee that the politics of looking become somewhat fraught. Cuarón overlooks Kee's perspective in this narrative about reproduction—a neglect of the mother symptomatic, perhaps, of the plot's fetishization of the child as the hope for the future. After all, the title of both the film and the novel it adapts, names "children" and "men"—with the glaring omission of mothers.

Cinematically, *Children of Men* follows the technical style Cuarón employed in *Y Tu Mamá También*, in which long, wide-shot takes constantly frame the characters against an equally detailed and significant environment. In a film that minimizes close-ups, the sociopolitical landscape becomes as much of a character as the individuals. Cuarón experiments with this technique in *Y Tu Mamá También*, which offers a resistant narrative of citizenship embedded in moments of detoured camera movement, in which the natural diagetic trajectory of the camera's gaze gets wrenched away from its more predictable path to allow for the disruption of distraction. These distractions often highlight the repressive authoritarian government and its subjection of its citizens to a range of policing acts. Whereas María Josefina Saldaña-Portillo understands this oscillation between the central and the peripheral narrative lines as working to "interrupt the filmic text," she also insists on the "interdependence between the peripheral and the consequential story lines," at least in the case of Y Tu Mamá También.[23] Slavoj Žižek, whose comments on Children of Men appear in the DVD's extra features, calls attention to the tension Cuarón cultivates between the foreground and the background. Žižek argues that "the true focus of the film is there in the background, and it's crucial to leave it as a background." Calling this technique a kind of "anamorphosis," Žižek suggests that "if you look at the thing too directly—the oppressive, social dimension—you don't see it; you can see it in an oblique way only if it remains in the background." The idea of activating the background is quite compelling, as is the potentiality Cuarón, as a Mexican auteur, sees in what the privileged, mobile subject (in this case, Theo) often overlooks, ignores, or passes by. But to what extent does a formulation of an anamorphic gaze decenter the white, male perspective? Theo could easily be characterized as an untrustworthy, unlikeable antihero. He is a coward, a broken soul, a man who uses the occasion of public mourning over the death of the youngest human alive to excuse himself from his dreary, dead-end desk job. Yet from the opening scene of the film, the camera and the narrative follow the emotional and physical journey of this disaffected, depressed ex-activist. We shadow Theo as he takes his morning coffee, watches the morning news, and goes to work. The film tethers us to his annoyance with the public weeping over the murder of Baby Diego, an eighteen-year-old boy, whose fame comes from his being the last baby born on earth. Though shaken by the bombing he has witnessed from feet away, Theo remains an unreliable and unlikeable protagonist, disconnected from and therefore complicit in the forms of state repression he passes on his way to work. By the end of the narrative, Theo emerges as a veritable hero, whose purpose has been restored through a recuperation of his fatherhood and masculinity, and it is this plot trajectory—still functioning according to a logic of development and progress—that Cuarón makes an effort to undercut and counterbalance with the perpetual intrusion of Theo's environment into his life.

Cuarón's use of anamorphosis works as a technology of haunting. In these anamorphic moments, Cuarón reveals a repressive police state, scenes of torture, and the ghostly specter of the camp. His films seem especially haunted by the surveillance state as a visual technology that possibly implicates film but also possibly facilitates the film's self-conscious critique of exploitative practices of looking. *Children of Men* stages a disruption of Fredric Jameson's definition of "spectrality" as "what makes the present waver" to theorize how haunting works: "The emphasis on the wavering present, on the propinquity of hard-to-touch, hard-to-see abstractions powerfully criss-crossing our concrete quotidian lives is key."[24] As Theo passes through the gates to the Bexhill Refugee Camp, a palimpsest of historical referents appears, as the gates themselves look remarkably like those outside of the Nazi concentration camps of World War II such as Auschwitz and Dachau, but the sign above the gates reads not "Arbeit Macht Frei" (Work shall set you free) but "Homeland Security." In this very detailed and carefully choreographed scene of entering the camp, Cuarón hints at the extrapolative process that led him to this grim near future. Nazi concentration camps and U.S.-backed detention centers haunt Bexhill's architecture as historical antecedents, and through these visual cues, Cuarón's film glances at the apparition of state-sanctioned torture and organized ethnic persecution. As Theo, Kee, and Miriam (Kee's doula) enter the camp, the camera takes our gaze over the shoulders of the main characters to look with them out the bus window to witness hooded, handcuffed prisoners kneeling in a line and dogs incited to terrorize and attack them.

Cuarón's audience has seen similar images before, specifically in April and May of 2004, when the abuse of prisoners at the Abu Ghraib prison in Iraq came to public attention both online and through major media outlets such as CBS's *60 Minutes II*, the *New Yorker*, ABC's *Nightly News*, and the *Washington Post*. One particularly chilling specter of the torture acts at Abu Ghraib lingers for an extra moment on screen in *Children of Men* as the bus pauses in front of a hooded detainee, standing on a box behind bars, arms extended to each side of his body, and rendered immobile because, as the audience already knows, he has been told that if he falls off the box, he will trigger the wires connected to him and be electrocuted. In this quick moment, the recent past and the near future collide, causing a rupture in the cinematic temporality of Theo's narrative — effectively causing the present to waver.[25] In this way, Cuarón makes critical use of the speculative fiction genre by imagining a future that nevertheless remains haunted by the past. By bringing the specter of torture at Abu Ghraib and Guantánamo home to

Bexhill, England, the film relocates the prison camp and the military detention center within domestic borders rather than allowing it to rest in the offshore imaginary.

In her stunning essay "Where Is Guantánamo?" Amy Kaplan lays out the stakes of such a move. She writes that "the legal space of Guantánamo today has been shaped and remains haunted by its imperial history. This complex history helps to explain how Guantánamo has become an ambiguous space both inside and outside different legal systems. Guantánamo's geographic and historical location provides the legal and political groundwork for the current violent penal regime."[26] In *Children of Men*, Cuarón effectively summons the specter of state-sponsored systems of disappearance by reproducing in Bexhill the chilling realities of offshore prison camps and "black site" detention centers of the twenty-first century. This cinematic technology may allow for a temporal haunting, but anamorphosis nevertheless requires a central gaze, around which the parameters of peripheral vision are delineated. The sidelong glance and the oblique look do not necessarily challenge the dynamics of spectatorship. Viewers must deal with the foreground even while the background compels our attention, and we remain primarily tethered to Theo's point of view throughout Cuarón's film. We follow Theo's footsteps and rarely come to inhabit Kee's perspective of being shuttled around by various groups who hope to capitalize on the significance of her pregnancy.

Furthermore, Theo can never fully disavow his privileged point of view. Smuggled into Bexhill, he even tries to feign foreignness when a prison guard threatens to compromise the secret of Kee's condition. The scene in which Theo attempts to speak in broken English to disguise his native tongue is one of the most awkward and least believable moments in the film. After all, Theo has access, through family connections, to the papers required for more mobility across a heavily surveilled and policed state. Before he meets Kee, he moves easily from one mode of transportation to the next as he passes before cages of detained subjects. Even when he is jumped and forcibly taken from the street—a gesture toward the apparently commonplace disappearances of other citizens—the whole event turns out to be somewhat of a charade, as his ex-wife Julian (Julianne Moore) has orchestrated the "theatrics," as she calls them, to arrange a clandestine meeting with him. The tension anamorphosis creates between center and periphery ultimately remains beholden to a framework that reproduces an imperialist dichotomy between a metropole (ostensibly home to order, modernity, and science) and a periphery (an imagined site of chaos, primitiveness, and irrationality). Even the film's setting moves from the metropole (London) to the countryside (a barn) and eventually to the shore (Bexhill), where those who have been deported from the metropole must now fight to survive.

Race and the Visual Iconographies of Futurity

The lack of attention to Kee's point of view becomes all the more troubling when one considers what symbolic work her body performs in Cuarón's screenplay and cinematic orchestration. The scene in which Kee reveals her pregnancy—to the camera, the audience, and Theo—demonstrates the film's conflicted politics of representing reproduction. Staged in a barn on a dairy farm, the scene places Kee, Theo, and a herd of dairy cows amid the mechanical apparatuses of industrialized milk extraction. Various tubes and pumps fill the confined space, and as we enter the barn along with Theo, Kee stands in a central pen surrounded by several calves. Surrounded, too, by the signs of industrial technology, Kee comments on the surgical cruelty these dairy cows undergo for the sake of the dairy industry: "You know what they do to these cows? They cut off their tits. They do. [Imitating slicing.] Gone. Bye. Only leave four. Four tits fits the machine. It's wacko. Why not make machines that suck eight titties?" On the one hand, Cuarón's barn scene connects the exploitation of black women's bodies and the exploitation of dairy cows, which live only twenty-three years, during which time their sole functions are to become pregnant, produce a fat calf immediately slated for the slaughterhouse, and produce milk. Kee's commentary on the violence committed against the dairy cows, whose udders are surgically removed to fit industrial milking apparatuses, points to capitalism's subjugation of reproductive bodies to profit-driven productivity. That Kee speaks from within the pen among the calves signifies a critical connection to the biopolitical mechanisms of excluding certain forms of life from the protections of modern liberal humanism, even as such exclusions participate in the production of a seemingly universal liberal subject.[27]

One might also be reminded of another scene of black motherhood in literary history. When in Toni Morrison's *Beloved*, Sethe enters a barn to take her baby's life, it is to save it from the institution of slavery, a system that relies on black women's reproduction to perpetuate itself. In this novel, readers enter the horrific barn scene through the perspective of the third-person omniscient, and we understand Sethe's drastic act as the ending of a biological life whose political life the institution of slavery has already terminated. When Schoolteacher laments the loss of Sethe's viability as a slave, he explains to his son that "you just can't mishandle creatures and expect success."[28] Cuarón's version of the barn scene differs from Morrison's narrative of a black fugitive woman desperate to spare her child from a future intent on capitalizing on that child's life by setting up the black mother as an object to be gazed at rather than as the subject through whom the audience experiences the scene. As Anthony Bogues notes, "We have not spent much time thinking about this question of who and what is a human being from the perspective of human beings who were considered to be non-humans."[29] In *Children of Men*, Cuarón replaces the scene of horror in the barn with a scene of hope, set to the angelic sounds of revelation orchestrated by John Tavener, the British composer known for combining Christian themes with 1970s minimalism. The moment becomes sacralized and transformed into a manger scene, alluding to miraculous birth. Kee stands in three-quarter view, covering her breasts with one arm and cupping her belly with the other, in a pose reminiscent of Sandro Botticelli's *Venus*. By directing Kee to pose in this way, Cuarón draws her into a visual lexicon of Renaissance art and a story about giving birth to an Age of Reason. He also subjects Kee to what Haraway—in her analysis of Albrecht Dürer's 1538 engraving *Draughtsman Drawing a Nude*—calls the disciplining "screen-grid" of perspectival looking, or the "virtual speculum," which "attests to the power of the technology of perspective to discipline vision to produce a new kind of knowledge of form."[30] Haraway's virtual speculum argument asks us to consider works like Dürer's *Draughtsman* as narrativizations of enlightenment and modernity that contribute to the production of "historical configurations conventionally called the 'Renaissance,' or in a later version of the birth of the modern, the 'Scientific Revolution,' or today's rendition called the 'New World Order' [...] as cradles of modern humanity." The visual technology itself, as speculum in Haraway's description, facilitates the birth of modernity, and in the case of Cuarón's *Children of Men*, the visual speculum of cinematic mastery delivers a promise of futurity, albeit a vexed one.

These overtures to both Christian iconography and Renaissance art, though, supplant white iconic womanhood with Kee, whose status as a refugee and fugitive in the narrative implicitly raises questions about the limits of these humanistic iconographies. In these directorial choices, Cuarón may invoke a European Enlightenment tradition, but he does so while pulling into the center of the frame the history of slavery and racial exclusion that subtend the very notion of what Jamaican philosopher Sylvia Wynter calls humanism under the Western order of Man.

But what exactly does Theo behold when he looks? What is the phenomenological effect of what he sees? Theo initially misunderstands what Kee's disrobing signals. "What are you doing? Don't do that," he implores as Kee begins to drop her shift off her shoulders. Momentarily misinterpreting the unveiling of her pregnancy as a sexual invitation, Theo begins to avert his eyes but is then, upon realizing that Kee is actually revealing the Future of Man, is permitted to fall headlong into another kind of looking. Panning slowly up from the calves in the pen to Kee's naked, pregnant torso, the camera invites viewers to inhabit a scopophilic spectator position that fetishizes the black pregnant body, projecting onto Kee Hope in the form of the Unborn Child.[31]

The barn scene in *Children of Men* serves primarily to signal the major turning point for Theo, who sheds his reluctance to become a hero because he finally realizes "what's at stake," as another character points out. But, whose future is at stake in *Children of Men* exactly? Kee's child will bear the name Dylan, after Theo's dead son, and the name of the boat that will ostensibly deliver them to safety is *The Tomorrow*. The reproductive technology at work here takes the shape of a narrative arc that writes a man's hopes and visions for the future across the body of a woman of color.[32] It is a surrogation of Theo's futurity and its investments are in the children of Man, in Wynter's sense of the word, of "our present ethnoclass (i.e., Western bourgeois) conception of the human, Man, which overrepresents itself as if it were the human itself."[33]

The narrative remains guided by what Lee Edelman has called "reproductive futurism," a drive that in this case asks the black female body to perform the labor of producing the figure of hope for Theo's continuing legacy. If Edelman objects to how the "universalized fantasy subtending the image of the child coercively shapes the structures within which the 'political' itself can be thought,"[34] then the example of *Children of Men* presents us with an intersectional version of that objection. The universalized fantasy that structures "the political itself," in the EuroAmerican Global North, at least, must also be whiteness, and the virtual speculum must also be understood as what Kobena Mercer identifies as a colonial fantasy of mastery over the technology of looking.[35]

This narrative of white, reproductive futurity relies on a form of racialized surrogation at a moment when reproductive technologies work to ensure the futures of wealthy, privileged subjects at the expense of the reproductive labor of poor women around the world. Kee's labor—aided not only by Theo's hands but also by the special effects that make the scene cinematically possible—delivers a promise of hope, but for whom and according to what terms?

Cuarón's deployment of anamorphosis works as a visual technology to signal a haunting, but this attempt to decenter the cinematic gaze is undermined by the narrative's continual return to Theo's point of view. The narrative remains structured around a drive toward reproductive futurity that restores white male heteropatriarchy by positioning Kee as a kind of surrogate mother. These two arguments are ultimately intertwined. The privileging of Theo's perspective and the racialized reproductive imperative at work in this film go hand in hand. Theo's ultimate heroic sacrifice ensures not only the survival of Kee and Dylan but also the reproduction of heteropatriarchal logic itself.

In the early to mid-1990s, feminist scholars of visual culture and science studies began to turn much-needed critical attention to reproductive discourses promoting ideologies around fetal personhood, a cultural construction beholden to advances in reproductive technologies and macro- and microphotography.[36] These studies made their interventions during the historical context of prolife campaigns that made use of fetal imaging, the emergence of the sonogram as a visual technology of reproduction, and critical attention to the work of biomedical photographer Lennart Nilsson.

Children of Men both instantiates and contemplates the relationship between reproductive technologies (in the Benjaminian sense) and the technologies of reproduction. In Cuarón's film, digital billboards remind citizens about state-mandated fertility tests and the criminalization of those who refuse such medical surveillance. Meanwhile, the DVD's extra features proclaim the special effects "triumph" of simulating Kee's birthing realistically on screen. Just as scientific technology such as electron micrographs and fetal imaging can be used to create narratives about life, so *Children of Men* capitalizes on cinematic special effects to orchestrate a science fiction about futures dependent on the reproductive labor of women of the Global South. Perhaps an inevitable irony of Cuarón's narrative of restored hope and rebirth is that the birth scene is computer-generated. The reproductive technologies that deliver Kee's baby as a cinematic event include the replacing of Ashitey's legs with prosthetic ones, the use of both an animatronic baby and a computer-generated one, and a completely choreographed single-shot scene that lasts three and a half minutes.

My reading of Cuarón's film is not a popular one. Naomi Klein and Žižek team up on the DVD's extra features to praise *Children of Men* for much of the work it does. But to hold up the metaphorical infertility of the Global North as embodied by Owen, Moore, and Caine and then hold up the possibility of redemption and deliverance of that infertility through the figuration of the Global South as mapped onto Ashitey's body is to make black lives matter in all the wrong ways, relegating Kee and her baby to the same kind of redemptive onus of "saving" capitalism through racism. By drawing *Children of Men* into conversation with the stories of Nadya Suleman and Alex Kuczynski, I mean to call attention to the global, racialized capitalist system that subtends the racialized reproductive futurity this chapter interrogates.[37]

The Racialization of Reproductive Futurity

In early 2015, I helped found the Ferguson Teaching Collective at Dartmouth College and launched a course called "10 Weeks, 10+ Professors: #BlackLivesMatter." Various news outlets picked up the story. In one outlet, Fox News, the comments section yielded some predictably vitriolic responses (see figure 3.1). The comments, posted by Internet trolls and regurgitated from the various talking points of the Christian Right, fetishize the life of the fetus to the neglect of sustaining black lives beyond infancy. "If black lives REALLY MATTER," writes jdelagado, "they should be stopping all the black baby ABORTIONS going on EVERYDAY." And docbugsy writes: "They can also teach about how over 13,000,000 black children have been aborted since 1973." The contradictory positions taken by the digital peanut gallery in relation to birth control and abortion rights are bewildering. When krbutler1947 writes "tell'em to get a job and use a con dom [sic]," Bamadog replies: "@krbutler1947 A what? They don't have those in the hood." Bamadog's response should not be mistaken for a call for wider access to birth control in publicly defunded neighborhoods, and krbutler1947's remark stops just short of making a full-blown eugenicist suggestion only to save the body for the purposes of work. The racist project of reducing black life to the function of labor can be seen elsewhere in contemporary circumstances, too. Consider the glaring discrepancy between the life expectancies of blacks and whites in the United States; the

nepa2500   Feb 4, 2015

BLACK LIVES MATTER END ABORTION TODAY RIGHT MARGERET SANGER

3 Like   Reply

justmary   Feb 4, 2015

@DopeAndMange margaret sanger's malice towards "undesirables" lives on at planned parenthood

Like   Reply

jdelagado   Feb 4, 2015

If black lives REALLY MATTER, they should be stopping all the black baby ABORTIONS going on EVERYDAY.....

3 Like   Reply

docbugsy   Feb 4, 2015

They can also teach about how over 13,000,000 black children have been aborted since 1973.

7 Like   Reply

dthillsr   Feb 4, 2015

Black lives matters as long as they get out of the womb.

2 Like   Reply

krbutler1947   Feb 4, 2015

tell'em to get a job and use a con dom..........

6 Like   Reply

Bamadog   Feb 4, 2015

@krbutler1947 A what? They don't have those in the hood.

FIGURE 3.1. Comments section of Fox News's report, "Dartmouth to Offer 'Black Lives Matter' Classes," February 4, 2015, accessed July 31, 2016, http://www.foxnews.com/us/2015/02/04/dartmouth-to-offer-black-lives-matter-classes.html. The comments section has since been taken down.

disproportionate number of people of color incarcerated in arguably the most industrious prison system on the planet; the uneven distribution of wealth, access to education, quality of health care, and so on—in short, the built environment of segregation in the United States that facilitates the foreshortening of black lives.

The double appearance of Margaret Sanger's name is what caught my attention in this slurry of racist commentary. How does Sanger—the promoter of birth control and reproduction as instruments of social reform, founder of Planned Parenthood, and author of works such as "The Eugenic Value of Birth Control Propaganda" and *The Pivot of Civilization*—become a metonym for abortion? U.S. feminists of color as well as women from the Global South have regularly critiqued Euro-American-centric conversations about reproductive rights that fail to consider the proto-eugenicist history of birth control movements led by Sanger and primarily white women in the early twentieth-century United States. In her 1982 essay "Racism, Birth Control, and Reproductive Rights," Angela Davis situates 1980s reproductive rights debates in a longer history, including nineteenth-century, largely white women's birth control movements, which were known to have advocated the involuntary sterilization of portions of the population deemed unfit to reproduce under the proto-eugenicist auspices of social reform. In this move, Davis interjects an account of racialized biopolitics that underwrites reproductive rights. By questioning for whom and in what way birth control is liberatory, she calls into question the ostensible universalism of "the human," "rights," and "life." Sylvia Wynter's work makes me think that reproductive rights, as they are formed around notions of human rights and Enlightenment constructions of "man" as the rights bearer, have already been compromised by the abjection of the slave and the migrant worker from the conditions of the human. Similarly, Dorothy Roberts suggests that the "notion of reproductive liberty . . . is limited by the liberal ideals of individual autonomy and freedom from government interference."[38] Roberts narrates a long history of denying black women's autonomy over reproduction, from the slave era through the sterilization of black women during the 1920s and 1930s and to the 1980s, when the distribution of Norplant in black communities and the cutting off of assistance to children born to women on welfare worked in tandem to curtail black women's birth rates.

Since the global proliferation of ARTs have dovetailed with speculative oocyte and surrogacy markets, the racialized biopolitics of reproduction have intensified at the IVF-IMF complex.[39] As Marie Jenkins Schwartz has demonstrated, the medicalization of slave reproduction in the antebellum U.S. South instantiates an earlier moment of biomedical and capitalist alignment. Chattel slavery's reliance on reproduction after the U.S. stopped importing slaves in 1808 occasioned the enmeshment of physician and plantation owner interests.[40] Slavery in the U.S. antebellum South produces through racial difference a biopoliticized population that renders slave women's bodies available for often violent, unanaesthitized surgical and medical experimentation. The surrogation of a labor force that facilitates U.S. plantation slavery provides an antecedent to the ongoing racialization of biopolitical reproduction after the advent of assisted reproductive technologies.

Calling on evidence from his other work on how the medical institution works to instill public hygiene, centralize information, and normalize knowledge, Michel Foucault identifies a shift in the eighteenth century toward thinking about humans at the scale of the "population."[41] Though Foucault delivered his now much-cited lectures on biopolitics at the Collège de France in the 1970s, that work does not enter into translation and wider U.S. scholarly discussions until the first decade of the twenty-first century. In the study of asymmetrical distributions of life chances, particularly in the context of U.S. racial formation and reproduction, I want to keep black feminist thought central. While the significant contributions of Angela Davis and Toni Morrison to the conversation about how black lives comes to matter have already been part of this chapter's ruminations, it's worth noting that their writings from the 1980s emerge in conjuncture with one another out of black, feminist, alternative intellectual space. While Morrison was a trade-book editor at Random House in the late 1960s and early 1970s, she worked with many black feminist authors, including Angela Davis. Davis would later bring to light how the two had sometimes commuted into Manhattan together.[42] This carpool constitutes a space for black feminist thought, wherein the story of Margaret Garner—the slave woman who took her infant's life to save it from enslavement—would eventually form the basis of Morrison's character Sethe in *Beloved* (1987) as well as Davis's pivotal 1982 essay on intersectional approaches to reproductive justice. This seemingly ancillary anecdote illustrates how the prehistories of race and reproduction as they come up through black feminist exchanges play an important role in understanding the connections between newer and older reproductive technologies. Seeing the continuities across the biopolitical histories of slavery and the ongoing practices of dispossession of reproductive agency in speculative biomarkets help identify the racialized systems of reproductive futurity. In the next section, I consider Nalo Hopkinson's *Midnight Robber*, which speculates on a vexed universe through which different stories about black lives, technology, and labor, navigate off-world fantasies of freedom and liberation.

Midnight Robber's Diasporic Constellations

Looking and looking back, black women involve ourselves in a process whereby we see our history as counter-memory, using it as a way to know the present and invent the future.
—bell hooks, *Black Looks*

Black people have always been masters of the figurative: saying one thing to mean something quite other has been basic to black survival in oppressive Western cultures.... This sort of metaphorical literacy, the learning to decipher complex codes, is just about the blackest aspect of the black tradition.
—HENRY LOUIS GATES, JR., *The Signifying Monkey*

There is no solid ground beneath us; we shift constantly to stay in one place.
—NALO HOPKINSON, "Speaking in Tongues"

In his article "Black to the Future," Mark Dery raises the question: "Why do so few African Americans write science fiction, a genre whose close encounters with the Other—the stranger in a strange land—would seem uniquely suited to the concerns of African-American novelists?"[43] Dery's article appears in a special issue of *The South Atlantic Quarterly* on "The Discourse of Cyberculture," published in 1993. Since then, this question has been revisited in various forms by a number of scholars, including Samuel Delany, Anna Everett, Walter Mosley, Alondra Nelson, Gregory Rutledge, Greg Tate, and Sheree Thomas.[44] Over the past decade or so, some academic journals—ranging from *Extrapolation*, which focuses on science fiction studies, to *Callaloo*, which emphasizes scholarly work on African diasporic studies—have dedicated more attention to black science fiction writers, especially Octavia Butler and Samuel Delany. One of these articles—Kalí Tal's "'That Just Kills Me': Black Militant Near-Future Fiction," in a special issue of *Social Text* titled "Afrofuturism"—begins with an anecdote about the author's 1977 experience in a science fiction writing course in Hollywood, during which she was asked to write a story about "why black people don't write science fiction."[45] Tal suggests that the instructor (and, by extension, Mark Dery) "asked the wrong question." Collectively, the essays in the Afrofuturism issue of *Social Text* suggest that black people have been excluded from technocultural discourse, despite always having had a relationship to and participating in technocultural production.

In several interviews, Hopkinson, whose novel *Midnight Robber* is the focus of this section, deplores the inadequacies of terms such as "science fiction," "fantasy," "horror," and "magical realism." She defines her work as speculative fiction, or "spec-fic," a genre that achieves the following: "We imagine what we want from the world; then we try to find a way to make it happen. Escapism can be the first step to creating a new reality, whether it's a personal change in one's existence or a larger change in the world. For me, spec-fic is a contemporary literature that is performing that act of the imagination . . . as fiction that starts from the principle of making the impossible possible."[46] For her, speculative fiction potentially performs the work of social change rather than just generating "adventure stories for white boys with high tech toys."[47] In doing so, it intervenes in the common misinterpretation of the genre as being "primarily by and about white men."[48]

Hopkinson's imaginings of the possibilities of collaboration take as their historical premise the intertwined labor histories of African and Asian migrations to the Americas. In what follows, I focus on *Midnight Robber* as one example of how extrapolative fiction can interrogate systems of labor, kinship structures, and power by shifting assumptions about modernity and technology. As in Octavia Butler's *Kindred*, space and time travel in *Midnight Robber*, which unfolds across multiple dimensions and worlds, allows for encounters with various historical traces and trajectories. Each time-space in Hopkinson's tale of the Midnight Robber Tan-Tan gives rise to another iteration of persistent labor abuses. What is more, *Midnight Robber* is also a prison narrative. The colony-planet Toussaint sends its carceral population to the prison-planet New Half-Way Tree — an exilic journey to another dimension in which prisoners must relearn how to rely on their own physical work, because New Half-Way Tree functions entirely without the help of artificial intelligence (AI). Space, it seems, is not the final frontier; Hopkinson's characters pass through dimensional veils to New Half-Way Tree, a trip suggestive of the multidimensional reverberations of slavery and incarceration that defy the progress narrative's tendency to imagine racial discrimination as something that lives only in the past.

Born in Jamaica and raised in Trinidad and Tobago, Hopkinson supplants Western myths of techno-origins with techno-networks that arise from overlapping diasporas and the intimacies among Chinese, Indo-, and

Afro-Caribbean migrations. In her imagined future, moments of crisis do not occasion a reversion to the nuclear, heteronormative family but rather yield collaborative communities of multiply displaced peoples who form coalitions across various formations of families that include gender-queer models of intimacy. One of my interests in Hopkinson's *Midnight Robber* lies in how this work of speculative fiction thereby queers notions of futurity. Hopkinson's formulation of futurity, however, not only looks forward but also thinks through alternative histories of technoscience. This doubly valenced view of the future emerges through a postcolonial critique of Western constructions of modernity. In these ways, *Midnight Robber* reminds us that storytelling itself, in its various forms of written and oral traditions, is a powerful technology capable of manipulating memories, charting multiple trajectories, and shifting the parameters of how we conceive of past, present, and future. I therefore examine how she understands the science fiction genre as a mode of writing that could stand to learn much from practices of storytelling beyond the Western canon.

Though both canonical science and science fiction proclaim their descent from Western origins, *Midnight Robber* imagines what kind of future would ensue from technocultural origin myths and rhetoric that emerge out of diasporic African roots.[49] For example, Hopkinson draws a parallel between the Middle Passage of African slaves to the New World and the arrival of Caribbean space colonists to Toussaint, a planet populated with people of mixed race who have banded together to escape Earth's longstanding patterns of exploitative labor practices. The novel both commences and concludes in Jonkanoo season, "when all of Toussaint would celebrate the landing of the Marryshow Corporation nation ships that had brought their ancestors to this planet two centuries before" (18).[50] Indeed, Hopkinson organizes the entire narrative around celebrations of diasporic movement. The original settlers of Toussaint arrived in rocket ships rather than tall ships, but the parallel between this fantastic voyage and the Middle Passage is reinforced by Ben, who has given the protagonist, Tan-Tan, a carnival hat in the shape of a ship. Ben says: "Long time, that hat would be make in the shape of a sea ship, not a rocket ship, and them black people inside woulda been lying packup head to toe in they own shit, with chains round them ankles. Let the child remember how black people make this crossing as free people this time" (21).

Ben draws an explicit connection between this future interplanetary journey and the transatlantic slave route, and Tan-Tan's Jonkanoo ship-hat also refers to other mass movements of diasporic communities. With the name "Black Star Line II" etched into its side, Tan-Tan's rocket ship alludes to Marcus Garvey's original Black Star Line, intended to facilitate a large-scale back-to-Africa movement in the 1920s. But more than supplanting one set of origin myths for another, Hopkinson suggests the ways diasporic movement itself functioned as Caribbean technoculture.

In this future world, spaceships recall an African diasporic past rather than Western classical legacies. In an interview with Dianne Glave, Hopkinson makes this argument very explicitly: "The current metaphors for technology and social behaviors and systems are largely from Greco-Roman mythology. We call our spaceships Apollo and our complexes Oedipus. We talk about cyberspace. So I wondered what metaphors we (Caribbean people) would create for technologies that we had made, how we would think about those technologies."[51] In this quotation, Hopkinson asks us to think critically about the names and metaphors people use to describe technology. She insightfully asserts that narratives about technology affect how we categorize "technology" and may even limit the process of conceiving of other kinds of technologies altogether. Naming spaceships after Greco-Roman mythology—or, for that matter, naming an early Space Shuttle orbiter prototype after the famous science fiction starship *Enterprise*—suggests a Western origin myth for technology that eclipses other points of technological origins and adaptations. Hopkinson adopts Caribbean myths as the creative basis for the names of and the logics behind the various technological innovations in *Midnight Robber* to alter common perceptions of what technology is, where it came from, and therefore who has a claim to it.

The image of the ship is equally central to Paul Gilroy's *The Black Atlantic*.[52] Gilroy emphasizes black transnational networks of social activism and cross-pollinating cultural production. Like Hopkinson, he establishes the Middle Passage as a sort of origin myth for future transoceanic crossings by the likes of W. E. B. Du Bois, Frederick Douglass, and Marcus Garvey. Through this same image of the ship, Hopkinson puts together these notions of diaspora and network to generate an alternative narrative about technology's relationship to projects of racial formation. The imaginative premise of *Midnight Robber* shifts the origins of a technofuture world from Greco-Roman, European Enlightenment roots to African routes—from an imperialist epistemology of amassed knowledge to a different model of information dispersal and circuitry. In her formulation of artificially intelligent *eshus*, tonal-based code resembling Caribbean patois, and nanomite-seeded Nation Worlds linked together by a digital network called Granny Nanny, Hopkinson speculates on an alternative genealogy of technology. Her imagination of an alternative genealogy from which a richly described world of technologies emerges is successful beyond just the superficial level of providing new names for existing technology. Conceived from an Afro-Caribbean trickster tradition, Toussaint's system of *eshus* and Anansi webs does not understand truth to be self-evident, universal, or beyond question. Rather, these artificially intelligent beings learn to tell partial truths and to manipulate historical narratives according to their audiences. This is how one character's wife is able to have an affair in her home without her husband finding out from the house *eshu* and how Tan-Tan's robot nurse is able to keep up with her insatiable appetite for alternative histories. In these ways, Hopkinson shows how intertwined cultural myths and technological innovations can be.

In *Midnight Robber*, technoscience does not take the form of Big Brother but of "Granny Nanny," whose name has three apparent sources: Granny Nanny of the Maroons, a legendary hero of Jamaica who led and organized the Maroons and other black dissidents against the British during the 1720s and 1730s; the nanotechnology that facilitates the human-machine interface on Toussaint, "the *Grande Nanotech* Sentient Interface" (10, emphasis mine); and Anansi, the trickster figure who takes the shape of a spider. "Granny Nansi's Web" reconfigures what we might think of as the World Wide Web, or the Internet, but the paradigm has shifted dramatically. Rather than emerging from William Gibson's conceptualization of "cyberspace" or from Bill Gates's corporate empire, this net earns its name from a web, or network, or even archipelago of cultural exchange throughout the African diaspora.

Though the cyberspace we know is based on a binary language, Granny Nanny's code is "tonal instead of text-based" (51). Navigating the web in Toussaint probably requires more familiarity with an oral tradition than with a written one. Indeed, "nannycode" or "nannysong" sounds most like the "warbling patwa" (221) of the douen women, whose nearly incomprehensible speech-song is so difficult to set down in type that Hopkinson captures it by using bold print, asterisks, and a different font from the rest of the text. She has already theorized her own use of creolized languages, but it is interesting to consider how the paradigm shift she discusses in her interview with Glave works to alter the etymological roots that shape our discourse and understanding of technoculture. By disassociating technology from its Greek and Latin roots, *Midnight Robber* aims at making the SF genre available to non-European writers whose cultural inheritance might include Yoruban mythology, Chinese folklore, or South Asian legends. The language that best expresses technoculture for Hopkinson is a kind of Caribbean patois, emblematic of the kind of "fusion of the genres" that she is after.[53]

At the end of the novel, Tan-Tan steps into the role of Robber Queen, the notorious trickster figure of the novel's title. The Midnight Robber at carnival time pretends to capture fellow revelers to terrify them with gory stories about death and destruction and to elicit coins from the audience in exchange for sparing their lives. Abducted into slavery, taken to a strange land filled with strange people, and forced to thieve in order to survive, the Midnight Robber works well as an SF hero or heroine who must earn his or her keep by being an excellent wordsmith.

The novel's opening poem, "Stolen Song," by David Findlay, celebrates signification practices and trickster finesse in its repetition of the line "I stole the torturer's tongue!" Creolization and signification serve as survival techniques in *Midnight Robber*. What Hopkinson refers to as the "word science" of the Robber Queen or Tan-Tan is what ultimately saves our heroine when she vanquishes Janisette in a verbal duel at the end of the novel (320). Dressed in full Robber costume, Tan-Tan "spat at Janisette—'no mercy!'—the traditional final phrase of the calypsonian who'd won the battle of wits and words. Tan-Tan gasped, put a hand up to her magical mouth" (326). Tan-Tan herself is a black SF writer. From an early age, she crafts "tales to pass the time" by extrapolating from bits of history available to her on the web: "So the minder would access the Nanny history from the web and try to adapt it to Tan-Tan's notions of how the story went" (17). Tan-Tan's ability to adapt historical narratives and create speculative fiction out of those variations points to the way in which Hopkinson uses historical revisions of technocultural origin myths to carve out a space for more alternative SF writers. "I'm fascinated with the notion of breaking an imposed language apart and remixing it," she writes. "To speak in the hacked language is not just to speak in an accent or a creole; to say the words aloud is an act of referencing history and claiming space."[54] This quotation most cogently reveals the way in which Hopkinson sees the creolization of language as a form of technology that can be "remixed" and "hacked" to claim space within an overly narrow definition of SF as a literary tradition. Because Tan-Tan's trickster speech saves her life, weaving fabulist tales (and writing speculative fiction) represents an integral survival technique, as Henry Louis Gates Jr. argues about "mastering the figurative" as an essential means of "black survival in oppressive Western cultures." Figuring Tan-Tan's linguistic prowess around the popular carnival character of the Midnight Robber, Hopkinson refers to the character's use of "Robber Talk," derived from the African griot tradition of storytelling. However, as the female protagonist who vanquishes her enemies with a performance of Robber Talk, Tan-Tan's Robber Queen also enacts a feminist appropriation of the male-dominated griot tradition—an intervention Hopkinson herself makes to the genre of science fiction.

Though many of the more overt signs of a diasporic literary inheritance are specifically African in origin, Hopkinson emphatically asserts the cross-ethnic circulation at work in the Caribbean. *Midnight Robber*'s heroes are figures of hybridity, heterogeneous bloodlines, and nomadic exile. Toussaint is already a planet of exiles, and it has established another dimension of exiles on the prison colony, worlds up the halfway tree. Going up this tree involves travel across several "dimensional veils" (74–75). Several scholars, including Hopkinson herself, have already made the connection between this phrase and Du Bois's use of the "veil" concept in his articulation of double consciousness in *Souls of Black Folk*.[55] Hopkinson also makes the connection to veils in an Indian experience of double consciousness in her online essay "Dark Ink," in which she cites Uppinder Mehan's essay "The Domestication of Technology in Indian Science Fiction Stories."[56] Tan-Tan suffers a sort of double exile over the course of the novel. She first becomes uprooted from her home on Toussaint when she follows her father, Antonio, into exile on New Half-Way Tree after he commits a murder. Then when Tan-Tan herself turns the knife on her father-turned-rapist, she must flee into the wilderness to live with the douen people: "She had had home torn from her again" (193). Tan-Tan's story of double exile, forced migration, and dislocation from home resonates with Caribbean history not only because of the halfway tree parallel to the forced migrations along the transatlantic slave route, but also because of its surprising connection to the Indian epic the Ramayana. Tracing the routes of this Indian cultural artifact, one notices how the Caribbean becomes one site where African and South Asian cultural routes intersect. Hopkinson's construction of this future world of exilic Caribbean peoples includes a reminder that a history of the Caribbean includes not only the African slave trade but also the migration of East Indian laborers to Trinidad and Tobago as well as Jamaica, following the abolition of slavery. Hopkinson is completely mindful of this convergence of two powerful oral traditions. For example, when Granny Nanny tells stories about Tan-Tan to several children, Hopkinson is careful to include one audience member named Sita, whose namesake in the Ramayana also suffers a double exile (78).[57] Some settlers of Toussaint, we learn, made their intergalactic voyage on a vessel named "Shipmate Shiva," which carried "longtime ago East Indians, the ones who crossed the Kalpani, the Black Water on Earth to go and work their fingers to the bone as indentured labour in the Caribbean" (49). Jonkanoo week, a celebration around Christmas time in the Caribbean, is another sign of Toussaint's heterogeneous ancestry. It is a "time to remember the way their forefathers had toiled and sweated together: Taino Carib and Arawak; African; Asian; Indian; even the Euro, though some wasn't too happy to acknowledge that there bloodline. All the bloods flowing into one river, making a new home on a new planet" (18). In this passage, Hopkinson points to the enmeshed bloodlines that constitute the population of Toussaint. It is a world in which hybridity and *créolité* are celebrated, overturning colonialist privileging of European bloodlines.

Midnight Robber not only names an Afro-Caribbean legacy to these space colonists but also recognizes the ways in which the African slave trade and the Asian coolie trade to the Caribbean remain linked and shared labor histories. In her depictions of Toussaint and New Half-Way Tree, Hopkinson renders the Caribbean archipelago a speculative space, in which diasporic movement works as a technology that travels covalently with other intensified global flows, including the conjuncture of African slave labor and Asian migrant labor to the Caribbean.

Though brought together by the common blood, sweat, and tears shed over the backbreaking work shared by all these racialized bodies, the multiethnic community of Toussaint enjoys a rather idyllic respite. No human bodies labor on Toussaint because various machines, AI, and "Granny Nanny" take care of most day-to-day conveniences. A robotic wetnurse provides Tan-Tan with milk from the moment she is born, and later a "minder" functions as Tan-Tan's primary caretaker, playmate, babysitter, and gentle disciplinarian: "[Tan-Tan] liked leaning against the minder's yielding chicle, humming along with the nursery rhymes it would sing to her. She had nearly outgrown the minder now, yes, but it did its level best to keep up with her" (17). The most visible acts of robot labor on Toussaint are forms of reproductive labor—precisely the kind of work that Caribbean migrant women perform in the Global North.

On the planet Toussaint, descendants of a slave exodus from Earth create an artificially intelligent class of servants who perform all acts of manual and domestic labor, from nursing human infants to running (or pulling) pedicabs and cleaning houses. As one character puts it, "backbreak ain't for people" (8). There is even a labor tax on humans who elect to perform manual labor. Mayor Antonio explains to a pedicab runner: "Is a labour tax. For the way allyou insist on using people when a a.i. could run a cab like this. You know how it does bother citizens to see allyou doing manual labor so" (8). Only one subset of human society on Toussaint refuses this dependence on AI, and Hopkinson uses this group to think through the relationship between technology and labor.

The pedicab runners of Toussaint are descendants of hackers who use their techno-savvy to maintain privacy, Toussaint's "most precious commodity" (10). Because Toussaint's buildings, tools, and "even the Earth itself" have been "seeded with nanomites," the "Nation Worlds were one enormous data-gathering system" monitored, regulated, and disseminated through one network (10). In such a data-fueled world, questions about labor arise alongside questions about information, history, and narrative. The pedicab runners "lived in group households and claimed that it was their religious right to use only headblind tools" (10). Organizing off the grid, these communities also form social networks that depart from normative familial structures. The pedicab runner Beata, whom Antonio encounters at the beginning of the novel, is a woman who lives with three wives and the father of her children in one home. As a pedicab runner, Beata creates her own routes that serve as ways to circulate information clandestinely, in a fashion similar to the strategy used by Toussaint's namesake Toussaint L'Ouverture, who, as a free black coachman, could disseminate information and organize the Haitian Revolution, the first successful slave revolt in the New World. Hopkinson's depiction of these queer pedicab communities models in speculative fiction the kinds of queer kinship formations elucidated in Martin Manalansan's work on "queer love."[58] Researching queer of color, makeshift communities in Jackson Heights, Queens, Manalansan focuses on how migrant, undocumented workers respond to the precarious conditions of their labor by altering notions of "family."[59] Hopkinson rewrites the developmental progress narrative as it pertains to not only technofutures but also to sexuality and thus emphasizes the importance of thinking through notions of futurity as inextricably linked to formulations of sexuality. In her incisive study of the policing of sexuality in Trinidad and Tobago and the Bahamas, M. Jacqui Alexander argues that in the postcolonial context, when the "nation" and its ideologies are in tumult, the criminalization of queer sex "functions as a technology of control, and much like other technologies of control becomes an important site for the production and reproduction of state power."[60]

The machine-human relationship on Toussaint purports to be nonabusive and benevolent, at first. The AI workers do not complain or revolt; they are eternally docile, subservient, and helpful. Nevertheless, Hopkinson undermines potential techno-utopian readings in at least two ways. First, the original denizens of Toussaint are comprised of refugees from Earth's Caribbean islands, where a history of slavery and hard, unpaid labor is actively remembered during every Jonkanoo season on Toussaint. Despite this history, people on Toussaint fail to think self-critically about this new generation of laboring, albeit mechanical, bodies. Hopkinson's invention of a multiethnic, diasporic community calls attention to the politics of nonhuman, so-called free labor.

Hopkinson's focus on Toussaint's overdependence on a subjugated labor force becomes readily apparent in the second half of the novel when she introduces readers to the prison-colony-world of New Half-Way Tree. This new world remains strangely familiar as we discover it is only Toussaint again in a parallel universe. In this alternate dimension, though, Toussaint/New Half-Way Tree is technologically impoverished; there are no "docile machines" to perform manual labor. The primary burden of work on New Half-Way Tree has been displaced onto the shoulders of the indigenous creatures of the planet. These forest dwellers are threatened by the impending onslaught of industrialization in the human sectors of the planet. Some are craftsmen, some work as gardeners, and some trade goods with the human colonists as merchants. The actual details of the labor they perform, though, remain rather vague, as Hopkinson's descriptions focus more on the power dynamics apparent in everyday encounters between groups. By juxtaposing New Half-Way Tree and Toussaint as employing different systems of labor, Hopkinson implicitly asks (in a similar vein as other SF stories such as Derrick Bell's "The Space Traders" and Sergio Arau and Yareli Arizmendi's 2004 film, *A Day without a Mexican*) what would happen to a place like Toussaint if all the workers suddenly disappeared. Hopkinson uses these parallel dimensions to posit alternative but repetitive systems of oppression. Even when sovereignty is no longer an issue—when slaves and prisoners escape across space and time—exploitative and violent social relations continue when masculinist paradigms remain in place.

On New Half-Way Tree, Tan-Tan discovers a preindustrial society in which everyone (human and nonhuman) must perform hard labor.[61] It is here that Hopkinson introduces readers to the douens, who are reptilian and birdlike creatures serving but living separately from humans. Though exiles themselves, the humans have become the colonizers of a new world. The human settlers find themselves in need of help from but threatened by the indigenous creature-peoples already there. Hopkinson's critique is of how quickly and readily a marginalized people will figure out a way to exploit another group once they themselves have access to power. Hopkinson's description of the everyday interactions between the humans and the douen recalls scenes from African American literature, including conjure tales and slave narratives by Charles Chesnutt and Frederick Douglass that emphasize linguistic adeptness bolstered by a trickster tradition. Infantilized within a paternalistic system of coerced subservience, the douens share somewhat in what is often considered to be an African American experience. Humans address Chichibud, Tan-Tan's first douen friend, as "boy," and Tan-Tan observes how men "spoke to Chichibud the way adults spoke to her" (120). Hopkinson casts Chichibud, in turn, as the consummate trickster figure whose witticisms delight Tan-Tan as an avid student of the double-voiced black vernacular he deploys. When a human challenges his laughter by asking, "You have something to say?" Chichibud replies, "No, Boss. Is tall-people business, oui?" (123). Though Tan-Tan arrives on New Half-Way Tree by hacking codes and manipulating time and space, she learns from Chichibud how to deploy such code sliding in everyday cultural practices of storytelling and dialogue. When Chichibud addresses the village men as "Master," Tan-Tan expresses her dismay and confusion: "Master? Only machines were supposed to give anybody rank like that. . . . Tan-Tan scolded, 'He not your boss, Chichibud.' . . . Shipmates all have the same status. Nobody higher than a next somebody. You must call he 'Compere,' she explained to the douen" (121).

According to the new human settlers of New Half-Way Tree, the douens, who practice "obeah magic," are "superstitious" (121) and "simple" (139). The douens reject industrialization and insist on working only with wood and natural materials; they "did everything with their hands and never thought to advance themselves any further" (139). In this way, Hopkinson levies a critique against the faulty correspondence between technological advancement and matter-of-course superiority that colonizers have deployed in their attempts to rationalize and justify their subjugation of indigenous peoples. The douens excel in handicrafts—carpentry, weaving, and the crafting of oral narratives. Here Hopkinson's postcolonial critique signals a challenge to the less troubled, more romantic picture of technology represented earlier in the novel on Toussaint.

Hopkinson cultivates an association between the function of the douen on New Half-Way Tree and the status of the AI in Toussaint in order to establish continuity across time and space—to emphasize the historical and ongoing politics of labor. Despite inhabiting different space-times, the douen and the AI both constitute laboring classes. On the one hand, technology has been a tool of colonization, oppression, and exploitation. On the other hand, one could claim (as Gates, Everett, and Gilroy do) that alternative technologies have always been necessary, integral, and useful tools for survival among those who are not readily granted access to dominant technologies. The inhabitants of New Half-Way Tree eventually erect iron forgeries that start to generate cars and weapons, which become the means of persecuting Tan-Tan and driving out the douens from their tree homes. The douens, sensing impending doom, do their best to learn the techniques of ironwork despite the villagers' profound efforts to keep the skills a secret, private trade. Chichibud explains: "If douens don't learn tallpeople tricks, oonuh will use them 'pon we" (230). This logic returns us to Gates's and Hopkinson's urgent advocacy of producing alternative technologies when it comes to language. These technolingual strategies of coding and signifying are particularly germane to the world of speculative fiction, and in this way, speculative fiction itself works as a form of trickster technology that takes the generic tools of science fiction and makes them available to communities whose members have previously been excluded from the genre.

In her revision of technocultural origin myths and her imagination of a technology emerging from a multiethnic Caribbean diasporic context, Hopkinson looks beyond Eurocentric technocultural discourse for alternative genealogies and more expansive understandings of technology. Furthermore, she not only extrapolates from this alternative genealogy a futuristic world of embedded AI and networked societies, but she also suggests that these technologies preexist in the forms of oral traditions and diasporic communications in their conceptual emergence. *Midnight Robber* thereby provides a countermemory of technology in ways that resonate with Gilroy's articulation of a "counterculture of modernity" in his formulation of the Black Atlantic.⁶²

Drawing from a vast reservoir of Caribbean culture and history, Hopkinson conjures up a speculative reality, and her explicit desire to imagine a techno-mythology specific to Caribbean communities attests to her narration of a technoculture that radically departs from Western Enlightenment traditions. Her visual representation of the warbling patwa of the douen women even constitutes an emergent form of language. Likewise, Tan-Tan's recognition of a similarity in these speech patterns to the nanny-song she learned as a child on Toussaint from communicating with AI suggests that hacking linguistic codes facilitates cross-cultural understanding. Once Tan-Tan cracks the code, she realizes that her adoptive douen mother Benta is not just chirping nonsense but in fact trying to communicate important messages to her.

Queer Families in Midnight Robber

In *Midnight Robber*, Tan-Tan forms an intimate relationship with Abitefa, a nongender-specific member of the indigenous species of the planet. It is a human/nonhuman intimacy that Hopkinson uses to explore alternative, queer formations of families and futurities that interrogate the reproductive futurity associated with strictly human, heteronormative families. The plot does not resolve with Tan-Tan finding solace in the invitation back into human and heteronormative society by marrying Melonhead. Rather, that childhood romance has been altered when they meet again, after Tan-Tan has come to understand the queerer kinship formations of the douen. On the brink of delivering her baby, Tan-Tan decides that she must leave the human settlement to give birth: "'Melonhead, I have to go home.' 'What home? Where?' 'I have to go back in the bush to Abitefa.' 'You mad or what? You turn bassourdie? You need to lie down and rest.' 'I will lie down when I reach back in the bush. I have to go right now.' Holding her belly protectively, she turned on her heel and started walking, with or without him" (327). Locating "home" for this doubly exiled woman, who has shifted across both time and space, means "shifting constantly to stay in one place," to put it in Hopkinson's words.⁶³ Tan-Tan's refusal to join normative society in the form of either the human settlement or a heteronormative wedding indicates Hopkinson's search for an alternative to a reproductive futurism that sustains heteropatriarchy. These queerings extend to narrative form, too.

Midnight Robber is a speculative fiction that considers language and narrative as technologies. It shifts across narrative points of view as frequently as it plays with shifts across time and space. Hopkinson begins, ends, and interrupts her narrative with short tales of Tan-Tan the Robber Queen, a mythic set of tales narrated by the AI nano-eshu who has found its way through Tan-Tan's bloodstream to communicate with her developing fetus. At other times, Hopkinson writes in the third person, with Tan-Tan as the focal character. Moving back and forth between these two narrative modes, one of them privileging a nonhuman point of view, Hopkinson emphasizes multiple perspectives.

Written as a narrative about labor in a structural form that emphasizes the labor of narrative production, *Midnight Robber* culminates and ends with the birth of Tubman, Tan-Tan's baby—whose name refers to Harriet Tubman, who helped many slaves escape their bonds in the U.S. South and find safe passage to the North, often going to Canada. The Underground Railroad, with which the name Tubman is closely associated, functioned as a network of secret routes and safe houses coordinated through a system of code words borrowed from the railroad terminology. By giving Tan-Tan's child the name Tubman, Hopkinson again alludes to another system of networks and linguistic codes used as tactical resistance to slavery. In this way, Hopkinson encodes her own text with multiple kinds of deliveries—the delivery of a child into the world, the delivery of slaves to freedom, and the delivery of a speech act that wins Tan-Tan the verbal battle against Janisette. Because Tan-Tan goes into labor precisely at the moment that she pronounces the winning words of the competition, and given the fact that part of *Midnight Robber* consists of an AI passing the stories of the mother on to her fetus, Tan-Tan's pregnancy also bears significance as a process of bringing stories into being.

The story of Harriet Tubman and the Underground Railroad is also a narrative that retells the origin story of network societies. The name Tubman invokes a network and perhaps specifically a fugitive framework that exceeds the borders of the United States, as do Hopkinson's own affiliations with Canada and the Caribbean. The Underground Railroad, which was comprised of not only free slaves but also white abolitionists and Native American activists, delivered runaway slaves to Canada and Mexico and thus connected the Americas in a hemispheric relation.

Hopkinson's *Midnight Robber*, like Cuarón's *Children of Men*, culminates in the birth of a child. Kee's baby girl, Dylan, will not only serve as a surrogation of patrilineal futurity but will also shoulder the responsibility of curing the world's infertility. She and her mother will immediately become subjects of medical experiments on board *The Tomorrow*, a vessel that might symbolize a future for mankind but that will, in practice, sustain a long history of subjecting black women to experiments in reproductive science. Meanwhile, Tan-Tan's delivery of Tubman not only refers us to a revolutionary activist but also occurs simultaneously with Tan-Tan's coming into her own voice: "Tan-Tan knew her body to be hers again, felt her mouth stretching, stretching open in amazement at the words that had come out of it" (325–26). Describing not Tubman's birth but the miraculous coming into being of Tan-Tan's story, Hopkinson shifts the site of accomplishment and hope to rest not solely on the shoulders of the child but also on the mother's victorious monologue. Hope for the future in *Midnight Robber* may ultimately reside in a birth, but Hopkinson's emphasis on the legacies and stories that get passed on to inform that future constitutes a feminist and queer account of reproductive futurism.

The history surrounding women of color and reproduction in the United States runs the gamut of some of the most egregious abuses of scientific power in the histories of science, including sterilization campaigns and medical experimentation on coerced subjects, not to mention the effects of slavery on the reproductive health and futures of black women. By analyzing *Children of Men* and *Midnight Robber*, I offer two contemporary science fictions that begin to interrogate a vexed history and politics of reproduction. In my consideration of the cinematography at work in Cuarón's film and the linguistic hacking prevalent in Hopkinson's writing, I also suggest the imbrications of science fictions of reproduction and reproductive technologies in formulations of futurity and argue that speculative fiction can unmoor futurity from the reproductive labor that is often exacted on women of color. Against the backdrop of tenacious moves to relegate black life to nonbeing, Hopkinson's speculative revisions of race and reproductive possibility offer an important alternative to the racialized surrogations of reproductive futurity.

4

THE CRUEL OPTIMISM OF
THE ASIAN CENTURY

> The really good news is that few Asians have lost their optimism about the future. They have no illusions about the crisis but are confident that they remain on the right trajectory to deliver the Asian century.
> —KISHORE MAHBUBANI, "Why Asia Stays Calm in the Storm"

The latest real estate and military developments in the Pacific Ocean feature brazen feats of building on sand. After thirty years of land reclamation efforts, Singapore's construction of the Marina Bay Sands casino and resort functions as the centerpiece to the city-state's reinvention. China's creation of new islands in the South China Sea—otherwise known as the West Philippines Sea—involves pumping massive amounts of sand from the ocean floor onto reef systems around the Spratly Islands. The land-grab for this resource-rich archipelago, hotly disputed among Vietnam, Taiwan, the Philippines, Malaysia, and Brunei, is all the more audacious as its primary developments include not only a military base but also a casino.

Even as gleaming skyscrapers, luxury hotels, and casinos present a futuristic vision of a New Asia, indentured Burmese workers eking out a life on shrimping boats off the coast of Thailand meet that future under vertiginously different circumstances. A Trans-Pacific Partnership, characterized by one reporter as "NAFTA on steroids"[1] continues to negotiate for US and European stakes in the "Asian Century," even as national frameworks yield to globalizing narratives that occlude the precipitous divide between the cosmopolitan elites and the continually displaced migrant workers of the world.

Transpacific futurities and precarities dwell on each other. Insofar as precarity names living in relation to an unknown future, it challenges the seeming inevitability of progress and development through profit-driven technoscience and entrepreneurship. At a moment when neoliberal enthusiasts in Asia excel in pushing notions like talent acquisition and human capital management as the path to the Asian Century, Asia's reconstitution through interest in the global marketplace and market-mediated subjectivities articulates an Asian futurity in which migrant workers, whose livelihoods have been the most decimated by the violence of finance capitalism, are rendered disposable and invisible. The cover of Kishore Mahbubani's 2008 *The New Asian Hemisphere: The Irresistible Shift of Global Power to the East* (figure 4.1) presents readers with what seems to be the global sign for financial growth: skyscrapers under construction.[2] Cranes perch atop every tower, suggestive of the "all-at-once-ness" of growth in Asia. The illuminated construction site stretching into the night sky highlights the unrelenting pace of growth, which proceeds even as the rest of the world sleeps. The scene is a familiar one, prefigured by the race for the tallest building that ran across parts of Asia—namely Singapore, Malaysia, and Taiwan—in the early 2000s.[3] But the unpainted, all white structures feel eerily hollow and decontextualized. There is no sign of the human laborers who welded and wired these structures. The parking lot in the foreground is all but empty, with the exception of one nondescript parked car. This scene of speculative building—construction predicted but not contracted to sell—feels like an already haunted future, in which New Asia has become an empty lot, evacuated of its denizens and prepared to signify the sheer potential of capital.

Published amid the financial crisis of 2008, Mahbubani's book and his piece in the *Financial Times*, which serves as this chapter's epigraph, declare an "Asian century" is realizable. Issued in forward-looking, prophetic tones, Mahbubani's declaration excites what Alan Greenspan once called

FIGURE 4.1. Cover of Kishore Mahbubani's *The New Asian Hemisphere*.

"irrational exuberance."[4] The phrase, uttered in a speech Greenspan gave in 1996, when he was chairman of the Board of Governors of the U.S. Federal Reserve System, characterized the "unduly escalated asset values" of Japan's economic bubble.[5] The next day, Tokyo's stock market fell sharply, closing down 3 percent, and Greenspan's speech was later seen as presaging the Asian financial crash a year later. The extent to which economic projections hang on the words of figures like Greenspan demonstrates how such speculations work as performative speech acts that call the future into being. Similarly, the optimism that Mahbubani announces will deliver the Asian Century structures the affective drive behind speculative investment in Asian futures. This vision of the new Asian hemisphere, colonized by empty high-rises reaching toward limitless horizons and built by deterritorialized workers, projects a future of automated speculative building, fueled by investment-hungry banks. If Greenspan and Mahbubani grasp how their respective declarations of pessimism and optimism will affect the global economy, they do so with two different Asias in mind: Japan of the late 1990s and Singapore at the dawn of a New Asia in 2008.[6] The Asian Century, toward which Mahbubani's optimism strains, functions as a large-scale speculative fiction spawned from neoliberal fantasies cultivated by the authors of the new world order.

The 2011 prospectus of the Asian Development Bank (ADB), *Asia 2050: Realizing the Asian Century*, declares Asia's future economic dominance on the world stage as "plausible but by no means preordained."[7] But in setting out to realize the Asian Century, the ADB—an international financial institution largely modeled on the International Monetary Fund and the World Bank—could not be more explicit about the relationship between imagining a general Asian futurity and the financial speculations in Asian futures and securities markets. As various members of the economic, political, and public policy communities attempt to locate the when and where of the Asian Century, something peculiar happens to how "Asia" is conceptualized. Peter Drysdale, editor of the *East Asia Forum*, refers interchangeably to nation-states and economic cluster entities as Asia: "Already the Asian economies, including Japan, South Korea, China and the other East Asian economies such as ASEAN and Australasia as well as South Asia, account for almost 40 per cent of global output. The Asian century is here."[8] By including the Association of Southeast Asian Nations (ASEAN) in this list, Drysdale does more than identify the Asian region as made up of multiple sovereign states. ASEAN is an international trade interest group of representatives from Brunei, Burma, Cambodia, Indonesia, Laos, Malaysia, the Philippines, Singapore, Thailand, and Vietnam that attempts to stimulate investment within and beyond the Southeast Asian region. Drysdale's conceptualization of the Asian Century revolves around market-mediated subject formations at the macro level. His language signals a shift in thinking from geopolitical regions to economic communities that resemble country clubs, where power is meted out to members according to their shares of ownership.

The Asian Century packages an Asia that has been reduced to signifying Asian capital. Asian people, geography, and culture recede to the backdrop of a global financial stage where the economy becomes the protagonist. Asia's future has been sold. While Asian political leaders, including Deng Xioping of the People's Republic of China and Indian Prime Minister Rajiv Gandhi, first proffered the term "Asian Century" in the 1980s, Mahbubani—Singapore's former ambassador to the United Nations—perpetuates the belief that Asia will take center stage in the world's economy. Drysdale's situating of the Asian Century in an economic region also acutely narrows the understanding of "Asia" and indicates clearly that in Asian futures, only global elites will matter. What does it mean to speak of the Asian Century in a celebratory or triumphalist manner? Drysdale's reduction of "Asia" to mean "Asian economies" signals a broader myopia in measurements of national wealth and affluence in terms of gross domestic product, which fails to account for great discrepancies in wealth among a nation's population.

Although the ADB declares that "Asia's future is in its own hands,"[9] the Bank is made up of sixty-seven member countries, of which only forty-eight are from "within Asia and the Pacific," while the remaining nineteen are from "outside."[10] Australia and New Zealand both count as "within Asia and the Pacific," whereas the United States and European countries are "outside." This sorting handily overlooks Guam and Hawaii as instances in which the United States could be considered to be "within" rather than beyond Asia. Reviewing the list of regional members (which include Bangladesh, Fiji, India, the Marshall Islands, Pakistan, the Philippines, Samoa, Sri Lanka, Vanuatu, and Vietnam, as well as Afghanistan—a founding member of the ADB in 1966, but tellingly absent from the bank's membership between 1980 and 2001), one reads the signs of centuries of U.S. and European imperialism in Asia that complicate the notion of discrete insides and outsides of the region. It is the unsettled dynamic that constitutes a transnational Asian/American space, which is precisely the in-between, both/and condition of the majority of the ADB's members that the framing of "within" versus "outside" works to disavow.[11] In its outlining of inside and outside members, the ADB occludes the transnational even as it deploys the neoliberal rhetoric of global (capitalist) cooperation. What facilitates and motivates this contradiction is the hope of delinking histories of U.S. and European imperialism in the Asia-Pacific region and the labor diasporas it created—delinking the aspirational orientations of self-improvement, optimization of life, and self-management of neoliberal reform from a reliance on invisible migrant labor to support the appearance of seemingly universal choice architecture.

The ADB also distributed a promotional video that proffers a contradictory theme of self-determination. What "Asia's future" in "its own hands" actually looks like is the bank's financial instruments such as equity investments and securities, pooled into the Asian Development Fund, which provides "opportunities for people to lift themselves out of poverty."[12] The bootstraps rhetoric of rugged individualism imagines Asia's future in the hands of what Aihwa Ong would call "educated and self-propulsive individuals" in the global circuit, who "claim citizenship-like entitlements and benefits, even at the expense of territorialized citizens."[13] Building on her earlier work on "flexible citizenship,"[14] in *Neoliberalism as Exception* Ong revisits the disaggregation of national populations into those with mobile entitlements and those whose often-forced displacements exclude them from the ostensible protections of national citizenship: "Low-skill citizens and migrants become exceptions to neoliberal mechanisms and are constructed as excludable populations in transit, shuttled in and out of zones of growth."

A critical analysis of Asian futurity as a discursive site can reveal points of contradiction in American neoliberalism as it travels abroad that have to do with earlier forms of racial and colonial subjugation nascent in the architecture of neoliberalism itself.[15] As Asia develops its own neoliberal rhetoric, articulating its aspirational orientations necessitates the revision of Asian futurity as projected through the racialized filters of the West.[16] Techno-Orientalism, as David Morley and Kevin Robins describe in their 1995 examination of the term, names the form of Orientalism shaped by U.S. and European fantasies of Japan and the shift in those imaginaries in the 1980s from an "exotic playground" to a land of emotionless automatons.[17] Perhaps epitomized by Western dystopian cyberpunk such as Ridley Scott's *Blade Runner* (1982) and William Gibson's *Neuromancer* (1984), techno-Orientalism figures the Japanese as "unfeeling aliens; they are cyborgs and replicants. But there is also the sense that these mutants are now better adapted to survive in the future."[18] While Morley and Robins understand techno-Orientalism as primarily born out of Western anxieties about Japan's challenge to U.S. economic hegemony, they also suggest more specifically how techno-Orientalism arises just as Japan emerges as "the largest creditor and the largest net investor in the world."[19] What Morley and Robins never fully develop, and what I explore in more depth here, is this coordinated turn toward Asian futures in both financial and cultural forms of speculation.

As Asia grasps at its own speculative language with which to narrate its own futurity, certain problems necessitate a disavowal of the racism of techno-Orientalism. As Asian capitalist interests attempt to harness the valuations of privatized worth that techno-Orientalism purveyed so efficiently, what other ideological frameworks are dragged into the narration of the Asian Century? And is there another way to imagine Asian futurity that is not always already working toward capitalist gain? This chapter offers a close examination of Asian futurity in its various forms.

The Asianization of Aspiration

[We] need to think "utopia" differently in terms of other forms of subjectivity,
work, and exploitation within the uneven conditions of globalization.
—LISA LOWE, "Utopia and Modernity"

In 2007, Philips Norelco launched an ad campaign to promote their moisturizing wet-shave system produced in collaboration with Nivea for Men.[20] Featuring a grooming robot fashioned in the style of a geisha (*nihongami*-esque hairdo, accentuation of the nape of the neck, elevated heels), the ad offers a revealing demonstration of the key mechanics of techno-Orientalism: the dehumanization of an Asian subject, a romance narrative between a feminized East and a masculinized West, and a broader preoccupation with Asia's rise to technocultural prowess in the global theater. Equipped with wrist-embedded, electric razor, the Philips Norelco geisha-bot prepares a futuristic bathroom, adjusting the automatically dimming windows and activating the gravity-defying shower with a wave of her hand. As the robot geisha and the white man awaiting his close but nonirritating shave meet in the shower, united in the miracle of wet-shave technology, the commercial rehearses an all-too-familiar scene of techno-Orientalism. The Robot Skin ad not only capitalizes on a fantasy of docile Asian technoscience, gendered and sexualized to perform a service role and rendered recognizable through a Western fetishization of geishas; it also—in its presentation of a seamless interface of the human body, technology, and the natural environment—promises insurance against potential friction (literal and figurative) at the contact zones of flesh and blade, water and electricity, East and West, past and future, local and global.[21]

A Netherlands-based multinational corporation, with factories across Southeast Asia and Latin America, Philips Norelco describes itself as a "Health and Well-being company, focused on improving people's lives through timely innovations."[22] Seeking to turn a profit by constructing a future that promises to deliver a better you with smoother skin and a nearly hairless existence, the geisha-bot ad instantiates a form of predatory speculation that capitalizes on vectors of improvement and notions of relentlessly modifiable selves. Philips Norelco proffers Robot Skin as the futuristic solution to needling insecurities about the ungroomed body. What would it mean to unsettle the smooth, well-managed world promised by Philips Norelco's predatory speculations? How might an alternative futurity disrupt the elegant fantasies of smooth, continuous time? Is it possible to take up techno-Orientalist tropes partially, selectively, and strategically to reinterpret and repurpose the narrative relation between Asia and technology?

In Philips Norelco's imagined futurescape of the shaver-wielding geisha-bot, the phallic threat of Asian technopower remains ensconced in a female casing made available for an interface on the terms of white, male, heterosexual desire. At once the sign of high *techne* and domesticated service, the geisha-bot can be read as supplemental, subservient, and even beholden to the West for her technological prowess. In this way, the Robot Skin ad cultivates an image of Asia as the dependent technological servant of Western economies and consumption. Asian modernity is represented as reliant on U.S. and European markets. Simultaneously ahead of the curve (with a high-tech robot) and behind the times (with a premodern geisha), Asia is never of the moment. Fixed in time as either pre- or postmodern, it does not exist in this narrative beyond two historical eras when the West stood to gain the most from a paternalistic relationship with Japan.[23] Borrowing the stylized accoutrements of the science fiction genre, the Philips Norelco ad campaign projects its fantasy of a future in which the perceived

Asian technological threat recognizes its indebtedness and obligation to the Western world.

The Robot Skin ad, which ran primarily in the United Kingdom and the United States at the end of 2007, remobilizes techno-Orientalism precisely at a moment when the so-called tiger economies—rapidly industrializing countries including South Korea, Singapore, Hong Kong, and Taiwan—stood at the precipice of a second financial crisis following the first, in 1997–98. In her keen analysis of the "Asianization" of financial crises, Laura Kang draws a revealing parallel between the characterization of newly industrializing Asian countries and the subprime borrowers of the U.S. housing market: "In both scenarios, the measure of economic ascent is greater indebtedness and exposure to the vagaries of capital markets rather than self-sufficiency and solvency. . . . By attributing the 1997–98 crisis to an untenable Asian permutation of an original and righteous 'Western capitalism,' the International Monetary Fund (IMF) and the U.S. Treasury Department compelled restructurings, which further buttressed the rightness of a specifically U.S.-dictated neoliberal program of deregulation, privatization, and financial liberalization."[24]

As Kang argues, rather than pointing to the dangers of unfettered speculations and the profiteering on financial instruments, the "Wall Street–Treasury–IMF complex"—rooted in U.S. empire in Asia—mapped preexisting racist ideas about Asians all looking the same onto the Asian financial crash by assuming a sameness of Asian markets.[25] Blaming the instability of the market on an errant "Asian" version of capitalism, Western economists emboldened a perceived difference between "Asian" and "American" capitalisms. Indeed, this bifurcation was vigorously reinforced by Asian politicians and pundits who, during the prosperous 1980s and 1990s, criticized neoliberalism as a particularly American form of capitalist imperialism to which Asian leaders should "say no."[26] But capitalism belongs to no one. It is all too eager to make itself at home and adapt to whatever ideological systems it needs to negotiate to set up shop. The adaptation, at least in the case of Singapore, unfolds across the terrain of Asian futurity.

Future•Singapore

Since the 1997–98 and 2007–8 financial crises, Singapore has probably emerged for the moment as the most triumphant Asian economy, cited as the fastest growing in the world with one of the highest gross domestic products per capita—an accomplishment often attributed to its aggressive and perhaps desperate turn toward financial liberalization after the 1997–98 crash. A key part of engineering this turn toward a radically more neoliberal economic policy involved the state reimagining itself as a city-state of the Future, which meant becoming an international hub of financial speculation, engineering, and biotechnology. Future•Singapore and its more recent speculative iteration Future-Ready Singapore are the names of two initiatives sponsored in the wake of the 2008 global financial crisis by the state's Economic Development Board (EDB) and clearly instantiate Singapore's active reinvention of itself as a neoliberal platform "designed to develop and test bed new ideas and solutions in the areas of urban living, wellness, ageing and healthcare, and lifestyle products and services."[27] Imagining itself as a testing ground, where foreign investment might "bed" down for future growth, the EDB mobilizes gendered, agricultural metaphors to connote financial growth. The Western fantasy of Asia as supplementary and disposable, as rehearsed in Philips Norelco's fetishization of the geisha-bot, plays out here in Southeast Asian policy and ideology, in somewhat altered form. While Singaporean business elites stand to profit from offering up the figuration of Singapore as a testing ground, the EDB does so to make Singapore indispensable to global futures rather than supplemental and disposable. Future•Singapore solicits international investments by positioning the city-state as a speculative geography: "Companies need somewhere to hatch ideas, a laboratory to test concepts, a facility where prototypes can be test-driven. We offer Singapore as that partner-location, as a living laboratory for innovative companies to experiment and develop world-class solutions."[28] This vision of Singapore as the world's laboratory for global development presents a sanitized environment, which the EDB suggests is fostered through a "pro-IP stance" and "competitive" tax rates and tax laws.[29] Critical science studies might be helpful in not only understanding the constraints of the laboratory's forms on its output but also in shedding light on the values, subjects, and interferences it disavows. Following Bruno Latour's injunction to examine the dirty underbelly of the laboratory—the monstrous leviathan that lurks below the promise of purification—let us pursue those anarchic variables that disturb the EDB's smooth projections of futurity.[30]

The fashioning of a worldly Singaporean as the idealized inhabitant of this Asian future involves the figurative disavowal as well as the actual evacuation of undesirable populations in Singapore, both of which have occurred since the turn toward neoliberalism. In her illuminating examination of Singapore's pursuit of "technopreneurialism"—the aggressive recruitment of foreign professors and researchers to add to its "store of expertise"—Ong describes how significant acts of dispossession are occurring as people are forced out of the fold to make room for massive biotech campuses filled with international experts and industry professionals.[31] To recruit such experts, as well as to pursue international institutional collaborations with the Massachusetts Institute of Technology, for example, the Singaporean state invests in foreign students who are promised high-paying jobs and fast-track permanent residency status. Whom do these newly recruited Singaporeans displace?

Singapore's investments in cosmopolitanism depend on carefully state-controlled movements of migrant laborers from other countries around Southeast Asia, including the Philippines, Indonesia, Sri Lanka, and Bangladesh. In addition to the disparities in flexibility afforded foreign care workers via the stringent work permit system, which segregates workers into high-skill and low-skill groups, Singapore also marginalizes its ethnic Malaysian population, whose members on average make only half the monthly income of Chinese Singaporeans and constitute only 2 percent of the nation's university graduates. In these ways, the promises of meritocracy and technofuturity touted by state officials and reiterated internationally fissure along national, ethnic, and class lines.

Future•Singapore culls and develops its flexible citizens not only by incentivizing foreign professionals to intermarry with local Singaporeans and streamlining their paths to citizenship, but also by pointing existing Singaporeans to "upgrade and upskill" toward professional, managerial, executive, and technical jobs ("Sustainable Population").[32] Feeling the strain on infrastructure and national identity caused by the booming population, the state released a white paper in January 2013 titled "Sustainable Population for a Dynamic Singapore," which reveals an unsustainable tension between the need to "support a dynamic economy . . . to meet Singaporeans' *hopes* and aspirations" and the need to "keep Singapore a good *home*" with a "strong Singaporean core." Witness here the state's neoliberal fantasies bumping up against its nationalist imaginary sustained by a (racially? ethnically? proto-Singaporean?) consolidated "core." Two demographic visions for Future•Singapore—of global business elites and of a homogeneous national body politic—compete without much regard for those whom both visions would readily displace.

In her compelling ethnography, *Desiring China*, Lisa Rofel argues that "neoliberalism in China is a *national* project about global reordering. The project is to remake national public culture."[33] The Future•Singapore initiative instantiates another example of neoliberal subjectification operating at the national level, but the white paper demonstrates the contradiction inherent in national campaigns of neoliberalism. If nationalisms have sustained themselves through racialized labor (even in postcolonial contexts in which racial mixing has been idealized into formulations of *mestizaje* or racial democracy), Singapore's reliance on an international circulation of research professionals and business elites might seem incommensurate with a nation-based imaginary. What Future•Singapore aims to do is displace a racially consolidated national imaginary with a new Singaporean futurity comprised of a multicultural, cosmopolitan elite. This new Singaporean future enables racialized divisions of labor to continue alongside National Day celebrations that emphasize the importance of reproducing Singaporeanness, while simultaneously holding the door open for a more flexible construction of future Singaporeans.

Of course, beneath the smooth surfaces of the global as a totality of interests, there are many glowing fissures: toxic waste dumps, misguided debt obligations, industrial disrepair, and secret prisons. But practices such as Future•Singapore work to stabilize such jagged terrain as one-world, standardizing protocols, procedures, and laws: a global civil society where liberal sovereign subjects can voice their demands, and rights and privileges are always on the way for those in the waiting room of history. What would an alternative fabulation of a Singaporean future — one that doesn't step even deeper into neoliberal fantasies that produce unsustainable, uneven, and unethical systems — entail?

Reparative Practices: Life in the Gutter with Malinky Robot

Sonny Liew's graphic narrative *Malinky Robot* (figure 4.2) intervenes in neoliberal discourses of constantly upgradeable lives. Published by Image Comics in 2011, the five short stories in the collection feature a motley crew of characters. Atari is a chain-smoking kid with a trenchant understanding of harsh realities: "Streetwise, with a world-weary air . . . [he] spends his time busking, shoplifting, stealing bicycles and reading comics."[34] His slightly more optimistic and notably alien — or at least nonhuman — companion, Oliver, is "as uncertain as anyone else where he came from or

FIGURE 4.2. Cover of Sonny Liew's *Malinky Robot* (France).

what he is."[35] Atari and Oliver have a middle-class friend, Misha, who lives on the fancier side of the tracks, buys them lunch, and passes along his games when he moves away. Finally, there is Little Robot, originally discounted by Atari as "more of an appliance,"[36] whose perspective nonetheless shapes the narrative arc of "New Year's Day," the fourth short story in the collection. Though the narrative voices are many, the reader primarily encounters the world of *Malinky Robot* through this interspecies assemblage of human, alien, and robot. Cultivating bonds of affiliation that cut across conventional categories of human and nonhuman, these life forms practice a living-in-common against a terrain jagged with joblessness, the apparent implosion of public education, and ecological devastation. Cast aside along with other discarded bits of a neoliberalized economy, they embody the fallout of Singapore's "reengineering" of its citizens.[37] The reader follows the protagonists as they make their way through their everyday encounters with poverty, despair, and boredom. Even amid severe conditions, though, Atari, Oliver, and their friends enliven worlds of possibility in everyday practices of care. They help each other relocate, pool resources, hatch plans to make money in unsanctioned ways, and—perhaps most significantly in the context of this book—they speculate together: pondering alternative histories and dreaming themselves into imaginative worlds that look, smell, and feel different from their immediate surroundings.

Set in a dilapidated urban landscape, *Malinky Robot* revisits the primal scene of techno-Orientalist fantasy: Tokyo. However, by focusing on Tokyo's day-laboring district of San'ya, which remains home to Tokyo's dispossessed, Liew shifts the origin point of Japan's economic success and underscores the vulnerability of those who were not folded into the prosperity of global capitalism.[38] Like the denizens of Tokyo's San'ya, Oliver and Atari "eke out a life" in a geopolitical context that works hard to eliminate them from the picture.[39] Together they scrape together bits and pieces of culture, currency, and materials from the discarded matter of the city. "Eking out a life"—one of Liew's favorite characterizations of Oliver and Atari's mode of engaging with the world around them—resonates profoundly with Eve Kosofsky Sedgwick's formulation of reparative practices, which illuminates "the many ways selves and communities succeed in extracting sustenance from the objects of a culture—even of a culture whose avowed desire has often been not to sustain them."[40]

Sedgwick's formulations of reparative versus paranoid modalities distinguish between ways of experiencing time—within and beyond narrative forms. Distinct from paranoid reading, which is motivated by an attempt to inure oneself to potentially horrible futures, reparative reading stays open and vulnerable to the radical possibilities of surprise.[41] Though called sequential art, comics as a literary form have a propensity for bending time across the page, wherein the space between panels—"the gutter"—could represent a fleeting moment or eons of time passing, not necessarily in chronological order. *Malinky Robot* flexes the possibilities of its graphic form to capture play and adventure in slow time at a moment when blockbuster films profit from ever more accelerated pacing. With sparse, unspectacularized story lines that amount to "a robot walks home," or "two kids borrow bikes to visit a friend," Liew's utopian visions—ephemeral and provisional—unfurl across the daily exploits and mundane, communal acts of these unlikely heroes of the future. *Malinky Robot* ruminates on forms of idleness that upend conceptions of wasted time, while simultaneously highlighting the waste of capitalist overproduction. Whereas the dystopian tenor of techno-Orientalist cyberpunk and the breakneck ambition of Future•Singapore both engender a paranoid relation to futurity by manifesting either foreboding about or securitization of it, *Malinky Robot* remains remarkably open to surprise and radical uncertainty. In this way, it articulates a reparative form of speculation—one that revels in the play of chance rather than the taming of it.[42]

Malinky Robot opens in 2024 atop a skyscraper (figure 4.3), where sunrise finds the protagonists on top of the world, not because they own or dominate it, but because they have made the rooftop their makeshift shelter. Atari and Oliver are homeless, making do with life in urban decay. Here, "mornings are . . . STINKY!!" (11). This is the surprising pronouncement that begins "Stinky Fish Blues," the first story in the collection. At dawn, Oliver encounters not the optimistic vista of sunlit horizons but the smell of a stagnant city, littered with signs of broken technological promises. Yet morning does bring surprising, if fleeting, moments of hope and unexpected opportunity. Oliver and Atari go fishing at the docks and discover rare life in the toxic waters—the nearly extinct *Foetidus piscis* (the stinky fish), which has persisted despite barrels of industrial sludge polluting its home. Their fortuitous catch fosters the hope of cashing it in for reward, but the fish ultimately falls prey to a friend's more pressing need to eat it. The kids are disappointed but not dejected, as prospects of cashing in recede to make allowances for the sharing of life in this contingent community. The stinky fish, living beyond all probability in pernicious condi-

FIGURE 4.3. Oliver atop a skyscraper (Sonny Liew, *Malinky Robot*, 22).

tions, serves as a fitting compatriot for Oliver and Atari, who manage to do more than just survive in a hostile environment. They dare to have dreams, foster friendships, and have adventures that actively extend the possibilities of the living conditions allotted to them, even if their dreams remain decidedly out of reach.

Likely destined to earn a living through tough, menial, and temporary work, Oliver and Atari might entertain brief moments of hope, but the fantasy to fly is not about ascendancy or mastery. The view from the top of Oliver's transient skyscraper haven differs from what Michel de Certeau describes in "Walking in the City." From the summit of the World Trade Center, de Certeau experiences being "lifted out of the city's grasp. . . . When one goes up there, he leaves behind the mass. . . . His elevation transfigures him into a voyeur."[43] But Oliver's prospects remain decidedly unchanged by this perspectival shift. He remains untransfigured, looking up like a homeless alien, not "looking down like a god." This difference reverberates profoundly across the context of Atari's and Oliver's likely futures working in the construction sites that emblematize New Asia and its speculative building frenzy. Indeed, when the two look upon a construction site, they consider their curtailed set of opportunities, and even Oliver's act of momentary ebullience ("I wanna fly a plane!") (figure 4.4) seems squelched as the frame zooms out to capture the dwarfing effects of the world around him.

The tops of skyscrapers yield only visions of unattainable aspirations and failed promises for Atari and Oliver, but they pursue adventure nonetheless and find in an arcade a virtual realization of Oliver's hopes to pilot a plane. In this closing frame of the story (figure 4.5), Liew leaves us with a stunning display of reparative practice, of engaging in fleeting acts of pleasure to carve out alternative ways of looking forward.

Together, Atari and Oliver explore alternative economies of exchange: they "borrow" bicycles that allow them to visit their friend Misha across town. Their mundane push toward collective ownership stands in stark contrast to the stealing-for-profit story Misha shares with them over lunch at "McDonnell's" about Obiyashi Takamashuru, an unscrupulous man who stole the design for cantilevered gears on bikes from their mentor Mr. Bon Bon. This short vignette about bicycle thievery turns sideways when it's revealed that bicycles themselves carry with them another story of stolen property.

As we learn from Misha's tale, the bicycle—as concept, design, and mode

FIGURE 4.4. "I wanna fly a plane!" (Sonny Liew, *Malinky Robot*, 21).

FIGURE 4.5. Flights of fancy (Sonny Liew, *Malinky Robot*, 29).

of transport—is always already stolen: the very mechanism that facilitates its locomotion turns out to be a lifted idea. Framed as the first in a series of comics within a comic, Misha's *Ingrown Nale* reveals the history of the bicycle as property privatized and patented in the shadiest of circumstances, throwing the world of propriety into ethical question. Drawn in the heavily cross-grained and stridently scraggy pen-and-ink style of graphic mavericks such as Robert Crumb, *Ingrown Nale* (ostensibly produced from Misha's hand but of course also a testament to Liew's creative range) takes the reader into Obiyashi's demented world of ruthless corporate competition, greed, and dishonesty. We follow Obiyashi to work on the day of his death and descent to a Dante-inspired hell, where he confesses how he stole the design of the cantilevered gear system. Though certainly incentivized to villainous action, Obiyashi turns out to be a dupe, trapped in the promise of a better future (figure 4.6). Before his fateful cardiac arrest, he reflects on his situation: "30 years! My life, a series of dwindling offices. I long for: the ocean, the trees, the breadth [sic] of my children as yet unborn. Today, though, will be a day different from days before" (45). We witness this corporate wonk's perpetually fruitless drive toward upward mobility in several key details. Obiyashi's namesake might ironically be Obayashi Global, the Japanese multinational construction corporation behind the building of Tokyo Sky Tree, the world's tallest broadcasting tower. Obiyashi's ascent in the corporate elevator leads him to a dead-end cube of an office. In his futile attempt to climb out of hell, he maniacally exclaims: "They gave me an office! They gave me a car! And a hat to wear for when it got windy!" (48). In these exclamations we hear the despair wrought by this subject's investments in "aspirational normativity":[44] a perpetually upskilled life, heteronormative reproductive futurity, and a drive toward individualistic achievement. Obiyashi has spent years subjected to the "good life" logics of neoliberal capitalism—the logics that rationalize financial and social speculations privileging profit for the few over more disposable lives that don't fit or aspire to the same narrative.

The astonishing and inspiring element of the *Malinky Robot* stories is their commitment to disarming the seduction of neoliberal ascension and individualism in favor of cultivating extended practices of care and more inclusive notions of family and collective responsibility. In figure 4.7, we see Oliver's comic strip embedded within the larger comic world of *Malinky Robot*. "Hi-Life" features two construction workers on their lunch break, sitting on a beam high up in a skyscraper, evocative of Charles Clyde

FIGURE 4.6. "A series of dwindling offices" (Sonny Liew, *Malinky Robot*, 45).

FIGURE 4.7. "Hi-life" (Sonny Liew, *Malinky Robot*, 54).

Ebbets's famous photograph, *Lunch atop a Skyscraper*, shot at New York City's Rockefeller Center in 1932. In both examples, the drama revolves around the precariousness of high-rise construction work. Without harnesses, the workers seem alarmingly casual about their safety. Unlike the Depression-era photo, though, the display of risk in Oliver's version has not been staged by corporate interest to promote the building of another Rockefeller skyscraper. Neither is the uncertainty of a person's future contained by a narrative about the importance of saving. Liew opts, instead, to stay with the awkwardness of uncertainty, as one of the workers admits that he spends all his money on alcohol. In *Malinky Robot*, a post–financial crash story, putting money in a savings or interest-bearing retirement account might actually be more foolish than squandering one's earnings on the pleasure of daily drinking. The snippet demonstrates Liew's purposive undercutting of the "good life" promise—a promise of better futures that the act of building skyscrapers would seem to deliver. However, in *Malinky Robot* technological inventions, whether in the form of skyscrapers or cantilevered bike gears, fail to deliver on their promises. Oliver's "Hi-Life" points to the irrelevance of whether these workers invest in the future or not; it recasts the tale of opportunity as a farce for those whom capitalism has deemed disposable, replaceable, and ultimately without a future.

Liew sabotages reproductive futurity in a similar comic within a comic that plays on the popular children's magazine activity of spotting the difference. Whereas a smiling child secures the happiness of the family portrait in the first panel, a tombstone supplants the child in the second and shatters the sunny disposition of reproductive futurity. Shattered also is the very exercise of spotting differences. These images make no pretense to similitude; with starkly contrasting color palettes—the first is in bright, mostly primary, colors, and the second is in macabre gray scale—spotting their differences hardly requires practiced sleuthing or careful discernment of the normal from the aberrant. Refusing to engage the familiar, normative apparatus, Liew puts pressure on *Highlights*'s slogan "fun with a purpose."[45] Oliver's morbid rendering of spotting differences interrogates and dramatically halts the instrumentalization of fun.

The critique of instrumentalized fun stands in direct contrast to Oliver's preference for "irrational exuberance" over edutainment's developmental games, designed to put kids on the dubious cutting edge of competitively tracked educational systems governed by quantitative evaluation and techno-positivist entrepreneurs. In this way, Oliver's "Spot the Difference" comic registers a complaint against what Lee Edelman has termed "reproductive futurism,"[46] a holding up of the figure of the child as the naturalized site of political incitement. The fraught case of imagining who shall inherit future Singapore, though, charts how capitalist development and ecological sustainability hold the question of reproduction and futurity in tension. Whereas a pronatalist movement in the 1980s led to a baby-bonus program with financial incentives for couples considering having second or third children, 1999 (on the heels of the financial crash of 1997–98) marked the launch of Singapore's international head-hunting program to recruit students and professionals primarily from India and China.[47] In 2001, the baby-bonus program was reinstated, awarding mothers $4,000 for each of the first two children born and $6,000 for the next two. More recently, at Singapore's 2008 National Day, Prime Minister Lee Hsien Loong dedicated more than 5,000 words of his speech to discussing the falling birth rate.[48]

Singapore's concern over its low birth rate—among the lowest in the world—was perhaps most overtly broadcast when a 2012 Mentos ad went viral, calling for a National Night wherein Singaporeans would enact their "civic duty" to make babies.[49] Set to a song in which a male vocalist raps: "It's National Night and I want a baby, boo, I know you want it, so duz the SDU," the commercial refers to the Social Development Unit (renamed the Social Development Network), a governmental body devoted to addressing the low birth rate and housed under the broader reaching Ministry of Social and Family Development. That state development includes such calls to reproduction as civic duty situates Singaporean futurity not in the figure of the child, but in actual children. The Mentos commercial, in its unapologetic overture to heterosexual baby making, makes clear the connections between reproductive futurity and other speculative futures. National Night, according to the video, also means getting aroused by the potential of buying a $900 stroller and taking a stroll through the Gardens by the Bay park—a billion-dollar, 103-acre public construction project that even looks like a giant bubble of speculative financing with all the aesthetic trappings of speculative futurity. It is against these financial forms of irrational exuberance that Atari and Oliver's flights of fancy and moments of ebullience stand in contrast.

Nevertheless, the exuberance Liew captures in his vibrant, dynamic, and wiggling lines also distinguishes itself from the imaginary of austerity and responsibility, marshaled by discourses of personal finance.[50] In another sidebar comic within a comic, Atari's imagined superhero Doctor

Midnight (Mr. Bon Bon in disguise) administers punishment to his foes even as he spouts after-school specials' canned statements about health and fitness. With each POW! KRAK! BIF! blow to the thugs who have come to claim the stolen bicycles, the doctor administers "medicine": "FLOSS after every meal!" "ALWAYS wear your seat-belt!" and "Maintain an ACTIVE lifestyle!" (60). Doctor Midnight's recitation of sound-bites about self-improvement and healthy living as civic virtue is decidedly ironic. For all of modern science's promises of its beneficial effects on the population, these pledged benefits have passed over Oliver and Atari, who seem wholly unmoved by overtures to longevity and prosperity. As the sworn defender of street urchins, Doctor Midnight interrogates for whom these logics of prolonging life are designed. After dispatching his adversaries, he rebukes the thin assurances of better tomorrows: "Who builds the **cities**? By whose sweat, by whose blood?? And in return to ask nothing but a **roof** over their heads. . . . Seeking merely to manage from day to day . . . in these times of **unending** change . . . and in the bitter end to shuffle into the darkness of this mortal coil that **binds** us all. What is it that **awaits** us beyond that final frontier? What **indignities**, what **sorrows**? What semblance of this **hell** that we have already tasted on this **cruel** earth?" (61). The city of the future does not provide a roof over the heads of those who built it. Oliver and Atari "manage from day to day" by squatting in makeshift shelters either on rooftops or in abandoned "McDonnell's" sites, making do with the materials of dilapidated futurity. Doctor Midnight's closing monologue alludes to the oscillatory quality of Hamlet's considerations "to be or not to be." The allusion helps illuminate the relationship between life and futurity— "perchance to dream"—and insists on the importance of thinking of the future as contested and critical terrain.

If they were to buy into the aspirations of upward mobility and the gleaming promises of Asian futurity, Oliver and Atari would partake in what Lauren Berlant has called "cruel optimism." Berlant investigates "what happens to fantasies of the good life when the ordinary becomes a landfill for overwhelming and impending crises of life-building and expectation whose sheer volume so threatens what it has meant to 'have a life' that adjustment seems like an accomplishment."[51] In many ways, *Malinky Robot* sketches out in haunting beauty the condition of "living in crisis,"[52] wherein we encounter Atari and Oliver negotiating "the impasse" of everyday crisis in their temporary shelters and tender socialities.[53] In Atari and Oliver's daily exploits, we find a sustained rumination on the caring re-

FIGURE 4.8. Doctor Midnight's soliloquy (Sonny Liew, *Malinky Robot*, 61).

lationship between two truant geeks who aspire "toward and beyond survival," but in ways that move "toward an opening that does not involve rehabituation, the invention of new normativities, or working through and beyond trauma."[54]

Rather than eschewing Asian futurity in the face of techno-Orientalism, *Malinky Robot* follows Berlant's injunction "to imagine better economies of intimacy and labor."[55] Launched from within a "McDonnell's" where Atari and Oliver have scored a free lunch from their friend Misha, this series of embedded comics, which include Misha's story of the theft of Mr. Bon Bon's intellectual property, Oliver's Sunday funnies about joblessness and curtailed futures, and Atari's Doctor Midnight superhero comic, allows incredible artistry and imaginative storytelling to unfurl against the backdrop of Super size french fries and the multinational reach of corporations like McDonald's. As the friends return to their neighborhood on their borrowed bicycles, they run into Mr. Bon Bon, whose backstory they've just learned over lunch. In the closing full-page panel of "Bicycles," we see Bon Bon crouch to inspect the cantilevered gear, the sign of all that could have been. But, as the ordinary hero, Mr. Bon Bon simply asks if the kids are hungry and suggests a new noodle place where they can eat, "his treat." In the cruel world of foreclosed opportunities, where Mr. Bon Bon works construction even though his invention could have gained him access to a life of financial security and relative comfort, Liew's story bears witness to the startling willingness to cultivate tender ties in precarious times. *Malinky Robot* posits an alternative to cruel optimism — call it a queer exuberance — that persists not only in the queer kinships Misha, Atari, Oliver, and Mr. Bon Bon form amid conditions of contingency and precarity, but also in Liew's ekphrastic exercise that restores texture to Asian futurity when techno-Orientalism works to smooth over the vicissitudes of neoliberalism. As Singapore relies increasingly on temporary migrant workers, its flexible accumulation trades on the cruelly optimistic drive toward a good life and the promise of an Asian futurity that will never arrive for the vast majority of the workers who sustain the wealth of the few. *Malinky Robot* imagines otherwise.

5

SALT FISH FUTURES *The Irradiated Transpacific and the Financialization of the Human Genome Project*

The pedigree of the clone is subaltern.
—SARAH FRANKLIN, *Dolly Mixtures*

The Irradiated Transpacific: Afterlives of the American Lake

Fish are the canaries in the coal mine of irradiated water. In 1946, scientists began studying the biological effects of America's fourth and fifth nuclear explosions (after Trinity, Hiroshima, and Nagasaki) on a wide variety of test animals in and around the Marshall Islands. To measure levels of radiation in the blast area of the Baker bomb, scientists developed what is called a fish radio-autograph, made by slicing a small fish in half, drying it, and then placing it insides-down on a photographic plate, which would register the radioactivity present in its tissues. The fish would essentially make its own x-ray, with the exposed film rendering the radioactive outline of its scales and organs.[1] Because almost all the fish in the area were found to be radioactive, and because their bellies gave off a concentrated glow, scientists were able to deduce that these fish were not only irradiated themselves but were also ingesting radioactive plankton and algae. Radiation sickness, they concluded, could be passed on from species to species like an epizootic. Another scene of pollution takes shape in the North Pacific Gyre, where plastic particulates outweigh plankton six to one, forming what has come to be known as the Great Pacific Garbage Patch. It is an aqueous wasteland also haunted by the specters of nuclear warfare—the afterlives of bomb detonations not only at Hiroshima and Nagasaki, but also at the Enewetak and Bikini Atolls, as well as Christmas and Johnston Islands.

This chapter looks to the horizon of the Pacific Ocean—the body of water, the aquatic organisms that inhabit it, the islands in it and their human denizens, as well as the nation-states and multinational corporations that parlay across it—to help shift imaginings of transpacific futures away from their current orientation toward economic profit and militarized occupation. If "future-ready" Singapore declares itself to be the new world order's laboratory (as discussed in chapter 4), it does so without acknowledging the calamitous ways in which the Pacific has already served as the site for actual U.S. military science laboratories since the 1940s (and as a location of European imperialist scientific exploration and fantastic speculation for hundreds of years prior to that). After World War II, many Pacific islands functioned as "radiation ecology" laboratories for the Atomic Energy Commission.[2] There were over forty nuclear weapons tests on the Enewetak Atoll, for example, during a ten-year period beginning in 1948.[3]

The transformation of the Pacific Ocean into a radiation laboratory occurred as part of the transfer of imperial power in the region from Japan to the United States following World War II. In April 1945, a new diplomatic form called a "strategic trust" took shape to provide internationally recognized legal grounds for the development of U.S. military bases all around Micronesia.[4] "This innovation," writes Kimie Hara, "would enable the USA to do legally what Japan had done illegally."[5] Unlike other trust territories, a *strategic* trust meant that the administration of the region would be overseen by the United Nations Security Council, where the United States had a veto, rather than the UN General Assembly, thus enabling "American control under a United Nations façade."[6] Born out of the contradictory needs for the U.S. to distinguish itself from older forms of imperialism while also establishing military domination in the region, the strategic trust invoked securitization and the "uncertainty of the future" in the face of rising tensions with the Soviet Union as the occasion for military fortification and cultural assimilation in the Pacific theater.[7] The strategic trust, in other words, was part of a broader turn to securitization at the outset of the Cold War and became an early instantiation of policy based on probable outcomes, preemptive impulses, and of speculation as modality.

When the UN Security Council officially established the Trust Territory of the Pacific Islands (TTPI) in April 1947, the strategic trust became the geo-political framework that would also provide the ideological and epistemological basis for the area of the U.S. nuclear testing initiative referred to as the Pacific Proving Ground. While there is much more to say about the strategic trust as a new, speculative, political form, for the sake of this chapter, I call attention to its emergence to signal how the transformation of the Pacific Ocean into a nuclear testing ground was parlayed into governmental projects for the remaking of life itself. Because of the nearly continuous nuclear weapons testing in the Pacific, trace elements of the Cold War nuclear project now saturate the biosphere and create an atomic signature found not only in organisms but also in soils and waterways. These elements constitute an irradiated transpacific, and it is from the perspective of this bio-ecological undercommons that this chapter attempts to imagine a future beyond the proliferation of military and economic domination.

More specifically, I examine the ways in which radiation and mutation have been key players in shaping the economic and ecological place of the transpacific in the world. First, I examine the rhetorical and ideological conversion of the Human Genome Project (HGP) from research on mutation to a project with promises of regeneration to reveal the financialization of genomics as it is tethered to U.S. imperialism in the Pacific. Then I turn to Larissa Lai's *Salt Fish Girl*, a twenty-first century work of queer, Asian Canadian speculative fiction that takes up questions about the future of genomics while also revisiting longer histories of transpacific movements of biocapital. By bringing these quite different sets of texts—historical, scientific, and literary—into conversation, I make a series of claims. The first is that the geopolitical context and ideological occasion for scientific research (be it anxieties about nuclear fallout after the bombing of Hiroshima and Nagasaki, or the post–Cold War race to map the human genome) matter. The second claim has to do with the changing infrastructure for scientific research funding and a turn toward measurable outcomes and accounting of scientific experiments that turns the orientation of scientific research always toward the future. In that shift in funding structures and temporal orientation, the historical narrative gets revised and sanitized in order to make the future projections seem logical. In other words, certain historical excisions and erasures occur to make the histories of mainstream science seem less messy. Official projections of the future too often obfuscate possible divergence or aberration. *Salt Fish Girl* takes up the project of revising the histories and projections of genomics, extrapolating from the perspectives of the discarded elements of transpacific global capitalism.

Set in a world shaped by predatory speculations that capitalize on the exploitation of biomatter, *Salt Fish Girl* calls attention to how disavowed histories of war trauma, labor exploitation, and ecological fallout inform a genetically modified future of corporate enclosures on the one hand and mutant assemblages on the other. Lai's queer, mutant-clone protagonists suffer from a "dreaming disease" that renders all genetically modified organisms susceptible to reliving historical traumas, and it is through this shared, transgenic experience that they come together to sabotage the ideological and material systems of genetic engineering that would excise them as unpredictable aberrations from corporate subjection (54).[8]

Set both in China before the Shang dynasty and in the Pacific Northwest of the near future, the novel structurally oscillates between past and future-present, eventually folding time and subject in on themselves, disrupting expectations of linear progression. I read these literary moves through the queer analytics of "genetic drag" and "temporal drag" as forms of antipositivist speculations that unsettle the financialized future.[9] As an extended rumination on transgenic life and as a literary experiment in transtemporal narrative, *Salt Fish Girl* imagines a postgenomic world that may very well configure a Deleuzian "dividual" of econometric calculation and biometric accounting, but that may also open onto unpredictable experiences of the sort that Dana Luciano and Mel Chen call "queer inhumanisms," through which the normative category of the human is called into question.[10] To write these bodies into the future, Lai must intervene in a neoliberal futurity that promises genetically modifiable lives for some while dispossessing others of a stakehold in that temporal geography.

I focus my analysis around the central figures of Lai's novel—the transgenic fish and the Asian clone worker—against the backdrop of the racialized histories of genomics, the financialization of science, and transpacific labor. To fill in that backdrop, I provide an interlude in which I put *Salt Fish Girl* in conversation with a different kind of speculative writing in the form of the 2011 strategic plan of the National Human Genome Research Institute (NHGRI) for the future of human genome research. I compare the plan to the key 1989 special issue of *Genomics* that crafted an origin story of the HGP particularly well suited to set up a progress narrative. In this comparison, I trace the rhetorical shifts in genomics research from a focus on mutation to one on regeneration and underline how funding for the HGP capitalized on a conversion of atomic age radiation trauma into the potential for gene therapy. By putting Lai's speculative fiction into conversation with these genomic speculative narratives, I approach genomic futurity as contested terrain, where *Salt Fish Girl* offers a revisitation of the "specters of the Pacific" that haunt the HGP's transpacific future.[11]

Speculating on Salt Fish Futures

Salt Fish Girl arose out of the confluence of several major events that Lai encountered in current events between roughly 1995 to 2000. These highly news-mediated occasions, as Lai recounts, include:

> the cloning of Dolly the sheep, the arrival of three rusty ships from China on the West Coast of British Columbia carrying around 600 Chinese migrant labourers, Monsanto's suing of a farmer whose canola crop, probably through natural pollination, had picked up some of Monsanto's altered DNA, the patenting of slightly modified basmati rice by a large Texas corporation, the construction of Celebration, a fully planned ur-American town, by Disney.[12]

Lai's list provides a curation of promiscuous movements of biomatter, any one of which could plausibly masquerade as science fiction elements: cloned sheep, aliens mysteriously washing ashore, and a plant species genetically modified to colonize indigenous crops. Furthermore, this range of life forms constitutes a transpacific undercommons, a pooling of abjected biomatter caught up in and displaced by the currents of transpacific exchange. In the late 1990s, that transpacific exchange is marked in particular by a global narrativization of Asia's financial "crisis" of 1997–98 and subsequent "recovery."[13] In the case of *Salt Fish Girl*, speculative fiction understands financial speculation as not just context, but as "co-text."[14]

Scientific speculation, technological forecasting, and promissory futures transform "basic science" (not to be mistaken for innocent or pure science) into an "entrepreneurial science," in which scientific inquiry follows an economy of deliverable outcomes and profitable goods rather than perhaps a less manufactured curiosity.[15] In an entrepreneurial approach to science, narratives of futurity function as scripts in laboratory protocols, military strategies of preemption, and economic extrapolations alike, instrumentalizing the speculative mode by attaching it to funding mechanisms that call on scientists to anticipate and project the potential impact, benefit, and even profit their research might have in the future.

These resulting prospectuses constitute forms of speculative narration, and as Colin Milburn suggests, "we have yet fully to take on the manifold ways these practices interrelate with the predominant mode of speculative narration in the modern era—namely, science fiction."[16] Milburn points out scientists' active disavowal of any substantive relationship their work might have to the literary genre of science fiction. Eschewed from the spatial construction of the pure and rational laboratory, science fiction seems nonetheless already part of the scientific process of imagining possibilities. If, however, the scientific, technological, engineering, and mathematical (STEM) fields remain oversaturated by white men, science fiction—with its possibly more successful recruitment of writers of color, queer thinkers, and women—might offer not only some explanation of historical exclusions and abuses of, say, imperial science, but also gesture toward how science itself might begin to imagine other kinds of possible futures.

In its counterimagining of genetic recombination's potential, *Salt Fish Girl* in particular proffers a politics of mutation rather than regeneration. Whereas regeneration's aim is to restore a body to an original or normative state, mutation finds its expression in changing the materiality of a thing, likely in ways that alter conceptualizations of bodies, differentiation, origins, and copies. Lai constructs a transgressive set of possibilities in mutation and its unpredictability in an era of rampant genetic modification (GM) that is marketed for its precision and control. Anchored by twin narrators located in different times—one in the past and the other in the future—the novel slips between temporal streams. For example, just when the year 2044 holds up the regenerative potential of bioengineered futurity, Lai's slipstream techniques point the reader to the histories of biocolonialism and even older forms of empire that have given rise to this dubiously manufactured future.[17] In this way, *Salt Fish Girl* as speculative fiction ruminates on two forms of future making: fabrication and fabulation, wherein the distinction and the tension seem to be their relationships to actualization—either the realizing of potential or the opening of possibility.

The Ghostly Matter of Transgenic Organisms

In Lai's speculative fiction, the future promised by advances in DNA recombination techniques is always already haunted by the past. Miranda Ching, one of the not-quite-human protagonists, is a "child afflicted by history" (70). She, like many of the other genetically modified inhabitants of this mutant future, exhibits symptoms of the "dreaming sickness," a mysterious malady speculated to be a "new breed of auto-immune diseases, related to genetic and other industrial modifications to our food supply," wherein people become consumed with the experience of traumatic histories of war, famine, and violence (69). Miranda relates the story of one girl "who smelled of cooking oil, who remembered all the wars ever fought. She could recall and recount every death, every rape, every wound; every moment of suffering that had ever been inflicted by a member of her ancestral lineage" (85). The dreaming sickness instantiates what Avery Gordon calls "memory as haunting," the return of the repressed, and in this case the ghostly matter has been spliced into one's DNA—a condition that renders the host a ghost, producing a primordial urge to drown rather than relive the disavowed experience of violence.[18] Also called the "drowning disease," this condition becomes so unbearable that its sufferers can find relief only when submerged underwater (85). The girl who smelled of cooking oil walked into the ocean and never returned. Miranda retreats to the bathtub. Traumatic experiences find their afterlives in transgenic forms, the constant undertow of such memories driving some to oblivion but others toward revolutionary pursuits.

People with dreaming sickness develop fistulas behind their ears. In medical discourse, a fistula often manifests at a site of trauma, forming "an abnormal connection between an organ, vessel, or intestine and another structure."[19] In *Salt Fish Girl*, fistulas "served the function of memory, recalling a time when we were more closely related to fish, a time when the body glistened with scales and turned in the dark, muscled easily through water" (107–8). As a symptom of the dreaming sickness, fistulas form at the site of a temporal rift, almost always behind the ears in this novel—which suggests some play on vestigial gills that might result from the "abnormal connection" of saltwater carp and human DNA in the trans-species genetic splicing that went into the genetic composition of the clone workers.

Fistulas also become a site of queer desire. Miranda describes her first kiss with Evie, the clone worker turned anarchist-activist: "I took her cold hand and pulled it under my T-shirt, pressed my nose and mouth to the soft space behind her ear. The smell of salt fish was unmistakable" (161). Lai transforms the fistula into a site of queer desire and transpecies connection. Because fistulas also recall the history of J. Marion Sims's surgical experimentation on slave women and the dubious origins of modern reproductive science,[20] black feminist critique of medical experimentation on the bodies of dispossessed, enslaved women and an attendant theorization of an insurgent, monstrous female social subject.[21]

These ghostly matters point to the ways in which the genomic dystopia of Miranda's world is a continuation of the necropolitical past.[22] Nextcorp, the multinational corporation that produces the clone laborers of the novel's near future, "bought out the Diverse Genome Project around the same time [Miranda] was born. . . . It focused on the peoples of the so-called Third World, Aboriginal peoples, and peoples in danger of extinction," and as a result all the factory workers have brown eyes and black hair (160). In *Salt Fish Girl*, the genetic engineering that produces clone workers of the future draws on the already racialized logics of the biobank. The dreaming sickness becomes Lai's vehicle for positioning the intertwined histories of war, labor, and the environment as the precondition for the age of genetic modification. In their discussion of dispossession and debt in the contemporary moment, Paula Chakravartty and Denise Ferreira da Silva articulate the "racial logic of global financial capitalism" and establish "how neoliberal architectures and discourses of dispossession act on earlier forms of racial and colonial subjugation."[23] Lai's novel recalls such a disavowed history of genomics and clarifies how futuristic scientific enterprise builds on neocolonial practices, from bioprospecting to racialized internment.

Miranda's girlfriend, Evie, belongs to a series of clone workers called the Sonias, who not only share DNA with freshwater carp but also have inherited some of their genetic material from a Chinese Canadian woman who chose to be interned with her Japanese Canadian husband during World War II.[24] This act of cross-ethnic solidarity, at a moment that might otherwise compel the assertion of difference, subtly but profoundly reintroduces the specter of nuclear warfare to the history of genomics. The initial interest in developing what would become the HGP took hold among scientists studying rates of inherited genetic mutations in the offspring of survivors of the nuclear bombings at Hiroshima and Nagasaki. By cultivating such elective affinities in the transgenic organism, Lai writes war, displacement, and trauma back into the cultural history of genomics.

*Specters of the Pacific: The HGP's Turn
from Mutation to Regeneration*

The stakes of *Salt Fish Girl*'s revisionist speculation on genomic futures become clearer when we investigate the HGP's often overlooked historical connection to the history of the atomic bomb.[25] Robert Cook-Deegan is one of the few people who relates that the HGP had its origins at the 1984 Alta Summit in the mountains of Utah.[26] In his original report on the Alta Summit, published in *Genomics* in 1989, Cook-Deegan clarifies that Alta "was not a meeting on mapping or sequencing the human genome. Through happenstance and historical accident, Alta links human genome projects to research on the effects of the atomic bombs dropped on Hiroshima and Nagasaki."[27] In this two-page report, Cook-Deegan makes explicit mention of Hiroshima and Nagasaki seven times, emphasizing in his narration how the Alta Summit signifies an important historical link between the Department of Energy's "traditional interest in detection of mutations"[28] and the HGP's focus on sequencing the human genome. In the concluding sentence of the report, Cook-Deegan asserts that the Alta Summit is just "one of several historical links between genome projects and . . . the Manhattan project."[29] By contrast, a report from the Santa Fe Workshop just two years later makes no explicit mention of the original Hiroshima and Nagasaki studies that led to the initial flurry of interest in improving DNA-sequencing technologies.

To look for the official history of the Human Genome Project, one might look to the NHGRI website, which proclaims the HGP to be "one of the great feats of exploration in history."[30] The website radically diminishes the project's origins in the atomic era. Instead, the historical narrative offered therein highlights flashpoints of invention, genius, and breakthrough. It places the HGP in a stunning patrilineal genealogy of genomic research beginning with Alfred Sturtevant's first mapping of the *Drosophilia* fruit fly in 1911, followed by the discovery of the double-helical structure of DNA by James Watson and Francis Crick; and on to Frederick Sanger's second Nobel Prize in chemistry in 1980 for his development of sequencing techniques in the mid-1970s. Organized around the discrete accomplishments of individual, prize-winning scientists, the history locates the intellectual roots of the HGP in these people and events while reducing the significance of a more nuanced history of science's relationship to the military's atomic research and its fallout. The positivist arc to the NHGRI's official history of the HGP presents a series of scientific innovations as the building blocks of technological progress. Meanwhile, the sequential timeline downplays the HGP's messier connections to the geopolitical contexts to which this research was attached, including but not limited to what Cook-Deegan called the "happenstance"[31] of Los Alamos, the Manhattan Project, and nuclear holocaust.

The NHGRI's selective forgetting of Hiroshima and Nagasaki also signals the instrumentalization of Japanese survivors of the nuclear blasts and their descendants on behalf of genomic science, which at its inception sought to align its interests with a more profitable demographic than the survivors of nuclear warfare. When Jodi Kim writes about the U.S. government prohibiting staff members of the Atomic Bomb Casualty Commission from treating the Japanese subjects whom they were studying, she recognizes the ways in which wartime targets become objects of state knowledge.[32] Such targeting and objectifying, I would argue, are twin functions of the same practice of biopolitical subjection, the "reducing of others to data."[33] This realignment included a reorientation of scientific research toward the financial sector, in which speculations on the HGP's potential to predict and preempt disease and genetic defects would ultimately become the source of prolific financial speculation—wherein venture capitalists could bet on scientific research and its conversion into private-sector enterprises like individualized genetic sequencing services such as those offered by 23andme.com.

To the extent that the HGP's official narrative attempts to fold the story of nuclear devastation into a narrative arc of the possibility of regenerative medicine, the renarrativization capitalizes on the proleptic logic the United States used to rationalize the dropping of atomic bombs to begin with. Hiroshima and Nagasaki were supposed to have, according to the narrative produced by American exceptionalism, liberated the rest of the world from the potential threat of Soviet nuclear imperialism. This "fantasmatic representation of nuclear holocaust in the future anterior" inaugurated the national security state that is now primed for all kinds of speculations on potential futures against which the nation can mobilize and militarize.[34] Similarly, the HGP presents itself as securitization against the onslaught of an uncertain mutagenic future, in which investment in genetic engineering hedges against potential risk. By emphasizing here the HGP's logics of financialization—investing, hedging, and forecasting—I signal the next move of this chapter, to interject the emergence of genomics research into a confluence of financial and military securitization.

In its attempt to informationalize biomatter and delink it from the feeling body, the HGP both subscribes to and is constituted by a strong turn toward quantification that helps convert biological life and sentiment into finance capitalism's terms of calculable, potential risk.

From the late 1970s through the late 1990s, basic science did not commercialize so much as it financialized, putting significantly more pressure on scientists to project the potential applications and utility of their research to sources of private funding with the purpose of fueling a derivatives market of betting on and hedging against the prospects of emerging technoscientific research.[35] Funding proposals and applications began to include a speculative section, usually in the concluding paragraphs, wherein scientists imagine a future application of their research.[36] Another genre of speculation, akin to these sections of grant applications, are strategic plans. The NHGRI published a series of overlapping five-year plans outlining the priorities and goals of the HGP. Plotting the trajectories and articulating the potential future benefits of research, these documents constitute forms of speculative writing. Reading the 2011 strategic plan reveals a striking shift in rhetoric. The plan opens with "optimism about the potential contributions of genomics for improving human health."[37] Optimism recurs as a point of emphasis in the document. The plan identifies the cell-biological models that have led to a better understanding of Crohn's disease and cancer as "examples [to] justify the optimism about genomics' potential to accelerate the understanding of disease."[38] The plan's conclusion names the "audacious vision" of what sequencing the human genome could mean for the "ultimate control of many human diseases."[39] The plan attributes this audacious vision to the origins of the HGP, but the origins the plan names (which include R. Dulbecco's 1986 article in *Science*, "A Turning Point in Cancer Research: Sequencing the Human Genome," and the National Research Council's 1988 *Mapping and Sequencing the Human Genome*) do not include the Alta Summit of 1984 and have already turned away from the study of radiation's effects on genetic mutation. The NHGRI's speculative vision can only come about via the repression of genomic research's ties to the Manhattan project. It is a "repetition-as-displacement" that, at the level of memory, anticipates the methodology of gene splicing.[40] Whereas the research on inherited genetic mutations garnered the attention and funding from the Japanese government and the U.S. Department of Energy (who worried about getting sued for the long-lasting and wide-reaching damage of radiation on anyone anywhere near either a bombing target or testing site), the NHGRI's more audacious priorities for biomedical research proclaim to reach "well beyond what any one organization can realistically support, and will (once again) require the creative energies and expertise of genome scientists around the world and from all sectors, including academic, government, and commercial."[41] If research on radiation seemed important primarily to people who perceived themselves to be immediately affected by the specific sites most commonly associated with the atomic age, the HGP's new directions were bound by no such geographical locations. The plan's new terrain would be the limitless future and its securitization of healthy, wealthy individuals from risk of disease, disaster, or accident.

The HGP's harnessing of financial backing by way of revolutionary promise helps explain a broader turn to regenerative medical science. Indeed, Susan Merrill Squier suggests that regenerative medicine was "even more potentially profitable than were the rejuvenation strategies of sixty years ago, and the culture of biomedical commodification has spawned an interesting new hybrid institution: the medical center that combines basic research with commercial and even medical-industrial application."[42] As Melinda Cooper's compelling account of the embryonic futures market of the late 1990s reminds us, "whole sectors of the economy were held aloft on a wave of media-induced expectation."[43] Venture capitalists funded scientific research long before there was an actual product to be sold to the public. In the twelve-month period between July 1991 and July 1992, for example, forty-six initial public offerings in biotechnology companies were filed, raising $1.4 billion.[44] Such speculations on regenerative medicine and precision-targeted designer drugs continue today, when investors extrapolate the endowed value of an experimental life form's "generative promise" based at least in part on how scientists narrate near-future projections of their research's impact.[45] Nowhere has the conversion of basic discovery to application been more dramatically accelerated than in the field of genetics. Cooper notes that stem-cell science in particular seeks to produce not just the potential organism, but "*biological promise itself, in a state of nascent transformability.*"[46] Both stem-cell science and the HGP constitute "markets and technologies specializing in biological promise [that] can in turn be understood as part of a larger trend toward the intensification of futures trading in both the US and world capital markets."[47] The HGP effectively brought together human genome sequencing with recombinant DNA techniques to produce an endless suite of biogenetically engineered products geared for the biomedical pharmaceutical industry.

The 2011 strategic plan's articulation of genomics research through the logics of speculative financing required not only the deployment of this narrative projection of futurity but also the translation of genetic material into statistical information. In its information-based approach to encoding, mapping, and "databasing" the genome, the HGP expresses its clear emphasis on studying genetic populations over and beyond a concern for individual bodies.[48] In this way, the HGP's emphasis on mapping and sequencing the genome dovetailed perfectly with the logic of financial datafication.

The promise of the genome's manipulability took deep root in its lexicality. As Judith Roof points out, "the uses and effects of textual metaphors, such as the book of life, the code, the blueprint, alphabet, or recipe employed to describe DNA . . . produce[d] a continued sense of human control and agency over genetic processes and provided the conceptual basis for turning genes into property via patents."[49] Roof suggestively puts Watson and Crick's 1953 articles on DNA in conversation with J. L. Austin's theorization of performative speech acts.[50] And if the performative utterance and DNA's alphabetical codes promised the magical delivery of materiality, genomic sequencing was also trained toward stability and normativity.

The rebranding of mutation as regeneration could proceed only with the collusion of a normative apparatus that could establish an ostensibly standard genome whose aberrations could be targeted and diseases identified. The 2011 strategic plan makes this relationship explicit. By "extending from basic research to health applications," the plan suggests that "the most effective way to improve human health is to understand normal biology (in this case, genome biology) as a basis for understanding disease biology."[51] Imagining the healthy body meant sequencing, reading, and editing the legible genome.

Heredity, as Michel Foucault explains in his lecture on biopower at the Collège de France in 1976, conceptually gives rise to a "theory of degeneracy" and sexuality, because it "represents the precise point where the disciplinary and the regulatory, the body and the population, are articulated" and become simultaneously disciplined and regulated.[52] "The norm," he continues, "is something that can be applied to both a body one wishes to discipline and a population one wishes to regularize."[53] Though Foucault delivered this lecture eight years before the Alta Summit, he already had some inkling that a genetic normativity would follow. In the subsequent paragraph, he cites atomic power as an example of "biopower that is in excess of sovereign right" and bioengineering ("when it becomes technologically and politically possible for man not only to manage life but to make it proliferate, to create living matter, to build the monster") as an example of biopower "beyond all human sovereignty."[54] Foucault's theorizations of biopower emerge precisely from thinking about the particular historical moment when the HGP makes its transition from the atomic age to the age of genetic modification.

The pathologization of genetic mutation in contemporary discourse is held over from only one side of an old debate in evolutionary biology between Hermann J. Muller and Theodosius Dobzhansky. This debate is helpfully rehearsed in Banu Subramaniam's 2014 book *Ghost Stories for Darwin*. "To Muller," writes Subramaniam, "all mutation was deleterious and thus an active eugenics program was necessary to foster the purifying effects of natural selection. . . . To Dobzhansky, genetic variation was critically important for evolution and genetic diversity was something we should cherish." Muller's research on mutation, one must note, took shape while he was studying the effects of radiation in the wake of Hiroshima and Nagasaki. Radiation, as Muller witnessed in the context of nuclear devastation in postwar Japan, produced mutations that were "inherently unstable"; whereas Dobzhansky saw genetic variation as "desirable and linked to a deep commitment to a diverse and egalitarian world." The NHGRI's plan for the future of human genome research takes Muller's view on mutation as its extrapolation point rather than Dobzhansky's. Conceiving mutation as deleterious and undesirable sets up a rhetorical shift in genomics research from "mutation" to "regeneration."

Mutant Assemblages and Queer Desire

In analyzing why the HGP turns from the study of mutation to the more profitable science of DNA recombination and genetic engineering, Jasbir Puar's formulation of "regenerative productivity" proves helpful: "Those 'folded' into life are seen as more capacious or on the side of capacity, while those targeted for premature or slow death are figured as debility," and while debility "is profitable to capitalism . . . so is the demand to 'recover' from or overcome it."[55] Gene therapy—the use of DNA to treat diseases from hemophilia to cancer by delivering therapeutic DNA into a patient's cells, often via some kind of vector—is a field fueled by its promises more than by its successful applications. The *Genetics Home Reference*, hosted online by the National Institutes of Health's Medline Plus portal, defines gene therapy as "inserting a normal gene to replace an abnormal gene," by swapping, repairing, or "altering the degree to which a gene is turned on or off."[56] This discourse of normal and abnormal genes, along with the practice among assisted reproductive technology clinics of sorting fertilized eggs into good and bad embryos.[57]

What is genetic mutation if not the disowned and unruly relative of genetic modification? In *Gender Trouble*, Judith Butler uses drag as an example of gender performativity, clarifying in *Bodies that Matter* that her point was not to suggest that gender is performed and elective by choice, but that drag disrupts the settling of gender on either a presupposed interior or exterior.[58] Therefore, "genetic drag"—a term Sarah Franklin introduces in *Dolly Mixtures*, her queer genealogy of transgenic organisms—works to reveal the production of genetic normativity, which assumes a certain stasis, wholeness, and originality of the genome through analogies that, as Roof also points out, configure DNA as the "blueprint" of life, consisting of "building blocks" of nucleic acids.[59] Practices such as gene therapy replace "faulty," mutated genes with "therapeutic" ones, even though those practices concurrently deploy DNA-recombination technologies that might be characterized as artificial.[60] Genetic drag upsets these natural-artificial, nature-culture binaries. *Salt Fish Girl* examines the tensions between genetic engineering and genetic mutation by looking at the differences between the two. Lai connects the violence used to punish nonconformity to predatory forms of financial speculation, which capitalize on the future "should" (holding the future hostage to an obligation or debt), rather than lingering in what "could" possibly come into being (holding the future open to a more radical uncertainty).

As *Salt Fish Girl* makes explicit, the clone, as biomatter forged in the fires of biocapital, is the offspring of the subaltern. The techno-Orientalized Asian clone in particular is a perfectly neoliberalized form of biomatter. Distant and forgotten kin to the irradiated bomb victim, it is all too undead. (Better to think of the Japanese as never having been alive than to remember the whole transpacific host of peoples—from the residents of Hiroshima and Nagasaki to the inhabitants of the Bikini Atoll—as rendered disposable in service of the atomic war machine.)

Though Lai's novel precedes the behavioral epigenetics studies of transgenerational genetic memory via DNA methylation, the dreaming sickness plays with the possibility of our recent ancestors' leaving the residue of their experiences of stress or trauma on our genetic scaffolding that scientists at Emory University would publish evidence toward in 2013.[61] *Discover* magazine describes the process as traumatic experiences leaving "molecular scars adhering to our DNA . . . like silt deposited on the cogs of a finely tuned machine after the seawater of a tsunami recedes."[62]

Lai's novel also performs a kind of "temporal drag" on genomic futurity. Elizabeth Freeman incites us to think about "'drag' as a *productive* obstacle to progress, a usefully distorting pull backward, and a necessary pressure on the present tense," emphasizing undertow as a simultaneously disruptive and productive force in the creation of waves.[63] While Freeman's arguments concern themselves primarily with feminist political movements, they also describe well how *Salt Fish Girl* evokes the necessary picking up of sediment from that which has been disavowed, the retrograde's formative relation to the progressive ("its forward movement is also a drag back").[64]

In *Salt Fish Girl*, the future folds into the past—a generic convention of speculative fiction (including time travel and quantum leaps) through which Lai creates a nonlinear complexity of temporal dimensions, facilitated not through wormholes but through fantastical and queer forms of reproduction. At the end of the novel, Miranda becomes Nu Wa, insofar as she remembers (perhaps through her transgenic material) that she has always been that mythological goddess of creation and figuration of entanglement. As a time-traveling snake goddess, Nu Wa instantiates what Karen Barad calls "the hauntological nature of quantum entanglements."[65] By cogitating on an electron's "quantum leap," which is not a leap at all but a discontinuous transgression of linear movement, Barad theorizes spacetime as diffracted and multiply threaded through a "nonlinear enfolding of spacetimemattering."[66] Nu Wa herself travels across time and space in movements that signal the ways in which speculative fiction can be used as a genre of migrant literature: abduction, alienation, and teleportation against the backdrop of indenture, displacement, and deportation.

Lai explains that *Salt Fish Girl* began with her interrogation of the Enlightenment notion of the individual subject and her inquiry into alternative renderings of embodiment and sensation that span geographical and generational space-times.[67] She writes: "Nu Wa is a hybrid goddess—half snake and half woman. So I'm not just dealing with travel and dislocation as social practices, I'm dealing with the hybridity and impurity of the body itself."[68] Lai's revision of the Nu Wa origin myth insists that we have always been transgenic and we have always been queer. *Salt Fish Girl* is a "founding myth about dislocation" that unravels "the patriarchal underpinnings of the founding myths of nation states."[69]

Whenever narratives of progress, development, and improvement seduce them, Lai's characters suffer the consequences. Nu Wa, who escapes the grind of factory work in nineteenth-century Canton, is duped by the alluring Edwina into traveling to the Island of Mist and Forgetfulness, which is suggestively abbreviated as "IMF" (also short for the International Monetary Fund). Taken in by the promises of "Progress" and "Democracy" inscribed on the gates to the IMF, Nu Wa begins working as a telemarketer, selling big chances to win lotteries in China, using her Chinese accent to lend credibility to the insider information she dispenses. Though the IMF promises opportunity—Edwina checks Nu Wa into a gilded hotel, which turns out to be a glorified prison—Nu Wa becomes embroiled in the indentured logics of predatory speculation and its empty promises. The financial scheme of Lai's fictional IMF strikingly resembles the Asian Development Bank's strategy of pooling financial instruments such as equity investments and securities into a fund, which provides "opportunities for people to lift themselves out of poverty."[70] Once she is blamed for fleecing pensioners of their retirement funds, Nu Wa is left jobless, destitute, and painfully aware of the precarity of her situation.

Other characters in the novel suffer the effects of such false assurances from financial institutions, too. Miranda's father, Stewart, works as a tax collector, and though "the bank promised adventure" (29) in the form of a first-person shooter game in which the protagonist protects destitute subjects by shooting down birds that burst into streams of digits, Stewart's job seems masochistic at best. The heroic savior narrative is a sham. Stewart as tax collector is not protecting people from a looming force but extracting money, which funnels to the Receivers General. In one of the game's scenarios, the Receivers General appear as policemen who bludgeon the collector. In another, they transform into a "gang of spindly tall children with mutilated faces" holding Stewart's head down in a cesspool while penetrating all his orifices with their long fingers. In these violent ways, the Receivers General dole out punishment under the auspices of fantastic play. The tax collector subjects himself to assault as part of his job, the violence folded into the bank's promise of adventure. Stewart works for the bank to secure a life in the suburban, corporate, GM-enclave Serendipity, but the novel makes clear that the sheen of this engineered life, which has taken the suburban ideal of manicured lawns and made them perpetually green, is undergirded with a form of violence.[71]

In Lai's Serendipity, the securitized city owned by the Saturna corporation, genetic recombination has given rise to apples genetically modified to feed a family of four, not to mention a clone labor force manufactured to clean buildings and work in factories. There, the Ching family feels that they really should mow the lawn, trim the hedges, and somehow expunge the stink of durian fruit from Miranda's pores.[72] When Miranda visits the home of her friend Ian Chestnut, she encounters the intensity of a genetically modified, augmented reality that a wealthy family can afford. On the table, there's "a bowl containing unnaturally large pink blossoms" (65). Ian's mom offers Miranda "a glass of brilliant blue liquid to drink. Her teeth gleamed white. Her eyes were both prosthetic and had a terrible piercing intelligence to them" (64). Ian's dad's "arm muscles ripple unnaturally" (64). While corporate enclosures like Serendipity promise perfect produce and pristine environs built on the controlled subjugation of these bioengineered organisms, the novel takes more interest in the possibilities of genetic mutation that belie the closed-system fantasy precision of laboratory life. The true uncertainty embodied by these forms of life is not to be contained by the security promised by the suburban bubble; instead, unpatented seeds germinate, and escaping workers slip beyond the purview of the corporate enclosure into the Unregulated Zone.

Despite an apparent acceleration of regulatory mechanisms, the GM future of *Salt Fish Girl* is nonetheless teeming with unbridled, queer life—queer in that transgenic and mutant life forms travel beyond normative conceptualizations of speciation, temporality, and communicability to form promiscuous bonds with one another. Clones produced by and for the factory assembly line find a way to reproduce themselves "offshore," on the banks of a magically fecund river whose reproductive power prolifically spawns mutation in the Unregulated Zone. The mutagenic conditions of the Unregulated Zone facilitate Miranda's conception. Though her mother, Aimee Ling, is "a good eight years past menopause" (15), her desire for a genetically rogue durian fruit growing in the Unregulated Zone compels her to reach beyond the seemingly safe and sterile enclave of Serendipity to satisfy her craving: "She wanted it so badly, she would have taken the risk, but my father said that wild things weren't safe. She knew that. She wanted it anyway" (14). This strange fruit—infused with the mythical powers of generation of the serpentine goddess of creation, who has coiled herself around its seed—fertilizes Miranda's mother's egg with Nu Wa's genetic essence. Conceived in a moment when her mother craved wild durian, Miranda embodies her mother's momentary rebellion against the privatization of food. "I should never have brought you that evil fruit," Stewart tells Aimee. "Only barbarians eat those kinds of things. You know if it doesn't have a Saturna sticker it isn't safe. Everything has been affected by these modified pollens. If it grows wild in the Unregulated Zone you have no idea what kinds of mutations have occurred" (32). Here, the discards from the lab experiment gone wrong, through fish genetics and through queer desire, hold wild assembly.

Nu Wa's attraction to Salt Fish Girl and Miranda's bond with the clone worker Evie traverse time, space, and heteronormative notions of propriety. In his formulation of a queer diaspora, David Eng provides "new methods of contesting traditional family and kinship structures — of reorganizing national and transnational communities based not on origin, filiation, and genetics but on destination, affiliation, and the assumption of a common set of social practices or political commitments."[73] Queer diaspora emerges in contradistinction to the concept of a nuclear family, with its attachments to neoliberal ideals of social respectability and personal responsibility, and the privatization of social reproduction.[74]

Salt Fish Girl refuses to demonize genetic manipulation as something to be feared or loathed. The queer GM family might even include a genetic engineer. The novel concludes in an aquarium, where Evie visits the DNA engineer Chang. The aquarium, a mimetic site of origin, marked by "an artificial stream that rushed into an artificial pond" (263), nonetheless serves as a primal scene that Evie warns Miranda not to disparage: "Many lives begin here" (261). Among the queer affiliations cultivated in the aquarium scene are the saltwater carp whose genetic material Evie shares and the transpecies bonds Miranda feels. Noticing a straight couple on the other side of a tank, Miranda observes: "They were not remotely as beautiful as the yellow, blue and orange fish that swam between us and them or as the vibrant, translucent corals that shivered with a strange, barely animate life" (262–63). In this moment, Miranda denaturalizes the reproductive futurity of the heterosexual couple and simultaneously recognizes the vibrancies of Evie's queerer genetic genealogies. Evie and Miranda seem happy enough to consider the queer kinship they share with the other genetically modified organisms of this inauthentic birthplace. Lai's novel focuses its critique not on genetic modification itself but on the securitization of genetically modified organisms (GMO) by a bioengineering industry whose leaders hope to profit from controlling, patenting, and privatizing genetic material.

Salt Fish Girl is a story of clones, fish, and mutants who enact a "queer improvisation of kinship" to intercede in the collusion of corporate greed and scientific ambition.[75] What brokers these alliances across species might be described best as queer desire. Queer theorizations of kinship, collectivity, and affinity-based politics become quite helpful in formulating the particularly queer ways that *Salt Fish Girl* reconceives transpacific futurity.

Miranda characterizes her desire for Evie as a primordial yearning for a radical intersubjectivity, a harkening back to a transgenic, already queer origin:

> Her fingers moved over my skin, cool and tingly as ice water. I wanted to turn into water myself, fall into her the way rain falls into the ocean. I moved through the cool dark with her, my body a single silver muscle slipping against hers, flailing for oxygen in a fast underwater current, shivering slippery cool wet and tumbling through dark towards a blue point of light in the distance, teeth, lip, nipple, the steel taste of blood, gills gaping open and closed, open and closed, mouth, breath, cool water running suddenly piss hot against velvet inner thighs and the quick shudder silver flash of fish turning above the ice-blue surface of the lake. (161)

Desire is transmutation—a falling into water, rain, ocean, and eventually fish, in a passage that renders the transpecies turn in terms evocative of fantastical lesbian erotica. Miranda's slippery tumbling between Evie's thighs moves the reader through what Amit Rai has called an "ecology of sensations" that opens sexual politics to "tactical but unpredictable experimentation."[76] That playful experimentation also manifests at the sentence level in Lai's orchestration of a slip from "rainfall" to "rain falls." Confusing even the automatic grammar check of word-processing programs, the structure produces an energy of connection between the two words, pulling multiple meanings into its quantum entanglement. Puzzling over the singular and plural articulations of rain, Lai uses this description of saltfishy, queer sex to explore interconnected modes of being in the world that call into question the force of individualism.

Improvisational life-forms and experimental practices form ad hoc community networks and resistance movements that coalesce spontaneously and ephemerally, on the fly, on the run, and cobbled together from recycled and repurposed materials. The Unregulated Zone is also home to all sorts of other mutant forms of commerce and life. Pirate television, backyard farming, and reconstructed bicycles offer alternative models of communing for workers fleeing the corporate compounds once "the stock market crisis and the further devaluation of the dollar" compel Saturna to start cutting pensions and firing workers (84). The clones who escape the Pallas shoe factory start making sneakers with revolutionary messages etched into their soles, sold on the black market to foment pedestrian speech acts in the mud. The artistic shoe impressions traverse unregulated space and indicate the hidden currents, the sudden, unexpected connections, unseen networks, and spontaneous associations that constitute the lived urban space beyond the frame of the blueprint and the planned city of Serendipity, or its Disney counterpart of Celebration, Florida. Insofar as they do the often anonymous work of disruption, these anarchic footprints instantiate *Salt Fish Girl*'s guerrilla tactics against the imagination of a neater, more compliant futurity. They participate in what Cooper calls a "creative sabotage of the future."[77]

Postscript: Transpacific Ecologies

The Pacific Ocean is occupied. An assemblage of mutagenic and discarded lifeforms helps us formulate transpacific futurity from below, by thinking speculatively from the perspective of the irradiated fish, the never-disintegrating bead of microplastic, the Asian migrant worker, the embryonic stem cell, and the disappearing coral reefs. This heterogeneous unmannerly crowd of indeterminate actors is bound together by a shared disenfranchisement. They have been cast as disposable service workers in global capitalism's transpacific speculations. By bringing together labor histories of Asian migration to, from, and between the Americas with projections of Asian biotech futures, I mean to tether twenty-first-century extrapolations about transpacific futurities in the era of global finance capitalism to earlier histories of U.S. imperialism across the Pacific. Thinking transpacific futurity from the extrapolation point of nuclear fallout demands a perspectival shift that disrupts the promissory optimism surrounding how genetically modified organisms, as well as other forms of biocapital exchanges, will deliver the so-called Asian Century. In my reading of *Salt Fish Girl* and the 2011 strategic plan of NHGRI, fallout serves as futurity's remainder, tugging at the sails of a more triumphant narrative of technoscientific progress.

After a six-month investigation in Thailand, the *Guardian* put together a report in 2014 on the "Supermarket Slave Trail,"[78] tracing the packages of frozen shrimp sold in the vast majority of supermarkets in the United States and Europe to the work of Burmese migrants coerced into indentured servitude on Thai shrimping boats, where their invisible free labor makes them feel "worthless." "The fish has more value than we do," one worker says. "We are less than human." He—like the Salt Fish Girl, who finds work in a factory assembling tin animal wind-up toys—expresses textbook alienation. Together, they and the fish constitute the flotsam and jetsam, the detritus, the imperial debris circulating in the Pacific Ocean, ground together into fishmeal to feed global capitalism. They are precisely the ones the Trans-Pacific Partnership renders disposable, even as it calls into being an Asian futurity.

Larissa Lai imagines transpacific futurity differently. *Salt Fish Girl* traces the biopolitical currents of the transpacific, bringing Asian/American labor histories into conversation with circulations of other forms of biocapital, including Monsanto seeds, embryonic stem cells, and irradiated fish. These human and inhuman assemblages point to an alternative apprehension of Asian futurity from the perspective of a transpacific undercommons. The novel's multiple forms of drag produce a number of interventions into the construction of speculative futurity. *Salt Fish Girl*'s interspecies "animacies,"[79] including but not limited to the genetic drag of Miranda's dreaming sickness and the clonal genealogies of Evie and the Sonias, also facilitate a temporal drag that dredges up the transpacific historiographies of wars in Asia and the collusion among military, industry, technology, capitalism, and scientific research and folds those histories back into the story of GM futures.

If the bombings of Hiroshima and Nagasaki and the atomic afterlives on the Bikini Atoll constitute the specters of the Pacific that haunt the era of genetic modification, Lai's invocation of them through the transgenic bodies of Miranda Ching and Salt Fish Girl—through the spliced DNA of saltwater carp and Asian migrant workers—suggests the queerness of a transpacific ecology. *Salt Fish Girl* is perhaps the most radical demonstration of the migrant futures collected in this book, and it seems fitting to offer Miranda's musings as a bookend to the epigraphs by Samuel Delany and Octavia Butler that preceded the introduction. In the final moments of *Salt Fish Girl*, Lai gives Miranda a closing soliloquy, which I am all too happy to use as the coda to this chapter:

> I thought, we are the new children of the earth, of the earth's revenge. Once we stepped out of mud, now we step out of moist earth, out of DNA both new and old, an imprint of what has gone before, but also a variation. By our difference we mark how ancient the alphabet of our bodies. By our strangeness we write our bodies into the future. (259)

EPILOGUE

SPECULATION AS DISCOURSE, SPECULATION AS EXUBERANCE

In an essay titled "The Rhetoric of Sex / The Discourse of Desire," Samuel Delany examines one possible etymology for "discourse" that stems from the Latin word for an ancient Roman oval racetrack, where spectators stood on the inside of the track, while the runners raced around the encircled spectators. These Roman discourses, Delany notes, "were places of much betting . . . , the touting up of odds, and the endless speculative conversation on the merits of the racers characteristic today of horse-racing tracks were a part of daily life at the discourse."[1] Building on Michel Foucault's theorizations of discourse in *Archaeology of Knowledge*, Delany understands discourse as a structuring mechanism that not only "tells us what is central and what is peripheral," but that also controls the entry and exit points of that facility.

Delany identifies the Roman discourse as an archaeology of knowledge that is simultaneously a primal scene for speculation. Discourse in this example presents itself as a mostly closed system that facilitates gambling by providing the conditions of manageable uncertainty without throwing itself over to chaos. The runners ostensibly never leave the track. What would happen, though, if they did? Like Foucault, Delany takes more interest in the multiplicity of discourses, discursive practices, and their relationships to the anomaly—that which falls beyond the purview of the discourse. For him, paying attention to the "anomalous and nonserious" discards of discourse reveals the exclusionary structuring mechanisms of the discourse itself.[2] Delany moves through these thoughts on discourse to arrive at his perhaps better known set of formulations on paraliterature, which includes speculative fiction and all sorts of other "anomalous and nonserious" forms of writing. And as Delany points out, "'anomalous and nonserious' is how the accomplishments of women, whether in the arts or in the world, were judged. And the writings of blacks in this country were, until very recently, considered even more of an accident."

"By our strangeness, we write our bodies into the future," Miranda says.[3] She's talking about genetic mutation, but Larissa Lai also invokes queer and migrant futurity. These are the anomalous futures that have run amok from the discourse of speculation. *Migrant Futures* has been a study of speculation not so much as a genre, but rather as a discursive practice. Migrant futures are epistemological anomalies. They are science fictions less interested in getting the science right than in interrogating the systems that produced that science.

Speculation becomes a colonizing mechanism when it attempts to capture, profit from, and realize the future. Predictions, premeditations, precautions, preparedness—these are all signposts of a speculative science working to colonize the future. This book has located several arenas in which speculation has met up with these imperialist logics: the financial derivatives market, military securitization, transnational surrogacy insurance, global development banking, as well as bio- and geo-engineering. Speculation as discourse has been around for some time in various guises. Consider, for example, the progress narrative that primes the funding rationale for Henry Ford's rubber plantation in Brazil. I have called attention to it in the figuration of homeland futurity at the U.S.-Mexico border. But it has been more interested in highlighting what it might mean to speculate otherwise.

In an article titled "Hope over Experience: Desirability and the Persistence of Optimism," a team of Yale economists concluded that people's desires direct them toward optimism over and against their so-called better judgment. Alan Greenspan denounced the "irrational exuberance" and blamed it for the Asian financial crisis in the 1990s. Through the work of queer theorists like Lauren Berlant and Jasbir Puar, we can see that capitalism thrives on the energy of this cruel optimism, pathologizing it only when the market collapses to save its idealized rational subject from reproach.

Migrant Futures addresses counterfactual futures as they are imagined in both apparent fictions—novels and films—as well as masked fictions such as economic forecasts, founding documents of scientific consortia, and development plans linked to structural adjustment loans. Rather than using the latter as background to understand the former, *Migrant Futures* places both types of extrapolative enterprises on an equal footing. Both generate cultural fictions that then produce material effects. If financialization is a project that turns human sentiment into data with the goal of predicting and mitigating risk for wealthy elites, *Migrant Futures* focuses on the speculative fictions of those populations shuttled in and out of zones of growth. The members of this undercommons refuse to participate in, and are denied access to, the ladder of corporate productivity and take comfort instead in forms of kinship and occupation that survive alongside and below the radar of freewheeling global entrepreneurialism. Their irrational exuberance serves them well in the struggle to enact an alternative economy of sharing amid destitution, love for others amid austerity, and collaboration amid incentivized competition.

To think of migrant futures is to posit that which may never come to pass but must nevertheless persist speculatively, against all odds. Perhaps the primary function of their existence is to hold open the aperture to the beyond, where the systems that seemingly dominate cease to overwhelm. The cultural texts assembled in this book explore a sense of wonder that exceeds or runs parallel to frameworks of the knowable. These speculations from below face uncertainty with exuberance, daring to stay open to chance, in part because that is all they have, but also because they are no longer playing the same game. They have left the track.

NOTES

Preface

1 Jervey Tervalon, "Sister from Another Planet: Remembering Octavia Butler," *LA Weekly*, March 1, 2006, accessed July 23, 2016, http://www.laweekly.com/news/sister-from-another-planet-2142238.
2 Mike Davis, *City of Quartz: Excavating the Future in Los Angeles* (New York: Verso, 1990), 55.
3 For example, Catherine Ramírez writes: "despite the genre's androcentrism and overwhelming whiteness, I found pleasure and meaning in science fiction. It beckoned me to imagine a world—indeed a universe—beyond the freeways, strip malls, and smog-alert days of my Southern California childhood. / More than mere escapism, science fiction can prompt us to recognize and rethink the status quo by depicting an alternative world, be it a parallel universe, distant future, or revised past" ("Afrofuturism/Chicanafuturism: Fictive Kin," *Aztlán: A Journal of Chicano Studies* 33:1 [Spring 2008], 185). N. K. Jemisin relates her experience of being affirmed in her interest in science fiction when she read Octavia Butler's *Dawn*, which features a black woman named Lilith Ayapo as a protagonist ("Celebrating Dawn by Octavia Butler," November 20, 2012, accessed July 23, 2016, https://youtu.be/aJKwxdsxklM). And Junot Diaz professes the extent to which reading *Pride and Prejudice* was science fiction to him (October 18, 2013).
4 Fredric Jameson, *Archaeologies of the Future: The Desire Called Utopia and Other Science Fictions* (London, New York: Verso, 2005), 199. Jameson revises this statement in an essay about Rem Koolhaas and the "future city," in which he interprets Koolhaas's Junkspace formulation of perpetual renovation as an "attempt to imagine capitalism by way of imagining the end of the world" ("Future City," *New Left Review*, vol. 21 [May-June 2003], 76).
5 I have one of the anonymous readers of this manuscript to thank for the apt characterization of the "starter archive" aspect of this project.

Introduction

1. This figure is according to the Bank for International Settlements, which has been charged by the Committee on the Global Financial System with collecting semi-annual derivatives statistics reports from the central banks of the eleven Group of Ten countries plus those of Australia and Spain. $710 trillion is a "notional" estimate that does not account for the measurement of credit and market risks. See Bank for International Settlements, "Semiannual OTC Derivatives Statistics," May 4, 2016, accessed July 23, 2016, http://www.bis.org/statistics/derstats.htm. See also Mayra Rodríguez Valladares, "Derivatives Markets Growing Again, with Few New Protections," *New York Times*, May 13, 2014, accessed July 23, 2016, http://dealbook.nytimes.com/2014/05/13/derivatives-markets-growing-again-with-few-new-protections/.
2. In his formulation of "hauntology," Jacques Derrida argues that "if the commodity-form is *not, presently*, use-value, and even if it is not *actually present*, it affects *in advance* the use-value of the wooden table. It affects and bereaves it in advance, like the ghost it will become, but this is precisely where haunting begins. And its time, and the untimeliness of its present, of its being 'out of joint.'" *Specters of Marx*, trans. Peggy Kamuf (New York: Routledge, 1994), 161.
3. Karl Marx, *Capital*, trans. Ernest Untermann (Chicago: Charles H. Kerr, 1909), 552.
4. Marx, *Capital*, 699.
5. For more on figurations of the vampire in Marx, see Gerry Canavan, "'We Are the Walking Dead': Race, Time, and Survival in Zombie Narrative," *Extrapolation* 51, no. 3 (2010): 431–53; Steven Shaviro, "Capitalist Monsters," *Historical Materialism* 10, no. 4 (2002): 281–90.
6. Donna Haraway, "Situated Knowledges: The Science Question in Feminism and the Privilege of Partial Perspective," *Feminist Studies* 14, no. 3 (1988): 581.
7. For a range of disciplinary approaches to the cultural studies of finance, see Aaron Carico and Dara Orenstein, eds., "The Fictions of Finance," special issue, *Radical History Review* 118 (Winter 2014); Karin Knorr Cetina and Alex Preda, *The Sociology of Financial Markets* (Oxford: Oxford University Press, 2004); Edward LiPuma and Benjamin Lee, *Financial Derivatives and the Globalization of Risk* (Durham, NC: Duke University Press, 2004); Donald A. MacKenzie, Fabian Muniesa, and Lucia Siu, eds., *Do Economists Make Markets? On the Performativity of Economics* (Princeton, NJ: Princeton University Press, 2007); Randy Martin, *The Financialization of Daily Life* (Philadelphia: Temple University Press, 2002).
8. LiPuma and Lee, *Financial Derivatives and the Globalization of Risk*, 24, 64.
9. LiPuma and Lee, *Financial Derivatives and the Globalization of Risk*, 26.
10. LiPuma and Lee, *Financial Derivatives and the Globalization of Risk*, 58.
11. Kathleen Woodward, *Statistical Panic: Cultural Politics and the Poetics of the Emotions* (Durham, NC: Duke University Press, 2009), 208. I am borrowing the term "datafication" from Wendy Hui Kyong Chun, "Orienting Orientalism, or How to Map Cyberspace," in *AsianAmerica.Net: Ethnicity, Nationalism, and Cyberspace*, edited by Rachel C. Lee and Sau-ling Cynthia Wong (New York: Routledge, 2003), 16, 34.

12 Uncertain Commons, *Speculate This!* (Durham, NC: Duke University Press, 2013) 2.
13 LiPuma and Lee, *Financial Derivatives and the Globalization of Risk*, 43–44.
14 Rodríguez Valladares, "Derivatives Markets Growing Again, with Few New Protections."
15 Jeffrey E. Garten, "The Future of the Global Financial System," accessed July 23, 2016, http://som.yale.edu/faculty-research/our-centers-initiatives/international-center-finance/research-initiatives/future-global-finance/project-overview.
16 Gilles Deleuze, "Postscript on the Societies of Control," *October* Vol. 59 (Winter 1992): 5.
17 Frank Knight, *Risk, Uncertainty and Profit* (Boston: Houghton Mifflin, 1921), 311. Writing in the immediate aftermath of World War I, the first major global crisis of the twentieth century, Frank Knight asserts that uncertainty is too quickly instrumentalized in risk calculations. He suggests that a "true Uncertainty" exists insofar as there can be an uncertainty that is never fully captured or completely capitalized by the speculative calculus that tries to make it profitable. Indeed, Knight reminds readers that approximations have been crucial to securing "our present marvelous mastery over the forces of nature" because "we know how to discount their incompleteness" (21, 5).
18 Dipesh Chakrabarty, *Provincializing Europe: Postcolonial Thought and Historical Difference* (Princeton, NJ: Princeton University Press, 2008), 8.
19 James C. Scott, *Seeing Like a State: How Certain Schemes to Improve the Human Condition Have Failed* (New Haven, CT: Yale University Press, 1998), 3.
20 Paisley Currah and Susan Stryker, introduction to "Making Transgender Count," edited by Paisley Currah and Susan Stryker, special issue, *TSQ* 2, no. 1 (2015): 4.
21 Paisley Currah and Susan Stryker, Introduction, 2.
22 Thanks to my mathematician colleague Craig Sutton, who bravely gave me a crash course in mathematical finance. For more on the turn to three-dimensional models in finance, see Pierre Henry-Labordère, *Analysis, Geometry, and Modeling in Finance: Advanced Methods in Option Pricing* (Boca Raton, FL: CRC, 2009).
23 Matthew G. Hannah, "Sampling and the Politics of Representation in US Census 2000," *Environment and Planning D: Society and Space* 19, no. 5: 516, as quoted in Paisley Currah and Susan Stryker, Introduction, 2.
24 Randy Martin, *The Financialization of Daily Life*, 3; Ulrich Beck, *Risk Society: Towards a New Modernity* (London: Sage, 1992).
25 In Muñoz's words, "for queers, the gesture and its aftermath, the ephemeral trace, matter more than many traditional modes of evidencing lives and politics." *Cruising Utopia: The Then and There of Queer Futurity* (New York: New York University Press, 2009), 81.
26 Muñoz, *Cruising Utopia*, 49.
27 Stefano Harney and Fred Moten, *The Undercommons: Fugitive Planning and Black Study* (Wivenhoe, NY: Minor Compositions, 2013).
28 Along similar lines, Ramón Saldívar identifies the emergence of a "transnational imaginary" in contemporary U.S. ethnic literatures such as Junot Diaz's *The Brief Wondrous Life of Oscar Wao* (Ramón Saldívar, "Imagining Cultures: The Transna-

tional Imaginary in Postrace America," *Journal of Transnational American Studies*, 4, no. 2 [2012]: 8, 9, 16). While *Migrant Futures*'s query is less concerned with the terms "postrace" and "post postmodern" as literary categories, I am grateful to find this work in conversation with Saldívar's cogitations.

29 Nalo Hopkinson, "Introduction," *So Long Been Dreaming: Postcolonial Science Fiction and Fantasy*, eds. Nalo Hopkinson and Uppinder Mehan (Vancouver, BC: Arsenal Press, 2004), 9.

30 See Jane Chi Hyun Park, *Yellow Future: Oriental Style in Hollywood Cinema* (Minneapolis: University of Minnesota Press, 2010); David S. Roh, Betsy Huang, and Greta A. Niu, eds. *Techno-Orientalism: Imagining Asia in Speculative Fiction, History, and Media* (New Brunswick, NJ: Rutgers University Press, 2015).

31 David Harvey, *The Condition of Postmodernity: An Enquiry into the Origins of Cultural Change* (Oxford: Blackwell, 1989), 12.

32 Terry Smith, "Visual Regimes of Colonization: Aboriginal Seeing and European Vision in Australia," in *Visual Culture Reader*, ed. Nicholas Mirzoeff, 2nd edition (London: Routledge, 2003), 491.

33 See Chet Van Duzer, *Sea Monsters on Medieval and Renaissance Maps* (London: The British Library, 2013); Joseph Nigg, *Sea Monsters: A Voyage around the World's Most Beguiling Map* (Chicago: University of Chicago Press, 2013). In a talk about his book, Van Duzer, a map historian at the Library of Congress, said: "The creatures look purely fantastic. They all look like they were just made up. But, in fact, a lot of them come from what were considered, at the time, scientific sources." Quoted in Tanya Lewis, "Here Be Dragons: The Evolution of Sea Monsters on Medieval Maps," *Live Science*, September 6, 2013, accessed July 23, 2016, http://www.livescience.com/39465-sea-monsters-on-medieval-maps.html.

34 Anne McClintock, *Imperial Leather: Race, Gender and Sexuality in the Colonial Contest* (New York: Routledge, 1995), 40; Mary Louise Pratt, *Imperial Eyes: Travel Writing and Transculturation*, 2nd ed. (London: Routledge, 2008). Though I reference Pratt's work more generally here, the actual phrase "mapping of progress" is taken from McClintock's *Imperial Leather* in which the author, like Pratt, considers colonial cartography, particularly through the gendered and racialized tropes of imperialist knowledge production.

35 Ian Hacking, *The Taming of Chance* (Cambridge: Cambridge University Press, 1990), 10.

36 Here I am following Anne McClintock's call to theorize "the *continuities* in international imbalances in imperial power" (*Imperial Leather*, 13). "Since the 1940s," she writes, "the U.S. imperialism-without-colonies has taken a number of distinct forms (military, political, economic, and cultural), some concealed, some half-concealed. The power of U.S. finance capital and huge multinational corporations to command the flows of capital, research, consumer goods and media information around the world can exert a coercive power as great as any colonial gunboat" (*Imperial Leather*, 13).

37 Fredric Jameson, *Archaeologies of the Future: The Desire Called Utopia and Other Science Fictions* (London: Verso, 2005), 228.

38 Darko Suvin, *Metamorphoses of Science Fiction: On the Poetics and History of a Literary Genre* (New Haven, CT: Yale University Press, 1979), 7. Suvin would later walk back his commitment to an "innocently and naively Formalist horizon" in a 2014 postscript to his "Estrangement and Cognition" essay from which this quotation is taken (Darko Suvin, "Estrangement and Cognition," *Strange Horizons*, November 24, 2014, accessed November 28, 2016, http://strangehorizons.com/non-fiction/articles/estrangement-and-cognition/#ps).

39 Gregory Benford, "Real Science, Imaginary Worlds," in *The Ascent of Wonder: The Evolution of Hard SF*, edited by David G. Hartwell and Kathryn Cramer (New York: Tom Doherty Associates, 1994), 15.

40 Benford, "Real Science, Imaginary Worlds," 16.

41 The process of generic differentiation itself, according to Mary Poovey, "belongs to the general history of specialization that we call *modernization*" (*Genres of the Credit Economy: Mediating Value in Eighteenth- and Nineteenth-Century Britain* [Chicago: University of Chicago Press, 2008], 1). In 1988, Sarah Lefanu argued that "the plasticity of science fiction and its openness to other literary genres allow an apparent contradiction, but one that is potentially of enormous importance to contemporary women writers: it makes possible, and encourages (despite its colonization by male writers), the inscription of women as subjects free from the constraints of mundane fiction; and it also offers the possibility of interrogating that very inscription, questioning the basis of gendered subjectivity." *In the Chinks of the World Machine: Feminism and Science Fiction* (London: Women's Press, 1988), 9.

42 Benford, "Real Science, Imaginary Worlds," 15.

43 Benford, "Real Science, Imaginary Worlds," 15–16.

44 Constance Penley, Andrew Ross, and Donna Haraway, "Cyborgs at Large: Interview with Donna Haraway," *Social Text*, no. 25/26 (1990): 9.

45 Donna J. Haraway, *Simians, Cyborgs, and Women: The Reinvention of Nature* (New York: Routledge, 1991), 174.

46 Donna J. Haraway, "Situated Knowledges: The Science Question in Feminism and the Privilege of Partial Perspective," *Feminist Studies* 14, no. 3 (1988): 581.

47 Haraway, "Situated Knowledges," 581. In addition to Haraway's work, some of the more foundational texts of the cultural studies of science and technology include: Anne Balsamo, ed., "Science, Technology and Culture," special issue, *Cultural Studies* 12, no. 3 (1998); Teresa de Lauretis, Andreas Huyssen, and Kathleen Woodward, eds., *The Technological Imagination: Theories and Fictions* (Madison, WI: Coda Press, 1980); Bruno Latour and Steve Woolgar, *Laboratory Life: The Construction of Scientific Facts* (Princeton, NJ: Princeton University Press, 1979); and Constance Penley and Andrew Ross, eds., *Technoculture* (Minneapolis, MN: University of Minnesota Press, 1991).

48 Nancy Leys Stepan, "Race, Gender, Science and Citizenship," *Gender and History* 10, no. 1 (1998): 33.

49 Samuel R. Delany, "Sword & Sorcery, S/M, and the Economics of Inadequation," 1989, in Samuel R. Delany, *Silent Interviews: On Language, Race, Sex, Science Fiction, and Some Comics: A Collection of Written Interviews* (Hanover, NH: University Press of New England, 1994), 152.

50 Donna J. Haraway, "SF: Science Fiction, Speculative Fabulation, String Figures, So Far," *Ada* no. 3 (2013).
51 Samuel R. Delany, "*Para·doxa* Interview: Inside and Outside the Canon," 1995, in Samuel R. Delany, *Shorter Views: Queer Thoughts & the Politics of the Paraliterary* (Hanover and London: University Press of New England, 1999), 210.
52 Jacques Derrida, "The Law of Genre," *Critical Inquiry* 7, no. 1 (Autumn 1980): 57.
53 Samuel R. Delany and Marilyn Hacker, "On Speculative Fiction," in *Quark* 4, eds. Samuel R. Delany and Marilyn Hacker (New York: Coronet Communications, 1971), 9.
54 Delany and Hacker, "On Speculative Fiction," 8.
55 LiPuma and Lee, *Financial Derivatives and the Globalization of Risk*, 19.
56 LiPuma and Lee, *Financial Derivatives and the Globalization of Risk*, 47.
57 Samuel R. Delany, "Critical Methods/Speculative Fiction," 1970, in Samuel R. Delany, *The Jewel-Hinged Jaw: Notes on the Language of Science Fiction*, 23, rev. ed. (Middletown, CT: Wesleyan University Press, 2009).
58 Delany, "Critical Methods / Speculative Fiction," 26.
59 Mark Fisher, "Capitalist Realism," *Strike!* June 3, 2013, accessed July 23, 2016, http://strikemag.org/capitalist-realism-by-mark-fisher/.
60 Lisa Lowe and David Lloyd, "Introduction," in *The Politics of Culture in the Shadow of Capital*, edited by Lisa Lowe and David Lloyd (Durham, NC: Duke University Press, 1997), 5.
61 Walter Benjamin, "Theses on the Philosophy of History," in Walter Benjamin, *Illuminations*, edited by Hannah Arendt and translated by Harry Zohn (New York: Shocken, 1968), 257–58. Benjamin famously writes: "A Klee painting named 'Angelus Novus' shows an angel looking as though he is about to move away from something he is fixedly contemplating. His eyes are staring, his mouth is open, his wings are spread. This is how one pictures the angel of history. His face is turned toward the past. Where we perceive a chain of events, he sees one single catastrophe which keeps piling wreckage upon wreckage and hurls it in front of his feet. The angel would like to stay, awaken the dead, and make whole what has been smashed. But a storm is blowing from Paradise; it has got caught in his wings with such violence that the angel can no longer close them. This storm irresistibly propels him into the future to which his back is turned, while the pile of debris before him grows skyward. This storm is what we call progress" (257–58).
62 See Geeta Patel, "Risky Subjects: Insurance, Sexuality, and Capital," *Social Text* 24, no. 4 (2006): 25–65.
63 Lisa Duggan, "The New Homonormativity: The Sexual Politics of Neoliberalism," in *Materializing Democracy: Toward a Revitalized Cultural Politics*, edited by Russ Castronovo and Dana D. Nelson (Durham, NC: Duke University Press, 2002), 175–94; Jasbir K. Puar, *Terrorist Assemblages: Homonationalism in Queer Times* (Durham, NC: Duke University Press, 2007); David L. Eng, *The Feeling of Kinship* (Durham, NC: Duke University Press, 2010).
64 Lisa Lowe, *Immigrant Acts: On Asian American Cultural Politics* (Durham, NC: Duke

University Press, 1996); Victor Bascara, *Model-Minority Imperialism* (Minneapolis: University of Minnesota Press, 2006); Mimi Thi Nguyen, *The Gift of Freedom* (Durham, NC: Duke University Press, 2012).

65 Kandice Chuh, *Imagine Otherwise: On Asian Americanist Critique* (Durham, NC: Duke University Press, 2003), 151.
66 Chuh, *Imagine Otherwise*, 10.
67 Chuh, *Imagine Otherwise*, 10–11.
68 David L. Eng, Judith Halberstam, and José Esteban Muñoz. "What's Queer about Queer Studies Now?," *Social Text* 23, no. 3 (2005): 3.
69 (Judith) Jack Halberstam, *In a Queer Time and Place: Transgender Bodies, Subcultural Lives* (New York: New York University Press, 2005), 2.
70 Halberstam, *In a Queer Time and Place*, 13.
71 Lee Edelman, *No Future: Queer Theory and the Death Drive* (Durham, NC: Duke University Press, 2004), 30.
72 Benjamin, "Theses on the Philosophy of History," 261.
73 Elizabeth Freeman, *Time Binds: Queer Temporalities, Queer Histories* (Durham, NC: Duke University Press, 2010), 3.
74 Dana Luciano, *Arranging Grief: Sacred Time and the Body in Nineteenth-Century America* (New York: New York University Press, 2007), 9.
75 Lauren Berlant, *Cruel Optimism* (Durham, NC: Duke University Press, 2011), 4.
76 Some of the more recent works on science and empire in the Americas that has been particularly helpful to me include: Michael Adas, *Dominance by Design: Technological Imperatives and America's Civilizing Mission* (Cambridge, MA: Harvard University Press, 2006); Carolyn de la Peña and Siva Vaidhyanathan, eds., "Rewiring the 'Nation': The Place of Technology in American Studies," special issue, *American Quarterly* 58, no. 3 (2007); James Delbourgo and Nicholas Dew, eds., *Science and Empire in the Atlantic World* (New York: Routledge, 2008); Richard Drayton, *Nature's Government: Science, Imperial Britain and the "Improvement" of the World* (New Haven, CT: Yale University Press, 2000); Julyan G. Peard, *Race, Place, and Medicine: The Idea of the Tropics in Nineteenth-Century Brazilian Medicine* (Durham, NC: Duke University Press, 1999); and Londa Schiebinger, *Plants and Empire: Colonial Bioprospecting in the Atlantic World* (Cambridge, MA: Harvard University Press, 2004).
77 Gloria Anzaldúa, *Borderlands/La Frontera: The New Mestiza* (San Francisco: Spinsters/Aunt Lute, 1987); Mary Pat Brady, *Extinct Lands, Temporal Geographies: Chicana Literature and the Urgency of Space* (Durham, NC: Duke University Press, 2002); María Josefina Saldaña-Portillo, *The Revolutionary Imagination in the Americas and the Age of Development* (Durham, NC: Duke University Press, 2003); José David Saldívar, *Border Matters: Remapping American Cultural Studies* (Berkeley University of California Press, 1997); Alicia R. Schmidt Camacho, *Migrant Imaginaries: Latino Cultural Politics in the U.S.-Mexico Borderlands* (New York: New York University Press, 2008).
78 Berlant, *Cruel Optimism*.

Chapter 1. Imperial Rubber

1. In a keen and complex analysis of the colonial gaze in both *Fitzcarraldo* and another Herzog jungle film, *Aguirre*, Lutz P. Koepnick argues that "both films stage colonial enterprises destined to fail due to the heroes' inability to escape their Western imagination. . . . The chaotic diversity of the rainforest exposes the systematic inappropriateness of Western routines of cognition and ordering. . . . Herzog at once comprehends the aporetic shortsightedness of the colonial gaze and yet in his role as an auteur director, he reproduces the instrumental logic of his hero" ("Colonial Forestry: Sylvan Politics in Werner Herzog's *Aguirre* and *Fitzcarraldo*," in Special Issue on German Film History, *New German Critique*, no. 60 [1993]: 135, 137). As his zany protagonist suggests, Herzog does make a spectacle of the jungle, and in doing so, does the making of the film, which relies on the exploitation of both indigenous actors and the local ecology to produce the spectacle, parallel some of the exploitative practices of the rubber industry? Even if the film hints at some awareness of its own participation in another form of Western cultural imperialism, it goes about its business anyway without much change to the political economy of its practices.
2. Mary Louise Pratt, *Imperial Eyes: Travel Writing and Transculturation*, 2nd ed. (London: Routledge, 2008), 20.
3. Charles-Marie de La Condamine, *A Succinct Abridgement of a Voyage made within the Inland Parts of South-America* (London: E. Withers, 1748), 24, quoted in Mary Louise Pratt, *Imperial Eyes*, 20.
4. For historical accounts of Ford's rubber plantations in Brazil, see Elizabeth Durham Esch, "Fordtown: Managing Race and Nation in the American Empire, 1925–1945," PhD diss., New York University, 2003; Richard P. Tucker, *Insatiable Appetite: The United States and the Ecological Degradation of the Tropical World* (Berkeley: University of California Press, 2000); Barbara Weinstein, *The Amazon Rubber Boom, 1850–1920* (Stanford, CA: Stanford University Press, 1983).
5. "The Ford Rubber Plantation of Brazil," brochure in box 1, "History and Cost," accession #74, Benson Ford Research Center, Dearborn, MI. All further references to this brochure, published by Companhia Ford Industrial do Brasil and other original documents found at the archives will be made parenthetically.
6. Anne McClintock, *Imperial Leather*, 40.
7. Ann Laura Stoler, *Race and the Education of Desire: Foucault's History of Sexuality and the Colonial Order of Things* (Durham, NC: Duke University Press, 1995), 61.
8. Lisa Lowe and David Lloyd, "Introduction," in *The Politics of Culture in the Shadow of Capital*, edited by Lisa Lowe and David Lloyd (Durham, NC: Duke University Press, 1997), 5.
9. Several Asian American scholars have examined Orientalist representations of Asians and Asianness in U.S. technocultural discourse. See, for example, Rachel C. Lee and Sau-ling Cynthia Wong, eds., *Asian America.Net: Ethnicity, Nationalism, and Cyberspace* (New York: Routledge, 2003); Lisa Nakamura, *Cybertypes: Race, Ethnicity, and Identity on the Internet* (New York: Routledge, 2002).
10. Kirsten Backstrom, "*Through the Arc of the Rain Forest*, Karen Tei Yamashita," in 500

Great Books by Women, edited by Erica Bauermeister, Jesse Larsen, and Holly Smith (New York: Penguin, 1994), 190.

11 Michael Harris, review of *Through the Arc of the Rain Forest*, by Karen Tei Yamashita, *Los Angeles Times*, September 9, 1990, accessed July 24, 2016, http://articles.latimes.com/1990-09-09/books/bk-363_1_karen-tei-yamashita.

12 Marita Sturken, *Tangled Memories: The Vietnam War, the AIDS Epidemic, and the Politics of Remembering* (Berkeley: University of California Press, 1997), 2.

13 This and future references to Karen Tei Yamashita, *Through the Arc of the Rain Forest: A Novel* (Minneapolis, MN: Coffee House Press, 1990), are made parenthetically.

14 See Frances R. Aparicio and Susana Chávez-Silverman, *Tropicalizations: Transcultural Representations of Latinidad* (Hanover, NH: University Press of New England, 1997).

15 See Rod Edmond, *Representing the South Pacific: Colonial Discourse from Cook to Gauguin* (Cambridge: Cambridge University Press, 1997); Patty O'Brien, *The Pacific Muse: Exotic Femininity and the Colonial Pacific* (Seattle: University of Washington Press, 2006). O'Brien writes that Gauguin, "whose vision of the Pacific has cast an enduring shadow on all that followed," spent time not only in Tahiti but also in Brazil, in Rio de Janeiro. She writes: "Like so many Occidental voyagers before him, Gauguin lusted for the mythologized halcyon days of Tahiti encapsulated by Bougainville. At first he was lacking any substantial knowledge of Tahiti, but what loomed largest in his imagination was a place of tropical fecundity, feminine beauty, and sexual emancipation that waited for immortalization. Gauguin's Tahiti was confected by more than a century of Occidental travel literature, anthropology, and art and half a century of photography. From the 1880s, Gauguin's formative artistic years, the long-standing South Seas myths woven from the earlier phases of colonization were revived and embellished for a popular audience of readers with a fresh interest in the empire" (*The Pacific Muse*, 216).

16 Claude Lévi-Strauss, *Tristes Tropiques* (Paris: Plon, 1955), 13.

17 Henri Bergson, *Creative Evolution*, translated by Arthur Mitchell (New York: H. Holt, 1911), 4.

18 Júnia Ferreira Furtado, "Tropical Empiricism: Making Medical Knowledge in Colonial Brazil," in *Science and Empire in the Atlantic World*, edited by James Delbourgo and Nicholas Dew (New York: Routledge, 2008), 129.

19 Nancy Leys Stepan asks: "As we look to the future, what place will tropical nature hold in the imagination? In an era of the commodification of nature on an unprecedented scale and of wholesale environmental destruction; when world travel and global networks make all places seem increasingly alike . . . —shall we then find that 'tropical nature,' as an imaginative construction, has itself become banal and trivialized? If so, what will the consequences be for our empathetic understanding of the natural world, especially the tropical world that we are so rapidly destroying?" *Picturing Tropical Nature* (Ithaca, NY: Cornell University Press, 2001), 240.

20 Rachel C. Lee, *The Americas of Asian American Literature: Gendered Fictions of Nation and Transnation* (Princeton, NJ: Princeton University Press, 1999), 118.

21 See Kathryn Kopinak, "Environmental Implications of New Mexican Industrial

Investment: The Rise of Asian Origin Maquiladoras as Generators of Hazardous Waste," *Asian Journal of Latin American Studies* 15, no. 1 (2002): 91–120.

22 See Karen Michelle Barad, *Meeting the Universe Halfway: Quantum Physics and the Entanglement of Matter and Meaning* (Durham, NC: Duke University Press, 2007); Donna J. Haraway, *When Species Meet* (Minneapolis: University of Minnesota Press, 2008).

23 Daniel Touro Linger, *No One Home: Brazilian Selves Remade in Japan* (Stanford, CA: Stanford University Press, 2001), xiv.

24 Linger, *No One Home*, 22.

25 Linger, *No One Home*, 23–25.

26 Avery Gordon, *Ghostly Matters: Haunting and the Sociological Imagination* (Minneapolis: University of Minnesota Press, 1997), 65.

27 A. Gordon, *Ghostly Matters*, 8.

28 George Ward Stocking and Myron W. Watkins explain how the attempt by the British to establish a cartel in the world rubber market through the Stevenson Plan backfired: between 1922 and 1928, the British share of the market dropped while "exports from the Dutch East Indies (and other far eastern sources) rose phenomenally in direct response to the market opportunities created by British restriction." *Cartels in Action: Case Studies in International Business Diplomacy* (New York: Twentieth Century Fund, 1946), 71.

29 Benjamin, "Theses on the Philosophy of History," 261. See also Benedict Anderson, *Imagined Communities: Reflections on the Origin and Spread of Nationalism* (London: Verso, 2006), 24; Bliss Cua Lim, *Translating Time: Cinema, the Fantastic, and Temporal Critique* (Durham, NC: Duke University Press, 2009), 11; Lloyd Pratt, *Archives of American Time: Literature and Modernity in the Nineteenth Century* (Philadelphia: University of Pennsylvania Press, 2010), 5.

30 "The Ford Rubber Plantation of Brazil" brochure, np. The quotations that follow in the paragraph are also from this brochure.

31 McClintock, *Imperial Leather*, 33.

32 Gilberto Freyre, *The Masters and the Slaves: A Study in the Development of Brazilian Civilization*, 1933, translated by Samuel Putnam (Berkeley: University of California Press, 1986). For a helpful history of the convergence of racial science and racialized labor practices used to manage the Ford rubber plantations in Brazil, see Elizabeth Durham Esch, "Fordtown: Managing Race and Nation in the American Empire, 1925–1945," PhD diss., New York University, 2003.

33 Esch, "Fordtown," 103.

34 France Winddance Twine, *Racism in a Racial Democracy: The Maintenance of White Supremacy in Brazil, 1997* (New Brunswick, NJ: Rutgers University Press, 2001), 87–88. See also Nancy Leys Stepan, *"The Hour of Eugenics": Race, Gender, and Nation in Latin America* (Ithaca, NY: Cornell University Press, 1991). In 1925, the Mexican philosopher José Vasconcelos published *La Raza Cósmica* (The cosmic race), which sets a trajectory of racial mixing with the eventuality of a utopian "fifth race of the future" in the Americas, comprised of a bronze people, so racially mixed and culturally consolidated that its members found a new civilization called "Universó-

polis." *The Cosmic Race: A Bilingual Edition*, translated and annotated by Didier T. Jaén (Baltimore, MD: Johns Hopkins University Press, 1997), originally published as *La Raza Cósmica: Misión de la Raza Iberoamericana Argentina y Brasil*, (Madrid: Agencia Mundial de Librería, 1925), 24, 25. "The world of the future," prophesies Vasconcelos, "will belong to whoever conquers the Amazon region" (25).

35 Weinstein refers to the influx of Syrian, Lebanese, and Jewish immigrants to the Brazilian state of Pará during the 1920s (*The Amazon Rubber Boom*, 259–60).

36 Greg Grandin documents the contributions of U.S. and European news media to this set of speculations. "It was billed as a proxy fight," he summarizes. "Ford represented vigor, dynamism, and the rushing energy that defined American capitalism in the early twentieth century; the Amazon the primal stillness, an ancient world that had so far proved unconquerable." *The Rise and Fall of Henry Ford's Forgotten Jungle City* (New York: Metropolitan, 2009), 4. Against the backdrop of recently disappeared British explorers, sixteenth-century stories of El Dorado, and Alexander von Humboldt's prophecy that the Amazon would become the world's granary, international news media characterized Ford's expedition in the Brazilian Amazon as bringing "white man's magic" to the wilderness. Their speculations predicted that "Black Indians armed with heavy blades will slash down their one-time haunts to make way for future windshield wipers, floor mats, balloon tires" (quoted in *Fordlandia*, 5). These predictions in the yellow journalism of the early twentieth century exemplify the racialized fantasies of a neocolonialist capitalism.

37 Tucker writes: "In the face of inefficiency, corruption, and ethnic antagonisms in the business of collecting wild rubber, British strategists attempted to grow *Hevea* in dense plantations. They never succeeded in conquering the tree's fatal disease, South American leaf blight, a fungus that had coevolved with *Hevea* in the forest. *Hevea* trees had survived over the millennia by growing widely dispersed among other species; capitalist concentrations of production demanded the opposite" (*Insatiable Appetite*, 233).

38 Tucker, *Insatiable Appetite*, 227.

39 Quoted in Cato Institute, "Hernando de Soto's Biography," accessed July 24, 2016, http://www.cato.org/friedman-prize/hernando-desoto/biography.

40 Quoted in Cato Institute, "Hernando de Soto's Biography." See also *Economist*, "The Mystery of Capital Deepens," August 24, 2006, accessed July 24, 2016, http://www.economist.com/node/7830209?zid=316&ah=2f6fb672faf113fdd3b11cd1b1bf8a77.

41 Quoted in Cato Institute, "Hernando de Soto's Biography."

42 Jeremy Clift, "Hearing the Dogs Bark: Jeremy Clift Interviews Development Guru Hernando de Soto," *Finance & Development*, December 2003, accessed July 24, 2016, https://www.imf.org/external/pubs/ft/fandd/2003/12/pdf/people.pdf.

43 Esch, "Fordtown," 7.

44 In her examination of how Chicana writers reconceptualize space, Mary Pat Brady suggests that authors such as Sandra Cisneros "twist realism as a representational strategy that too easily solidifies oppressive spatial alignments by hiding the processual quality of space. Out of such twisting frequently emerge whole new conceptualizations of spatiality and sociality that are revolutionary in their implication." *Extinct*

Lands, Temporal Geographies: Chicana Literature and the Urgency of Space (Durham, NC: Duke University Press, 2002), 7.

Chapter 2. Homeland Futurity

1. Quoted in Mimi Hall, "Sci-Fi Writers Join War on Terror," *USA Today*, May 31, 2007.
2. For more on scenario thinking see Annie McClanahan, "Future's Shock: Plausibility, Preemption, and the Fiction of 9/11," *symploke* 17, no. 1 (2009): 41–62.
3. Andrew Lakoff, "The Generic Biothreat, or, How We Became Unprepared," *Cultural Anthropology* 23, no. 3 (2008): 402.
4. Quoted in Lakoff, "The Generic Biothreat," 416.
5. Lakoff, "The Generic Biothreat," 401.
6. Lakoff, "The Generic Biothreat," 416.
7. Lakoff, "The Generic Biothreat," 417.
8. Patricia L. Dunmire, "Preempting the Future: Rhetoric and Ideology of the Future in Political Discourse," *Discourse Society* 15, no. 4 (2005): 488.
9. Jean Baudrillard, *Simulacra and Simulation*, translated by Sheila Faria Glaser (Ann Arbor: University of Michigan Press, 1994), 124. In this era of the hyperreal, science fiction's process "will be to put decentered situations, models of simulation in place and to contrive to give them the feeling of the real, of the banal, of lived experience, to reinvent the real as fiction, precisely because it has disappeared from our life" (ibid.). Originally published in 1981, Baudrillard's *Simulacra and Simulation* may overdramatize the disappearance of the real from our lives—the immediate threat of police violence for some and the constant state of precarity for others, for example, contradict Baudrillard's projections of the state of the real in the contemporary moment—but he nevertheless describes well the ways in which securitization has adapted the imaginary potential of science fiction to the demands of applied policy based on quantifiable outcomes.
10. Lakoff, "The Generic Biothreat," 417.
11. Randy Martin observes this self-fulfilling property of risk management in both financial and military contexts: "Derivatives both anticipate and encourage volatility" and "the anticipation of risk is always meant to be self-fulfilling, a preemptive action that makes its imagined future come to pass." *The Empire of Indifference: American War and the Financial Logic of Risk Management* (Durham, NC: Duke University Press, 2007), 11, 63.
12. See Martin, *The Empire of Indifference*.
13. See Colleen Lye, "The Literary Case of Wen Ho Lee," *Journal of Asian American Studies* 14, no. 2 (2011): 249–82; Joseph Masco, *Nuclear Borderlands: The Manhattan Project in Post–Cold War New Mexico* (Princeton, NJ: Princeton University Press, 2006).
14. Quoted in National Public Radio, "Film Examines 'A Day without a Mexican,'" May 1, 2006, accessed July 24, 2016, http://www.npr.org/templates/story/story.php?storyId=5372878.

15 Optioned for TV's *Cosmic Slop* in 1994, the story was adapted for the screen by Trey Ellis and Chester Himes, both established black detective fiction authors.
16 For more comprehensive genealogies of Afro futurism and Chicana futurism, see Alondra Nelson, ed., "Afrofuturism," special issue, *Social Text* 20, no. 2 (2002); Lysa Rivera, "Future Histories and Cyborg Labor: Reading Borderlands Science Fiction after NAFTA," *Science Fiction Studies* 39, no. 3 (2012): 415–36.
17 For an excellent analysis of the Electronic Disturbance Theater, see Rita Raley, *Tactical Media* (Minneapolis: University of Minnesota Press, 2009), 31–64.
18 In *The Revolutionary Imagination in the Americas and the Age of Development* (Durham, NC: Duke University Press, 2003), María Josefina Saldaña-Portillo suggests that development imaginaries can too easily fantasize that a supposedly premodern subject need only become a hacker to secure her deliverance from a subsistence economy to a global future.
19 Donald E. Pease, *The New American Exceptionalism* (Minneapolis: University of Minnesota Press, 2009), 174.
20 Amy Kaplan, *The Anarchy of Empire in the Making of U.S. Culture* (Cambridge, MA: Harvard University Press, 2002), 1.
21 Kaplan, *The Anarchy of Empire*, 3.
22 My references to time-space compression and flexible accumulation here deliberately invoke the work of David Harvey, particularly in *The Postmodern Condition* and *The Limits to Capital*.
23 See, for example, the somewhat incendiary op-ed by Ronald Steel (a professor of international relations at the University of Southern California), "Peel Me a Poison Grape," *New York Times*, March 21, 1989, accessed July 25, 2016, http://www.nytimes.com/1989/03/21/opinion/peel-me-a-poison-grape.html.
24 "U.S. Will Permit Fruit From Chile To Enter Market," *New York Times*, March 18, 1989.
25 This and future references to Karen Tei Yamashita, *Tropic of Orange: A Novel* (Minneapolis, MN: Coffee House, 1997), are made parenthetically.
26 Curtis Marez, *Drug Wars: The Political Economy of Narcotics* (Minneapolis: University of Minnesota Press, 2004), 2.
27 Marez, *Drug Wars*, 5.
28 Fernando Romero, *Hyper-Border: The Contemporary U.S.-Mexico Border and Its Future* (New York: Princeton Architectural Press, 2008), 140.
29 George Lipsitz, *The Possessive Investment in Whiteness: How White People Profit from Identity Politics* (Philadelphia: Temple University Press, 1998), 47.
30 Lipsitz, *The Possessive Investment in Whiteness*, 47.
31 Timothy J. Dunn, *The Militarization of the US-Mexico Border, 1978–1992: Low-Intensity Conflict Doctrine Comes Home* (Austin: CMAS Books, University of Texas at Austin, 1996).
32 Saldaña-Portillo, *The Revolutionary Imagination*, 754–58.
33 Saldaña-Portillo, *The Revolutionary Imagination*, 757.
34 Molly Rauch, "Fruit Salad," *Nation* (March 2, 1998), 28.

35 See Kirsten Silva Gruesz, "The Mercurial Space of 'Central' America: New Orleans, Honduras, and the Writing of the Banana Republic," in *Hemispheric American Studies*, edited by Caroline F. Levander and Robert S. Levine (New Brunswick, NJ: Rutgers University Press, 2008), 140–65; John Soluri, *Banana Cultures: Agriculture, Consumption, and Environmental Change in Honduras and the United States* (Austin: University of Texas Press, 2005); Steve Striffler and Mark Moberg, eds, *Banana Wars: Power, Production and History in the Americas* (Durham, NC: Duke University Press, 2003).

36 See Jean Vengua Gier and Calra Alicia Tejeda, "An Interview with Karen Tei Yamashita," *Jouvert* 2, no. 2 (1998): 4; Guillermo Gómez-Peña, *The New World Border: Prophecies, Poems and Loqueras* (San Francisco: City Lights, 1996). *Tropic of Orange* makes multiple allusions to Gómez-Peña's oeuvre, particularly *The New World Border*, a portion of which appears in the epigraph to Yamashita's book. These allusions put *Tropic of Orange* in conversation with a vibrant Chican@ movement to remap the borderlands, to "see through the colonial map of North, Central, and South America, to a more complex system of overlapping, interlocking, and overlaid maps. Among others, we can see Amerindia, Afroamerica, Americamestizaymulata, Hybridamerica, and Transamerica—the 'other America' that belongs to the homeless, and to nomads, migrants, and exiles" (Gómez-Peña, *The New World Border*, 6). Gómez-Peña takes issue with the utopian cartography produced by neoliberal trade agreements such as NAFTA: "We try to imagine more enlightened cartographies" (Gómez-Peña, *New World Border*, 6). His insistent presence in *Tropic of Orange* is an instantiation of productive cross-ethnic collaboration in the rewriting and rewiring of the borderlands.

37 Karen Michelle Barad, "Quantum Entanglements and Hauntological Relations of Inheritance: Dis/continuities, SpaceTime Enfoldings, and Justice-to-Come," *Derrida Today* 3, no. 2 (2010): 240–41.

38 Barad, "Quantum Entanglements," 240.

39 Barad, "Quantum Entanglements," 248–49.

40 Mary Louise Pratt, *Imperial Eyes: Travel Writing and Transculturation*, 2nd ed. (London: Routledge, 2008).

41 See Estelle Lau, *Paper Families: Identity, Immigration Administration, and Chinese Exclusion* (Durham, NC: Duke University Press, 2007), 169n1: "Immigration officers on the border concentrated primarily on enforcement of the Chinese exclusion laws." See also Erika Lee, "Enforcing the Borders: Chinese Exclusion along the U.S. Borders with Canada and Mexico, 1882–1924," *The Journal of American History* 89, no. 1 (2002): 54–86.

42 Claudia Sadowski-Smith, "Reading across Diaspora: Chinese and Mexican Undocumented Immigration across U.S. Land Borders," in *Globalization on the Line: Culture, Capital, and Citizenship at U.S. Borders*, edited by Claudia Sadowski-Smith (New York: Palgrave, 2002), 72. Sadowski-Smith sees "the role of Chinese immigrants as predecessors of the Mexican *indocumentado*" (75).

43 Marita Sturken writes: "The preoccupation with establishing American technology's ability to see can be directly traced to the representations of American technology in the Vietnam War. The 'impenetrable' jungle foliage of Vietnam has

been consistently blamed for the inability of American military technology to win the war (hence the campaign of massive defoliation by Agent Orange perpetrated by the US in Vietnam)." *Tangled Memories: The Vietnam War, the AIDS Epidemic, and the Politics of Remembering* (Berkeley: University of California Press, 1997), 131–32.
44 Lisa Lowe, *Immigrant Acts: On Asian American Cultural Politics* (Durham, NC: Duke University Press, 1996), 28.
45 Alex Rivera, dir., *Why Cybraceros?* (1997).
46 Jacques Lacan, "The Split between the Eye and the Gaze," in *The Four Fundamental Concepts of Psychoanalysis*, translated by Alan Sheridan (New York: Norton, 1978), 73.
47 Michel de Certeau, "Walking in the City," *The Practice of Everyday Life* (Berkeley: University of California Press, 1984), 91–110.
48 de Certeau, "Walking in the City," 93.
49 Alex Lubin, "Welcome to Albuquerque," *American Studies Association Annual Meeting Program: Back Down to the Crossroads: Integrative American Studies in Theory and Practice* (Albuquerque, NM: American Studies Association, 2008), 30.
50 Masco, *The Nuclear Borderlands*.
51 Since 2006, the University of California (UC) has shared operational responsibility for Los Alamos with, among others, Bechtel, the largest engineering firm in the world. Robert C. Dynes, chancellor of UC San Diego from 1996 to 2007, maintained extensive ties to Los Alamos, as vice-chair of the UC President's Council on the National Labs and also as a member of UC's five-person Board of Oversight for Los Alamos.
52 Quoted in Naomi Klein, *The Shock Doctrine: The Rise of Disaster Capitalism* (Toronto, ON: Knopf Canada, 2007), 300.
53 Klein, *The Shock Doctrine*, 300.
54 Klein, *The Shock Doctrine*, 301.

Chapter 3. Speculation and the Speculum

Epigraph: http://www.vulture.com/2017/01/alfonso-cuaron-children-of-men-tran script.html, accessed February 11, 2017.
1 Alex Kuczynski, "Her Body, My Baby: My Adventures with a Surrogate Mom," *New York Times Magazine*, November 2008, 42–49, 64, 74, 78.
2 Judith Newman, Letter, "Her Body, My Baby," *The New York Times Magazine*, December 14, 2008. Last accessed November 4, 2016, http://www.nytimes.com/2008/12/14/magazine/14letters-t-HERBODYMYBAB_LETTERS.html.
3 Alex Kuczynski, "Her Body, My Baby," 64.
4 Bindu Shajan Perappadan, "A Setback for Surrogacy in India?" *Hindu*, November 29, 2015, accessed July 31, 2016, http://www.thehindu.com/opinion/op-ed/a-setback-for-surrogacy-in-india/article7927730.ece.
5 Avery Gordon, *Ghostly Matters: Haunting and the Sociological Imagination* (Minneapolis: University of Minnesota Press, 1997), 8.
6 Nalo Hopkinson, "A Conversation with Nalo Hopkinson," *SF Site*, May 5, 2007, accessed July 25, 2009, http://www.sfsite.com/03b/nh77.htm.

7   Ruth Wilson Gilmore, *Golden Gulag: Prisons, Surplus, Crisis, and Opposition in Globalizing California* (Berkeley: University of California Press, 2007), 28; Nikolas Rose, *The Politics of Life Itself* (Princeton: Princeton University Press, 2007), 3.
8   Joseph Roach, *Cities of the Dead: Circum-Atlantic Performance* (New York: Columbia University Press, 1996), 3–5.
9   Rob Mitchell and Cathy Waldby, "National Biobanks: Clinical Labour, Risk Production, and the Creation of Biovalue," ST&HV 35, no. 3 (2010): 330–55.
10 Abigail Haworth, "Surrogate Mothers: Womb for Rent," *Marie Claire Magazine*. World Reports, International News, accessed March 26, 2009, http://www.marieclaire.com/world-reports/news/international/surrogate-mothers-india.
11 Kalindi Vora, "Indian Transnational Surrogacy and the Disaggregation of Mothering Work," *Anthropology News* 50, no. 2 (2009): 9.
12 Vora, "Indian Transnational Surrogacy," 9.
13 Wife's name never indicated. This whole booklet is rather suspiciously authored, in fact. Originally hosted on their website ourindiaivf.com, the URL of which remains linked to from various IVF blogs and chat rooms, the booklet itself has vanished from the internet since 2011 or so when I last came across it. Other traces of its former existence have been captured on a SlideShare.net link: dmiller3, "Our India IVF Experience—IVF and Surrogacy with Dr. Nayna Patel in Anand and Kiran IVF in Hyderabdad [sic] India," accessed February 22, 2017, https://www.slideshare.net/dmiller3/our-india-ivf-experience-ivf-and-surrogacy-with-dr-nayna-patel-presentation; and a single YouTube video hosted by "dmiller3377": https://www.youtube.com/channel/UC5u5n22DbZGLj4otO8diX-Q.
14 Dana Ain Davis, "The Politics of Reproduction: The Troubling Case of Nadya Suleman and Assisted Reproductive Technology," *Transforming Anthropology* 17, no. 2 (2009): 108.
15 NBC Los Angeles, Gordon Tokumatsu, "Mom's Publicist Sets Record Straight," accessed March 26, 2009: http://www.nbclosangeles.com/news/local/Mom_s_Publicist_Sets_Record_Straight_Los_Angeles.html.
16 Eli Clare, "Comment from the Field: Yearning toward Carrie Buck," *Journal of Literary & Cultural Disability Studies* 8, no. 3 (2014), 335.
17 Laura Briggs, *Reproducing Empire: Race, Sex, Science, and U.S. Imperialism in Puerto Rico* (Berkeley: University of California Press, 2003), 51.
18 "OctoMom—It Was a Very Goodyear," TMZ, accessed March 20, 2009, http://www.tmz.com/2009/02/12/octomom-it-was-a-very-goodyear/.
19 Anne Balsamo, "Public Pregnancies and Cultural Narratives of Surveillance," in *Technologies of the Gendered Body: Reading Cyborg Women* (Durham, NC: Duke University Press, 1995), 80–115. Balsamo argues that pregnant women "cannot easily avoid the scrutiny of a fascinated gaze" and that the biomedical gaze, as produced through visualization technologies such as laparoscopy and ultrasound scans, further reduces the reproductive body to an object of "scientific management of fertilization, implantation, and pregnancy more broadly" (80, 81).
20 "PR Exec: Death Threats Forced Firm to Drop Octuplet Mom," CNN: Entertainment,

February 17, 2009, accessed October 9, 2009, http://www.cnn.com/2009/SHOWBIZ/TV/02/17/killeen.qanda/index.html.

21 Kathryn Krase, "History of Forced Sterilization and Current U.S. Abuses," Our Bodies Ourselves, October 1, 2014, accessed October 9, 2014, http://www.ourbodiesourselves.org/health-info/forced-sterilization/.

22 Cuarón mentions in an interview that among the visual references he used for the portrayal of the refugee camp in the film were in the Balkans, Calais and outside of Syria. See Abraham Riesman, "The Vulture Transcript: Alfonso Cuarón on *Children of Men*," *Vulture*, January 6, 2017, http://www.vulture.com/2017/01/alfonso-cuaron-children-of-men-transcript.html.

23 María Josefina Saldaña-Portillo, "In the Shadow of NAFTA: *Y tu mama tambien* Revisits the National Allegory of Mexican Sovereignty," *American Quarterly* 57, no. 3 (2005): 752.

24 A. Gordon, *Ghostly Matters*, 168.

25 Matthew Beaumont asserts that science fiction in particular makes use of the anamorphic image as an estranging device, as it "posits the coded presence of an almost unimaginable reality that momentarily obtrudes on an almost unimaginable reality that momentarily obtrudes on ideologically constituted reality, thereby rendering it arbitrary, ontologically inconsistent" (33–34).

26 Amy Kaplan, "Where Is Guantánamo?" *American Quarterly* 57, no. 3 (2005): 833.

27 See Lisa Lowe, *The Intimacies of Four Continents* (Durham, NC: Duke University Press, 2015).

28 Toni Morrison, *Beloved* (New York: Plume, 1988), 149–50.

29 Anthony Bogues, *Empire of Liberty: Power, Desire, and Freedom* (Hanover, NH: University Press of New England, 2010), 109.

30 Donna J. Haraway, "The Virtual Speculum in the New World Order," *Feminist Review* 55 (Spring, 1997): 29–30. Haraway's argument follows the feminist art historian Lynda Nead's analysis of the engraving as a key example of gendered practices of looking and the ways in which technologies of visual representation participate in this uneven relationship between artist and subject, auteur and actor. (Lynda Nead, *The Female Nude: Art, Obscenity and Sexuality* [New York: Routledge, 1992]).

31 Rebekah Sheldon, "Somatic Capitalism: Reproduction, Futurity, and Feminist Science Fiction," *Ada: A Journal of Gender, New Media, and Technology*, no. 3 (2013).

32 Rosa Linda Fregoso makes a similar argument in her analysis of John Sayles's film *Lone Star*: "My profound ambivalence toward this film has something to do with Sayles's willingness to complicate the nation's racial imaginary.... If Sayles's multicultural project is to truly represent a new social order and make a dent in the predominant mono-cultural, ethnocentric vision of society, it must de-center whiteness and masculinity" (*MeXicana Encounters: The Making of Social Identities on the Borderlands* [Berkeley: University of California Press, 2003], 55–56).

33 Sylvia Wynter, "Unsettling the Coloniality of Being/Power/Truth/Freedom: Towards the Human, After Man, Its Overrepresentation—An Argument," CR: *The New Centennial Review* 3, no. 3 (Fall 2003): 260.

34 Lee Edelman, "The Future Is Kid Stuff: Queer Theory, Disidentification, and the Death Drive," *Narrative* 6, no. 1 (January 1998): 19.
35 Kobena Mercer, *Welcome to the Jungle: New Positions in Black Cultural Studies* (London: Routledge, 1994), 176. Mercer argues that in Mapplethorpe's *Black Males* (1983) and *The Black Book* (1986), "the black man's flesh becomes burdened with the task of symbolizing the transgressive fantasies and desires of the white gay male subject. The glossy, shining, fetishized surface of black skin thus serves and services a white male desire to look and to enjoy the fantasy of mastery precisely through the scopic intensity that the pictures solicit" (ibid.).
36 See Anne Balsamo, *Technologies of the Gendered Body: Reading Cyborg Women* (Durham, NC: Duke University Press, 1995); Haraway, "The Virtual Speculum in the New World Order"; Valerie Hartouni, *Making Life Make Sense: New Technologies and the Discourses of Reproduction* (Minneapolis: University of Minnesota Press, 1996); Karen Newman, *Fetal Positions: Individualism, Science, Visuality* (Stanford, CA: Stanford University Press, 1997); Carol A. Stabile, "Shooting the Mother: Fetal Photography and the Politics of Disappearance," *Camera Obscura* 10, no. 1 (1992): 178–205.
37 See Heather Latimer, "Bio-Reproductive Futurism: Bare Life and the Pregnant Refugee in Alfonso Cuaron's *Children of Men*," *Social Text* 29, no. 3 (2011): 54.
38 Dorothy Roberts, *Killing the Black Body: Race, Reproduction, and the Meaning of Liberty* (New York: Pantheon Books, 1997), 6.
39 For more on oocyte markets and where IVF and the IMF intersect, see Catherine Waldby and Melinda Cooper, "The Biopolitics of Reproduction," *Australian Feminist Studies* 23:55 (May 2008): 57–73.
40 Marie Jenkins Schwartz, *Birthing a Slave: Motherhood and Medicine in the Antebellum South* (Cambridge: Harvard University Press, 2010), 1–4.
41 Michel Foucault, *"Society Must Be Defended": Lectures at the Collège de France, 1975–1976*, translated by David Macey. Edited by Mauro Bertani and Alessandro Fontana, General Editors: François Ewald and Alessandro Fontana, English Series Editor: Arnold I. Davidson (New York: Picador, 2003), 243–44.
42 Dan White, "Toni Morrison and Angela Davis on Friendship and Creativity," University of California, Santa Cruz NewsCenter, October 29, 2014, accessed June 29, 2015, news.ucsc.edu/2014/10/morrison-davis-q-a.html.
43 Mark Dery, "Black to the Future: Interviews with Samuel R. Delany, Greg Tate, and Tricia Rose," ed. Mark Dery, "Flame Wars: The Discourse of Cyberculture," special issue, *South Atlantic Quarterly* 92, no. 4 (1993): 736–37.
44 See, for example, Alondra Nelson, ed., "Afrofuturism," special issue, *Social Text* 20, no. 2 (2002). Many articles in this special issue of *Social Text* call into question the implied opposition between blackness and technology that inflects Dery's line of inquiry.
45 Kalí Tal, "'That Just Kills Me': Black Militant Near-Future Fiction," ed. Alondra Nelson, "Afrofuturism," special issue, *Social Text* 20, no. 2 (2002): 65.
46 Nalo Hopkinson and Alondra Nelson, "Making the Impossible Possible: An Interview with Nalo Hopkinson," ed. Alondra Nelson, "Afrofuturism," special issue, *Social Text* 20, no. 2 (2002): 98.

47 Dianne D. Glave and Nalo Hopkinson, "An Interview with Nalo Hopkinson," *Callaloo* 26, no. 1 (2003): 148.
48 Glave and Hopkinson, "An Interview with Nalo Hopkinson," 148. In another interview, Hopkinson proposes that science fiction need not participate in the fairly common trope of colonization, saying that such a practice would be dangerous for a people who have "been on the receiving end of colonization, and for [whom] it's not an entertaining adventure story" (Gregory E. Rutledge and Nalo Hopkinson, "Speaking in Tongues: An Interview with Science Fiction Writer Nalo Hopkinson," *African American Review* 33, no. 4 [1999]: 590).
49 The manifestations of this non-Eurocentric utopian vision are multiple and too many to cite comprehensively here. Hopkinson does much of this work herself in her interviews with Nelson, Rutledge, and Glave, cited in notes 46, 47, and 48.
50 This and future references to Nalo Hopkinson, *Midnight Robber* (New York: Grand Central, 2000) are made parenthetically.
51 Glave and Hopkinson, "An Interview with Nalo Hopkinson," 149.
52 For Paul Gilroy, "the image of the ship—a living, micro-cultural, micro-political system in motion is especially important" (*The Black Atlantic: Modernity and Double Consciousness* [Cambridge, MA: Harvard University Press, 1993], 4).
53 Hopkinson and Nelson, "Making the Impossible Possible," 99. Hopkinson goes on to say: "when my work is coming from a Caribbean context, fusion fits very well; that's how we survived."
54 Nalo Hopkinson, "Code Sliding: About *Midnight Robber* and My Use of Creole in the Narrative," accessed December 7, 2006. http://www.sff.net/people/nalo/writing/slide.html.
55 W. E. B. Du Bois, *The Souls of Black Folk*, 1903 (New York: Dover, 1994), 8–9.
56 "Dark Ink" essay, accessed July 2017, https://web.archive.org/web/20080723171139/http://www.nalohopkinson.com/writing/on_writing/dark_ink/essay_dark_ink.html.
57 Sita, the heroine of the Ramayana and a paragon of wifely duty, first follows her husband, Rama, when his father commands him to go into exile. While in the wilderness, a villainous monster, Ravana, abducts Sita and tries unsuccessfully to seduce her. She is rescued and can accompany Rama home after their period of banishment has elapsed. After their return, Sita is subjected to a trial by fire to prove her purity, because her abduction gives rise to the suspicion that Ravana raped her. Despite emerging from the fire unscathed, Sita still cannot escape the fate of a second exile. Rama sends her out of the country again because, regardless of her having passed the test, her mere association with potential rape taints her reputation. In *Midnight Robber*, Sita occupies only the margins of the story. Sita, as a goddess figure who is ostensibly never raped, has a very different story from that of Tan-Tan, who expresses revenge as one of her primary motivations to continue to be a disruptive voice of interjection.
58 Martin F. Manalansan IV, "Feeling Our Way through the Crises: Embodied Belongings and Asian American Studies," keynote address at "Acts of Elaboration: A Symposium on Asian American Studies in the Northeast," Boston College, May 29, 2009.

59 Manalansan IV, "Feeling Our Way through the Crises"; see also Martin Manalansan, "Race, Violence, and Neoliberal Spatial Politics in the Global City," *Social Text* 23, no. 3 (2005): 141–55.

60 M. Jacqui Alexander, "Not Just (Any) Body Can Be a Citizen: The Politics of Law, Sexuality and Postcoloniality in Trinidad and Tobago and the Bahamas," *Feminist Review* no. 48 (Autumn, 1994): 6.

61 New Half-Way Tree bears a striking resemblance to the antebellum South and to the colonial sugarcane plantations of the Caribbean. One village Tan-Tan stumbles across later in her escapades as the Robber Queen operates on a plantation system. She quickly runs the other direction after encountering a woman chained in the cane fields.

62 Gilroy, *The Black Atlantic*, 36.

63 Gregory E. Rutledge and Nalo Hopkinson, "Speaking in Tongues: An Interview with Science Fiction Writer Nalo Hopkinson," *African American Review* 33, no. 4 (1999): 599.

Chapter 4. The Cruel Optimism of the Asian Century

1 Lori Wallach, "NAFTA on Steroids," *The Nation*, June 27, 2012, https://www.thenation.com/article/nafta-steroids/.

2 Kishore Mahbubani, *The New Asian Hemisphere: The Irresistable Shift of Global Power to the East* (New York: PublicAffairs, 2008).

3 See Jini Kim Watson, *The New Asian City: Three-Dimensional Fictions of Space and Urban Form* (Minneapolis: University of Minnesota Press, 2011). See also and *Worlding Cities: Asian Experiments and the Art of Being Global*. Eds. Ananya Roy and Aihwa Ong (2011), in which Ong quotes Rem Koolhaas' 2004 statement: ". . . the skyline rises in the East."

4 Alan Greenspan, "Remarks by Chairman Alan Greenspan" (presentation, Annual Dinner and Francis Boyer Lecture of The American Enterprise Institute for Public Policy Research, Washington, DC, December 5, 1996. https://www.federalreserve.gov/boarddocs/speeches/1996/19961205.htm.

5 Greenspan, "Remarks by Chairman Alan Greenspan."

6 It is particularly important to remember Japan's occupation of Singapore (1942–45), which marks Singapore not only as a former British colony but also as a city-state with multiple imperialisms in its history. As this chapter is especially interested in the relationship between a Singaporean text relationship and techno-Orientalism, which is most conventionally associated with Japan, we must consider the postcolonial context of Singapore as we witness neoliberal ideology and policy taking shape in that context.

7 Asian Development Bank, *Asia 2050: Realizing the Asian Century* (Singapore: Asian Development Bank, 2011), 1; accessed December 9, 2016, https://www.adb.org/publications/asia-2050-realizing-asian-century. Headquartered in the Philippines, the ADB has a Japanese president. Of its 67 members, Japan and the United States have

the most investments in the bank—15.6 percent each. There should be no mistaking that the bank's push for regional cooperation means the continued neoliberalization of postsocialist and postindependence economies.

8 Peter Drysdale, "Coming to Terms with the Asian Century," *East Asia Forum*, June 10, 2013, accessed July 31, 2016, http://www.eastasiaforum.org/2013/06/10/coming-to-terms-with-the-asian-century/.

9 Rajat M. Nag, "The Asian Century: Plausible but not Preordained" (speech, School of Public Policy and Management, Tsinghua University, Beijing, People's Republic of China, June 20, 2011).

10 "About ADB: Members," *Asian Development Bank*, accessed December 10, 2016, https://www.adb.org/about/members.

11 See David Palumbo-Liu's productive formulation of Asian/American that "marks *both* the distinction installed between 'Asian' and 'American' *and* a dynamic, unsettled, and inclusive movement" (*Asian/American: Historical Crossings of a Racial Frontier* [Stanford, CA: Stanford University Press, 1999], 1).

12 "Key Facts," *Asian Development Bank*, last accessed December 10, 2016, https://www.adb.org/about/key-facts.

13 Aihwa Ong, *Neoliberalism as Exception: Mutations in Citizenship and Sovereignty* (Durham, NC: Duke University Press, 2006), 16.

14 Aihwa Ong, *Flexible Citizenship: The Cultural Logics of Transnationality* (Durham, NC: Duke University Press, 1999).

15 In this discussion, the special issue of *American Quarterly* on "Race, Empire, and the Crisis of the Subprime" (64, no. 3 [2012]), coedited by Paula Chakravartty and Denise Ferreira da Silva, has been helpful.

16 See Jane Chi Hyun Park, *Yellow Future: Oriental Style in Hollywood Cinema* (Minneapolis: University of Minnesota Press, 2010); David S. Roh, Betsy Huang, and Greta A. Niu, *Techno-Orientalism: Imagining Asia in Speculative Fiction, History, and Media* (New Brunswick, NJ: Rutgers University Press, 2015).

17 David Morley and Kevin Robins, "Techno-Orientalism," *Spaces of Identity: Global Media, Electronic Landscapes, and Cultural Boundaries* (London: Routledge, 1995), 153.

18 Morley and Robins, "Techno-Orientalism," 170.

19 Morley and Robins, "Techno-Orientalism," 153.

20 Philips Norelco launched an ad campaign to promote their moisturizing wet-shave system produced in collaboration with Nivea for Men http://youtu.be/dAuvyqvN3Uo.

21 Anna Lowenhaupt Tsing's formulation of "friction" as an integral component of movement (what makes a wheel turn when it encounters a road) is instructive here. Friction, writes Tsing, "refuses the lie that global power operates as a well-oiled machine" and asks us to think about universals "not as truths or lies but as stick engagements" (*Friction: An Ethnography of Global Connection* [Princeton, NJ: Princeton University Press, 2005], 6).

22 See the Philips Company Profile online, accessed July 2017, http://www.philips.com/a-w/about/company/introduction.html.

23 Wendy Hui Kyong Chun offers a thorough analysis of how this juxtaposition of primitive artifacts and exoticizing futurisms facilitates a "high-tech Orientalism" that renders digital landscapes available for conquest by styling the future as Orientalized empty space: "These anachronistic signs of Japaneseness are not chosen randomly. Rather, samurais, ninjas, and shonen are drawn from Japan's Edo period and they confine the Japanese past to the period of first contact between the West and Japan. Cyberpunk thus mixes images of the mysterious yet-to-be-opened Japan (which eventually did submit to the West) with the conquering corporate Japan of the future" ("Orienting Orientalism: How to Map Cyberspace," in *AsianAmerica.Net: Ethnicity, Nationalism, and Cyberspace*, edited by Rachel C. Lee and Sau-ling Cynthia Wong [New York: Routledge, 2003], 12). Kumiko Sato writes that "images of Japan manifest in two contrary stereotypes, which are the premodern traditionalism (geisha, samurai, etc.) and the supremacy of high-technology" (355n1).
24 Laura Kang, "The Uses of Asianization: Figuring Crises, 1997–98 and 2007–?" "Race, Empire, and the Crisis of the Subprime," edited by Paula Chakravartty and Denise da Silva, special issue, *American Quarterly* 64, no. 3 (2012): 411–36.
25 Kang, "Uses of Asianization," 413.
26 Shintaro Ishihara, *The Japan That Can Say No: Why Japan Will Be First among Equals* (1989), translated by Frank Baldwin (New York: Simon & Schuster, 1992).
27 "Building Blocks for New Businesses: Trust," *Future•Ready Singapore*, Singapore Economic Development Board, last updated December 14, 2016, http://www.edb.gov.sg/content/edb/en/why-singapore/about-singapore/values/trust.html.
28 *Future•Singapore: The Future in Singapore, and Singapore in the Future*, Singapore Economic Development Board, 3; accessed July 2017, https://www.edb.gov.sg/content/dam/edb/en/resources/pdfs/publications/Annual%20Reports/AnnualReport-2007-2008.pdf.
29 "Building Blocks," Singapore Economic Development Board.
30 Bruno Latour, *We Have Never Been Modern*, 1991, translated by Catherine Porter (Cambridge, MA: Harvard University Press, 1993), 10–12, 28–43.
31 Ong, *Neoliberalism as Exception*, 181.
32 National Population and Talent Division, "A Sustainable Population for a Dynamic Singapore," Prime Minister's Office, January 2013, accessed January 8, 2017. "Upgrading" and "upskilling" are iconic neoliberal concepts, the counterpoints to the mobility of global elites who exercise what Ong has called "flexible citizenship" (Aihwa Ong, *Flexible Citizenship* [Durham, NC: Duke University Press, 1999]).
33 Lisa Rofel, *Desiring China: Experiments in Neoliberalism, Sexuality, and Public Culture* (Durham, NC: Duke University Press, 2007), 20.
34 Sonny Liew, "Character and Story Synopsis Cards," in *Box of Things: Mementoes from a Dusty City*, limited edition box set.
35 Liew, "Character and Story Synopsis Cards," in *Box of Things*.
36 This and future references to Sonny Liew, *Malinky Robot: Collected Stories and Other Bits* (New York: Image Comics, 2011) are made parenthetically.
37 Ong, *Neoliberalism as Exception*, 185.

38 Liew learned about San'ya from Edward Fowler's *San'ya Blues* (Ithaca, NY: Cornell University Press, 1996), which he found in a bargain book bin at Brown University's bookstore. Fowler's ethnography of day laborers in Tokyo offers an alternative narrative to the history of the Japanese economic boom from 1989 to 1991.
39 Sonny Liew, *Box of Things: Mementoes from a Dusty City*. Press Kit for *Malinky Robot*. Printed and distributed by Sonny Liew, 2012. In the box, Liew includes a small carton containing trading cards for each character of *Malinky Robot*. "Eke out a life" is a phrase Liew uses to describe Atari on his character card.
40 Eve Kosofsky Sedgwick, *Touching Feeling: Affect, Pedagogy, Performativity* (Durham, NC: Duke University Press, 2003), 150–51.
41 Sedgwick, *Touching Feeling*, 146.
42 Ian Hacking, *The Taming of Chance* (Cambridge: Cambridge University Press, 1990), 10. Hacking's argument points to the regulation of populations through laws of chance. This statistical turn took root in the idea "that one can improve — control — a deviant subpopulation by enumeration and classification" (3).
43 Michel de Certeau, "Walking in the City," in *The Practice of Everyday Life*, translated by Steven Randall (Berkeley: University of California Press, 1984), 92.
44 Lauren Gail Berlant, *Cruel Optimism* (Durham, NC: Duke University Press, 2011), 164.
45 "Company History: 1946," *Highlights*, last accessed February 18, 2016, https://www.highlights.com/about-us/history. "Fun with a Purpose" has been the *Highlights* slogan since its inception in 1946.
46 Lee Edelman, *No Future: Queer Theory and the Death Drive* (Durham, NC: Duke University Press, 2004), 3.
47 Ong, *Neoliberalism as Exception*, 185–86.
48 Shibani Mahtani, "Thursday's the Day to Go All the Way for Civic Duty in Singapore: New Ad Campaign Urges Locals to Help Spike Birthrate; 'Make Fireworks Ignite,'" *The Wall Street Journal*, August 10, 2012.
49 Thanks to Catherine Fung for calling my attention to the Mentos National Night ("Mentos National Night," August 1, 2012, accessed August 1, 2016, https://youtube/8jxU89x78ac) and National Day Proposal ads ("Mentos National Day Proposal," July 31, 2013, accessed August 1, 2016, http://youtu.be/xvKLcQKoETU).
50 Randy Martin, *The Financialization of Daily Life* (Philadelphia: Temple University Press, 2002), 160.
51 Berlant, *Cruel Optimism*, 3.
52 Berlant, *Cruel Optimism*, 63.
53 Berlant, *Cruel Optimism*, 4–5. Berlant's formulation of the impasse is more fully developed in chapter 6 of *Cruel Optimism*. My use of the word here is perhaps best glossed by Berlant in her introduction, in which she describes an "impasse shaped by crisis in which people find themselves developing skills for adjusting to newly proliferating pressures to scramble for modes of living on" (16).
54 Berlant, *Cruel Optimism*, 9, 256.
55 Lauren Berlant, "On Her Book *Cruel Optimism*." Cover Interview. Rorotoko.com.

June 5, 2012. http://rorotoko.com/interview/20120605_berlant_lauren_on_cruel_optimism/.

Chapter 5. Salt Fish Futures

1 Joseph Masco, *Nuclear Borderlands: The Manhattan Project in Post–Cold War New Mexico* (Princeton, NJ: Princeton University Press, 2006), 304–5.
2 Elizabeth DeLoughrey, "Heliotropes: Solar Ecologies and Pacific Radiations," in *Postcolonial Ecologies: Literatures of the Environment*, edited by Elizabeth DeLoughrey and George B. Handley (Oxford: Oxford University Press, 2011), 238.
3 DeLoughrey, "Heliotropes," 238.
4 Hal M. Friedman, *Governing the American Lake: The US Defense and Administration of the Pacific, 1945–1947* (East Lansing: Michigan State University Press, 2007). Friedman provides a history of the TTPI, wherein American policy makers, planners, and strategic thinkers were "concerned enough about the United States' future position in the Pacific Basin to be willing to weaken the United States' commitment to UN principles and argue for predominant US control in the area, whether by strategic trusteeship or annexation" (210).
5 Kimie Hara, *Cold War Frontiers in the Asia Pacific: Divided Territories in the San Francisco System* (New York: Routledge, 2007).
6 Hal M. Friedman, "The Beast in Paradise: The United States Navy in Micronesia, 1943–1947," *Pacific Historical Review*, 52, no. 2 (1993): 173.
7 Friedman, "The Beast in Paradise," 177.
8 This and future references to Larissa Lai, *Salt Fish Girl: A Novel* (Toronto, ON: Dundurn, 2002) are made parenthetically.
9 I borrow from Sarah Franklin and Elizabeth Freeman, respectively, and will develop them later in the chapter.
10 Gilles Deleuze, "Postscript on Societies of Control," *October* 59 (Winter 1992): 5; Dana Luciano and Mel Y. Chen, "Introduction: Has the Queer Ever Been Human?," in "Queer Inhumanisms," special issue, edited by Dana Luciano and Mel Y. Chen, *GLQ* 21, nos. 2–3 (2015): 182–207.
11 By titling this chapter, "Specters of the Pacific," I am riffing off of Ian Baucom's *Specters of the Atlantic: Finance Capital, Slavery, and the Philosophy of History* (Durham, NC: Duke University Press, 2005). Baucom himself is quoting Toni Morrison in the phrase "specters of the Atlantic" and mobilizes this haunting to recognize not only the disposability but also the insurability of slaves thrown overboard from the 1781 British slave ship *Zong* as an early instantiation of the financialization of biomatter. I understand the atomic devastations in the Pacific theater of war in the mid-twentieth century as a significant turning point that set up the financial apparatus that would help fund the age of genomic sequencing and genetic engineering.
12 Larissa Lai, "Future Asians: Migrant Speculations, Repressed History & Cyborg Hope," *West Coast Line* 38, no. 2 (2004): 168–75.
13 Laura Kang, "The Uses of Asianization: Figuring Crises, 1997–98 and 2007–?," in "Race, Empire, and the Crisis of the Subprime," edited by Paula Chakravartty and

Denise da Silva, special issue of *American Quarterly* 64, no. 3 (2012): 412, 413. Kang's critical attention to the racialization of these financial narratives is key. For an example of the Asianization of crises, see Christopher Wood, *The Bubble Economy: Japan's Extraordinary Speculative Boom of the '80s and the Dramatic Bust of the '90s* (New York: Atlantic Monthly Press, 1992). Wood's characterization of Japan's speculative "frenzy" (6) in the late 1980s that led to the Tokyo stock market crash of 1990 anticipates Alan Greenspan's description of the speculative bubble in Japan as a case of "irrational exuberance" in 1996.

14 Donna J. Haraway, *Simians, Cyborgs, and Women: The Reinvention of Nature* (New York: Routledge, 1991), 214. "Context," writes Haraway, "is a fundamental matter not as surrounding 'information', but as co-structure or co-text."

15 See the work of Paula E. Stephan, especially *How Economics Shapes Science* (Cambridge, MA: Harvard University Press, 2012). The tension between basic science and entrepreneurial science as it relates to genomics in particular was the topic of a 2001 special issue of *Nature* on the HGP. The introduction to that issue considered the burgeoning commercial sector based on publication of genome information (Paula E. Stephan, "Human Genomes: Public and Private," in special issue, *Nature* 409, no. 6822 [2001]: 745).

16 Colin Milburn, "Modifiable Futures: Science Fiction at the Bench," *Isis* 101, no. 3 (2010): 568.

17 Bruce Sterling defines "slipstream" as a genre related to speculative fiction, fantasy, and literary fiction, in which books "tend to sarcastically tear at the structure of 'everyday life.' . . . Slipstream tends, not to 'create' new worlds, but to *quote* them, chop them up out of context, and turn them against themselves" ("CATSCAN 5: Slipstream," *SF Eye* 5 [July 1989], 4). See also Bruce Sterling, "Slipstream 2," *Science Fiction Studies* 38, no. 1 (2011): 6–10.

18 Avery Gordon, *Ghostly Matters: Haunting and the Sociological Imagination* (Minneapolis: University of Minnesota Press, 1997), 185. Gordon's psychoanalytic approach to "ghostly matters" makes for a productive frame through which to read Hiroshima and Nagasaki in the history of the HGP.

19 "Fistula," *MedlinePlus*, A.D.A.M. Medical Encyclopedia, U.S. National Library of Medicine, page last updated: November 1, 2016, https://medlineplus.gov/ency/article/002365.htm.

20 Thanks to Rebekah Sheldon for pointing out this connection. Sims's controversial practices are documented in Harriet Washington, *Medical Apartheid* (New York: Anchor, 2007).

21 Hortense J. Spillers, "Mama's Baby, Papa's Maybe: An American Grammar Book," *Diacritics* 17, no. 2 (1987): 80. In Spillers's conclusion, she writes that out of the context of slavery, "only the female stands *in the flesh*, both mother and mother-dispossessed. This problematizing of gender places her, in my view, *out* of the traditional symbolics of female gender, and it is our task to make a place for this different social subject. In doing so, we are less interested in joining the ranks of gendered femaleness than gaining the *insurgent* ground as female social subject. Actually *claiming* the monstrosity (of a female with the potential to 'name'), which her cul-

ture imposes in blindness, 'Sapphire' might rewrite after all a radically different text for a female empowerment" (80).

22 Washington, *Medical Apartheid*, 69.
23 Paula Chakravartty and Denise Ferreira da Silva, "Accumulation, Dispossession, and Debt: The Racial Logic of Global Capitalism—An Introduction," in "Race, Empire, and the Crisis of the Subprime," edited by Paula Chakravartty and Denise Ferreira da Silva, special issue, *American Quarterly* 64, no. 3 (2012): 369.
24 Thanks to Tamara Ho for reminding me of this crucial detail and for offering her own insightful reading of *Salt Fish Girl* in "Larissa Lai's 'New Cultural Politics of Intimacy': Animal. Asian. Cyborg," in "Speculative Life," special issue, *Social Text: Periscope* (2012).
25 I would like to thank Yoo Jung Kim for her excellent undergraduate research paper on this topic for my class, "Science, Fiction, and Empire," Spring 2014.
26 Robert Mullan Cook-Deegan, "The Alta Summit, December 1984," *Genomics*, 5, no. 3 (1989): 661.
27 Cook-Deegan, "The Alta Summit," 661.
28 Cook-Deegan, "The Alta Summit," 662.
29 Cook-Deegan, "The Alta Summit," 662.
30 National Human Genome Research Institute, "All About the Human Genome Project (HGP)," accessed June 24, 2014, http://www.genome.gov/10001772.
31 Cook-Deegan, "The Alta Summit," 661.
32 Jodi Kim, *Ends of Empire: Asian American Critique and the Cold War* (Minneapolis, University of Minnesota Press, 2010), 117.
33 Wendy Hui Kyong Chun, "Orienting Orientalism, or How to Map Cyberspace," paper presented at the Matters of Representation: Feminism, Theory and the Arts Conference, University of Buffalo, Buffalo, New York, March–April 2000.
34 Donald E. Pease, *The New American Exceptionalism* (Minneapolis: University of Minnesota Press, 2009), 49.
35 See Stephan, "Human Genomes: Public and Private," 745. Stephan's work documents this shift in the years immediately following World War II. See also Sheila Slaughter, "Beyond Basic Science: Research University Presidents' Narratives of Science Policy," *Science, Technology, and Human Values* 18, no. 3 (1993), 278–302. Slaughter argues that during this period, the relation of university science to government and to industry also changed markedly, as part of an increasingly ubiquitous model of "academic capitalism" (278).
36 Milburn, "Modifiable Futures," 568.
37 Eric D. Green and Mark S. Guyer, "Charting a Course for Genomic Medicine from Base Pairs to Bedside," *Nature* 470, no. 7333 (2011): 204.
38 Green and Guyer, "Charting a Course for Genomic Medicine," 207.
39 Green and Guyer, "Charting a Course for Genomic Medicine," 211.
40 A. Gordon, *Ghostly Matters*, 45.
41 Green and Guyer, "Charting a Course for Genomic Medicine," 212.
42 Susan Merrill Squier, *Liminal Lives: Imagining the Human at the Frontiers of Biomedicine* (Durham, NC: Duke University Press, 2004), 234.

43 Melinda Cooper, *Life as Surplus: Biotechnology and Capitalism in the Neoliberal Era* (Seattle: University of Washington Press, 2008), 131.
44 Paula E. Stephan and Sharon G. Levin, "Property Rights and Entrepreneurship in Science," *Small Business Economics* 8 (1996): 181.
45 Cooper, *Life as Surplus*, 130.
46 Cooper, *Life as Surplus*, 140.
47 Cooper, *Life as Surplus*, 141. See also Kaushik Sunder Rajan, ed., *Lively Capital: Biotechnologies, Ethics, and Governance in Global Markets* (Durham, NC: Duke University Press, 2012). In his introduction to that edited volume, Sunder Rajan highlights "the convergence of the life sciences with systems and regimes of capital. In that register, the title [of the volume] refers concretely to the ways in which the life sciences are increasingly incorporated into market regimes. This is an institutional movement, away from the university and toward the market, which has been particularly marked in the American context since the late 1970s and early 1980s, and has, in the process, seen the university itself become a more entrepreneurial institutional space, one that explicitly encourages the commercialization of 'basic' research conducted within its confines" (2). Whereas Sunder Rajan elucidates the commercialization of university research and the collusion between market and university, Cooper focuses even more intently on the "tight institutional alliances between the arts of speculative promise and risk-taking and the actual cultures of life science experimentation" (*Life as Surplus*, 142).
48 Eugene Thacker, *The Global Genome: Biotechnology, Politics, and Culture* (Cambridge, MA: MIT Press, 2005), 138.
49 Judith Roof, *The Poetics of DNA* (Minneapolis: University of Minnesota Press, 2007), 28. See also Lily Kay, *Who Wrote the Book of Life? A History of the Genetic Code* (Palo Alto, CA: Stanford University Press, 2000); Evelyn Fox Keller, *The Century of the Gene* (Cambridge, MA: Harvard University Press, 2000).
50 Roof, *The Poetics of DNA*, 3.
51 Green and Guyer, "Charting a Course for Genomic Medicine from Base Pairs to Bedside," 204.
52 Michel Foucault, *"Society Must Be Defended": Lectures at the Collège de France, 1975–1976*, translated by David Macey, edited by Mauro Bertani and Alessandro Fontana (New York: Picador, 2003), 252.
53 Foucault, *"Society Must Be Defended,"* 253.
54 Foucault, *"Society Must Be Defended,"* 254.
55 Jasbir K. Puar, "Coda: The Cost of Getting Better: Suicide, Sensation, Switchpoints," *GLQ* 18:1 (2011): 153, 154.
56 MedLine Plus, "Genes and Gene Therapy."
57 See, for example, Charis Thompson, *Making Parents: The Ontological Choreography of Reproductive Technologies* (Cambridge, MA: MIT Press, 2005), 79–116, 245–76.
58 Judith Butler, *Gender Trouble: Feminism and the Subversion of Identity* (New York: Routledge, 1990), and *Bodies That Matter: On the Discursive Limits of "Sex"* (New York: Routledge, 1993).
59 Roof, *The Poetics of DNA*, 85.

60 Sarah Franklin, *Dolly Mixtures: The Remaking of Genealogy* (Durham, NC: Duke University Press, 2007), 29–30. Franklin approaches the concept of genetic drag through the iconic example of Dolly the cloned sheep, whose story was one of the events that influenced Lai in the writing of *Salt Fish Girl*. Franklin situates the circulation of Dolly's story as a narrative and phenomenon within a history of cloning that is oddly textured with insecurities about genealogical normativity. The cloning technology that produced Dolly performed "genetic drag" insofar as it "enabled adult DNA to 'pass' as newly youthful." Dolly, according to Franklin, reads as biologically queer and disruptive of the dividing line between animal and human.

61 Brian G. Dias and Kerry J. Ressler, "Parental Olfactory Experience Influences Behavior and Neural Structure in Subsequent Generations," *Nature Neuroscience* 17, no. 1 (2014): 89–96.

62 Dan Hurley, "Grandma's Experiences Leave a Mark on Your Genes," *Discover*, May 2013, accessed June 20, 2014, http://discovermagazine.com/2013/may/13-grandmas-experiences-leave-epigenetic-mark-on-your-genes.

63 Elizabeth Freeman, *Time Binds: Queer Temporalities, Queer Histories* (Durham, NC: Duke University Press, 2010), 64.

64 Freeman, *Time Binds*, 65.

65 Karen Michelle Barad, "Quantum Entanglements and Hauntological Relations of Inheritance: Dis/continuities, SpaceTime Enfoldings, and Justice-to-Come," *Derrida Today* 3, no. 2 (2010): 241. Like Lai, Barad uses the atomic bomb as a site of exploding preconceived formulations of human experience.

66 Barad, "Quantum Entanglements and Hauntological Relations of Inheritance," 241.

67 L. Lai, "Future Asians," 171.

68 L. Lai, "Future Asians," 174.

69 L. Lai, "Future Asians," 173, 174.

70 Asian Development Bank, "Key Facts," accessed June 14, 2014, www.adb.org/about/key-facts.

71 This textual example also speaks to the broader phenomenon of gamification that has long tethered the video-game industry to military training and Wall Street speculations. See Hayles-Jagoda-LeMieux, "Speculation: Financial Games."

72 Paul Lai reads the novel's theme of smelliness (recall that one of the indicators of dreaming sickness is a pungent odor) as the text's critique of punishing difference, especially nonnormative reproduction. He argues that "the novel's focus on stinky bodies emphasizes the materiality and biology that undergird social relations even as biotechnological control promises a transcendence of the biological" ("Stinky Bodies: Mythological Futures and the Olfactory Sense in Larissa Lai's *Salt Fish Girl*," in "Alien/Asian," edited by Stephen Sohn, special issue, MELUS 33, no. 4 [2008]: 167).

73 David Eng, "Transnational Adoption and Queer Diaspora," *Social Text* 21, no. 3 (2003): 4.

74 Eng, "Transnational Adoption and Queer Diaspora," 6–7. In a close reading of a commercial for mutual funds, annuities, and life insurance, Eng demonstrates that the invention of the nuclear family supplants a social commons and coerces investments in privatized futures instead.

75 Jackie Stacey, *The Cinematic Life of the Gene* (Durham, NC: Duke University Press, 2010), 131.
76 Quoted in Puar, "Ecologies of Sex, Sensation, and Slow Death," *Social Text*, 18. November 22, 2010. http://socialtextjournal.org/periscope_article/ecologies_of_sex_sensation_and_slow_death/.
77 Cooper, *Life as Surplus*, 99.
78 Chris Kelly, dir. "Supermarket Slave Trail," *Chris Kelly Film*, http://chriskellyfilm.com/film/journalism/supermarket-slave-trail/, accessed February 22, 2017; also available on *The Guardian*'s YouTube Channel: The Guardian, "Slave Ships & Supermarkets: Modern Day Slavery in Thailand | Guardian Investigations," *YouTube*, June 11, 2014, https://youtu.be/PB9gTbLGTN4, accessed February 22, 2017. See also: Kate Hodal, Chris Kelly, and Felicity Lawrence, "Revealed: Asian Slave Labour Producing Prawns for Supermarkets in US, UK," *The Guardian*, June 10, 2014, https://www.theguardian.com/global-development/2014/jun/10/supermarket-prawns-thailand-produced-slave-labour, accessed February 22, 2017.
79 Mel Chen, *Animacies: Biopolitics, Racial Mattering, and Queer Affect* (Durham, NC: Duke University Press, 2012), 9.

Epilogue

1 Samuel R. Delany, *Shorter Views: Queer Thoughts and the Politics of the Paraliterary* (Hanover, NH: University Press of New England, 1999), 13.
2 Delany, *Shorter Views*, 11.
3 Larissa Lai, *Salt Fish Girl: A Novel* (Toronto, ON: Dundurn, 2002), 259.

BIBLIOGRAPHY

Adas, Michael. *Dominance by Design: Technological Imperatives and America's Civilizing Mission*. Cambridge, MA: Harvard University Press, 2006.

Alexander, M. Jacqui. "Not Just (Any) Body Can Be a Citizen: The Politics of Law, Sexuality and Postcoloniality in Trinidad and Tobago and the Bahamas." *Feminist Review*, no. 48 (1994): 5–23.

Anderson, Benedict. *Imagined Communities: Reflections on the Origin and Spread of Nationalism*. London: Verso, 2006.

Anzaldúa, Gloria. *Borderlands/La Frontera*. San Francisco: Aunt Lute Books, 1987.

Aparicio, Frances R., and Susana Chávez-Silverman. *Tropicalizations: Transcultural Representations of Latinidad*. Hanover, NH: University Press of New England, 1997.

Arau, Sergio and Yareli Arizmendi. *A Day without a Mexican*. 2004. Santa Monica, CA: Xenon Pictures, 2004. DVD.

Backstrom, Kirsten. "*Through the Arc of the Rain Forest*, Karen Tei Yamashita." In *500 Great Books by Women*, edited by Erica Bauermeister, Jesse Larsen, and Holly Smith, 190. New York: Penguin, 1994.

Bahng, Aimee. "Specters of the Pacific: Salt Fish Drag and Atomic Hauntologies in the Era of Genetic Modification." *Journal of American Studies* 49, no. 4 (Fall 2015): 663–83.

Balsamo, Anne, ed. "Science, Technology and Culture." Special issue, *Cultural Studies* 12, no. 3 (1998).

———. *Technologies of the Gendered Body: Reading Cyborg Women*. Durham, NC: Duke University Press, 1995.

Barad, Karen Michelle. *Meeting the Universe Halfway: Quantum Physics and the Entanglement of Matter and Meaning*. Durham, NC: Duke University Press, 2007.

———. "Quantum Entanglements and Hauntological Relations of Inheritance: Dis/continuities, SpaceTime Enfoldings, and Justice-to-Come." *Derrida Today* 3, no. 2 (2010): 240–68.

Bascara, Victor. *Model-Minority Imperialism*. Minneapolis: University of Minnesota Press, 2006.

Baucom, Ian. *Specters of the Atlantic: Finance Capital, Slavery, and the Philosophy of History*. Durham, NC: Duke University Press, 2005.

Baudrillard, Jean. *Simulacra and Simulation*. Translated by Sheila Glaser. Ann Arbor: University of Michigan Press, 1994.

Beaumont, Matthew. "The Anamorphic Estrangements of Science Fiction." In *Red Planets: Marxism and Science Fiction*, edited by Mark Bould and China Miéville, 29–46. Middletown, CT: Wesleyan Press, 2009.

Beck, Ulrich. *Risk Society: Towards a New Modernity*. London: Sage, 1992.

Bell, Derrick. "The Space Traders." In *Dark Matter: A Century of Speculative Fiction from the African Diaspora*, edited by Sheree R. Thomas, 326–55. New York: Warner Books, 2000.

Benford, Gregory. "Real Science, Imaginary Worlds." In *The Ascent of Wonder: The Evolution of Hard SF*, edited by David G. Hartwell and Kathryn Cramer, 15–23. New York: Tom Doherty Associates, 1994.

Benjamin, Walter. "Theses on the Philosophy of History." 1940. In *Walter Benjamin, Illuminations*, edited by Hannah Arendt and translated by Harry Zohn, 253–65. New York: Shocken, 1968.

Bergson, Henri. *Creative Evolution*. Translated by Arthur Mitchell. New York: H. Holt, 1911.

Berlant, Lauren Gail. *Cruel Optimism*. Durham, NC: Duke University Press, 2011.

Bogues, Anthony. *Empire of Liberty: Power, Desire, and Freedom*. Hanover, NH: University Press of New England, 2010.

Bould, Mark, and China Miéville, eds. *Red Planets: Marxism and Science Fiction*. Middletown, CT: Wesleyan University Press, 2009.

Brady, Mary Pat. *Extinct Lands, Temporal Geographies: Chicana Literature and the Urgency of Space*. Durham, NC: Duke University Press, 2002.

Briggs, Laura. *Reproducing Empire: Race, Sex, Science, and U.S. Imperialism in Puerto Rico*. Berkeley: University of California Press, 2003.

Butler, Judith. *Bodies That Matter: On the Discursive Limits of "Sex."* New York: Routledge, 1993.

———. *Gender Trouble: Feminism and the Subversion of Identity*. New York: Routledge, 1990.

Butler, Octavia. "Octavia Butler on Charlie Rose—Part 1/2." November 12, 2008. Accessed July 23, 2016. https://www.youtube.com/watch?v=66pu-Miq4tk.

———. *Kindred*. Boston: Beacon Press, 1988.

Canavan, Gerry. "'We Are the Walking Dead': Race, Time, and Survival in Zombie Narrative." *Extrapolation* 51, no. 3 (2010): 431–53.

Candelaria, Matthew, and James E. Gunn. *Speculations on Speculation: Theories of Science Fiction*. Lanham, MD: Scarecrow, 2005.

Cardozo, Karen, and Banu Subramaniam. "Truth Is Stranger: The Postnational 'Aliens' of Biofiction." In *The Postnational Fantasy: Essays on Postcolonialism, Cosmopolitics and Science Fiction*, edited by Masood Ashraf Raja, Jason W. Ellis, and Swaralipi Nandi, 30–45. Jefferson, NC: McFarland, 2011.

Carico, Aaron, and Dara Orenstein. "Editors' Introduction: The Fictions of Finance." "The Fictions of Finance," special issue, *Radical History Review* 118 (Winter 2014): 3–13.

———, eds. "The Fictions of Finance," special issue, *Radical History Review* 118 (Winter 2014).
Chakrabarty, Dipesh. "The Climate of History: Four Theses." *Critical Inquiry* 35, no. 2 (2009): 197–222.
———. *Provincializing Europe: Postcolonial Thought and Historical Difference*. Princeton, NJ: Princeton University Press, 2008.
Chakravartty, Paula, and Denise Ferreira da Silva. "Accumulation, Dispossession, and Debt: The Racial Logic of Global Capitalism—An Introduction." "Race, Empire, and the Crisis of the Subprime," edited by Paula Chakravartty and Denise Ferreira da Silva, special issue, *American Quarterly* 64, no. 3 (2012): 369–85.
———, eds. "Race, Empire, and the Crisis of the Subprime." Special issue, *American Quarterly* 64, no. 3 (2012).
Chen, Mel. *Animacies: Biopolitics, Racial Mattering, and Queer Affect*. Durham, NC: Duke University Press, 2012.
Chen, Nancy N. "Feeding the Nation: Chinese Biotechnology and Genetically Modified Foods." In *Asian Biotech: Ethics and Communities of Fate*, edited by Aihwa Ong and Nancy N. Chen, 81–94. Durham, NC: Duke University Press, 2010.
Chow, Rey. *The Age of the World Target: Self-Referentiality in War, Theory, and Comparative Work*. Durham, NC: Duke University Press, 2006.
Chuh, Kandice. *Imagine Otherwise: On Asian Americanist Critique*. Durham, NC: Duke University Press, 2003.
———. "Of Hemispheres and Other Spheres: Navigating Karen Tei Yamashita's Literary World." *American Literary History* 18, no. 3 (2006): 618–37.
Chun, Wendy Hui Kyong. "Orienting Orientalism, or How to Map Cyberspace." In *AsianAmerica.Net: Ethnicity, Nationalism, and Cyberspace*, edited by Rachel C. Lee and Sau-ling Cynthia Wong, 3–36. New York: Routledge, 2003.
Clare, Eli. "Comment from the Field: Yearning toward Carrie Buck." *Journal of Literary & Cultural Disability Studies* 8, no. 3 (2014): 335–44.
Cook-Deegan, Robert M. "The Alta Summit, December 1984." *Genomics* 5, no. 3 (1989): 661–63.
———. *The Gene Wars: Science, Politics, and the Human Genome*. London: W. W. Norton, 1996.
Cooper, Melinda. *Life as Surplus: Biotechnology and Capitalism in the Neoliberal Era*. Seattle: University of Washington Press, 2008.
Cuarón, Alfonso, dir. *Children of Men*. Los Angeles, CA: Universal Studios Home Video, 2006.
———, dir. *Y Tu Mamá También*. Mexico City, State of Mexico: 20th Century Fox, 2001.
Currah, Paisley, and Susan Stryker. Introduction to "Making Transgender Count," edited by Paisley Currah and Susan Stryker, special issue, *TSQ* 2, no. 1 (2015): 1–12.
Cvetkovich, Ann. *An Archive of Feelings: Trauma, Sexuality, and Lesbian Public Cultures*. Durham, NC: Duke University Press, 2003.
———. "Public Feelings." *South Atlantic Quarterly* 106, no. 3 (2007): 459–68.
DasGupta, Sayantani. "(Re)Conceiving the Surrogate: Maternity, Race, and Reproductive Technologies in Alfonso Cuarón's *Children of Men*." In *Gender Scripts in Medicine*

and Narrative, edited by Marcelline Block and Angela Laflen, 178–211. Newcastle, UK: Cambridge Scholars, 2010.

Daston, Lorraine. *Classical Probability in the Enlightenment*. Princeton, NJ: Princeton University Press, 1988.

Davis, Angela. "Racism, Birth Control, and Reproductive Rights." *Women, Race and Class*, 202–7. New York: Random House, 1982.

Davis, Dana Ain. "The Politics of Reproduction: The Troubling Case of Nadya Suleman and Assisted Reproductive Technology." *Transforming Anthropology* 17, no. 2 (2009): 105–16.

Davis, Mike. *City of Quartz: Excavating the Future in Los Angeles*. New York: Verso, 1990.

De Certeau, Michel. "Walking in the City." In *The Practice of Everyday Life*, translated by Steven Rendall, 91–110. Berkeley: University of California Press, 1984.

De Goede, Marieke. *Speculative Security: The Politics of Pursuing Terrorist Monies*. Minneapolis: University of Minnesota Press, 2012.

De la Peña, Carolyn, and Siva Vaidhyanathan, eds. "Rewiring the 'Nation': The Place of Technology in American Studies." Special issue, *American Quarterly* (March 2007).

De Lauretis, Teresa, Andreas Huyssen, and Kathleen Woodward, eds. *The Technological Imagination: Theories and Fictions*. Madison, WI: Coda Press, 1980.

De Soto, Hernando. *The Other Path: The Invisible Revolution in the Third World*. New York: Harper and Row, 1989.

Delany, Samuel R. "Critical Methods / Speculative Fiction." 1970. In Samuel R. Delany, *The Jewel-Hinged Jaw: Notes on the Language of Science Fiction*, 17–28. Rev. ed. Middletown, CT: Wesleyan University Press, 2009.

———. "The Necessity of Tomorrows," *Starboard Wine: More Notes on the Language of Science Fiction*. Pleasantville, NY: Dragon Press, 1984.

———. "Racism and Science Fiction." 1999. In *Dark Matter*, edited by Sheree R. Thomas, 383–97. New York: Warner/Aspect, 2000.

———. "The Para•doxa Interview: Inside and Outside the Canon." 1995. In Samuel R. Delany, *Shorter Views: Queer Thoughts and the Politics of the Paraliterary*, 186–217. Hanover, NH: University Press of New England, 1999.

———. "The Rhetoric of Sex/The Discourse of Desire." 1993. In Samuel R. Delany, *Shorter Views: Queer Thoughts and the Politics of the Paraliterary*, 3–40. Hanover, NH: University Press of New England, 1999.

———. "Sword & Sorcery, S/M, and the Economics of Inadequation." 1989. In Samuel R. Delany, *Silent Interviews: On Language, Race, Sex, Science Fiction, and Some Comics: A Collection of Written Interviews*, 127–63. Hanover, NH: University Press of New England, 1994.

———. *Times Square Red, Times Square Blue*. New York: NYU Press, 1999.

——— and Carl Howard Freedman. *Conversations with Samuel R. Delany*. Jackson: University Press of Mississippi, 2009.

——— and Marilyn Hacker. "On Speculative Fiction." In *Quark* 4, eds. Samuel R. Delany and Marilyn Hacker. New York: Coronet Communications, 1971: 7–9.

Delbourgo, James, and Nicholas Dew, eds. *Science and Empire in the Atlantic World*. New York: Routledge, 2008.

Deleuze, Gilles. "Postscript on Societies of Control." *October* 59 (Winter 1992): 3–7.

DeLoughrey, Elizabeth. "Heliotropes: Solar Ecologies and Pacific Radiations." In *Postcolonial Ecologies: Literatures of the Environment*, edited by Elizabeth DeLoughrey and George B. Handley, 238. Oxford: Oxford University Press, 2011.

Dery, Mark. "Black to the Future: Interviews with Samuel R. Delany, Greg Tate, and Tricia Rose." In *Flame Wars: The Discourse of Cyberculture*, 179–222. Durham, NC: Duke University Press, 1994.

Desai, Jigna. "Homo on the Range." *Social Text* 20, no. 4 (2002): 65–89.

Derrida, Jacques, and Avital Ronell. "The Law of Genre." *Critical Inquiry* 7, no. 1 (1980): 55–81.

———. *Specters of Marx: The State of the Debt, the Work of Mourning and the New International*. Translated by Peggy Kamuf. New York: Routledge, 1994.

Dias, Brian G. and Kerry J. Ressler. "Parental Olfactory Experience Influences Behavior and Neural Structure in Subsequent Generations." *Nature Neuroscience* 17, no. 1 (2014): 89–96.

Drayton, Richard. *Nature's Government: Science, Imperial Britain and the "Improvement" of the World*. New Haven, CT: Yale University Press, 2000.

Du Bois, W. E. B. *The Souls of Black Folk*. 1903. New York: Dover, 1994.

Duggan, Lisa. "The New Homonormativity: The Sexual Politics of Neoliberalism." In *Materializing Democracy: Toward a Revitalized Cultural Politics*, edited by Russ Castronovo and Dana D. Nelson, 175–94. Durham, NC: Duke University Press, 2002.

Dunmire, Patricia L. "Preempting the Future: Rhetoric and Ideology of the Future in Political Discourse." *Discourse Society* 16, no. 4 (2005): 481–513.

Dunn, Timothy J. *The Militarization of the U.S.-Mexico Border, 1978–1992: Low-Intensity Conflict Doctrine Comes Home*. Austin: CMAS Books, University of Texas at Austin, 1996.

Edelman, Lee. *No Future: Queer Theory and the Death Drive*. Durham, NC: Duke University Press, 2004.

———. "The Future Is Kid Stuff: Queer Theory, Disidentification, and the Death Drive." *Narrative* 6, no. 1 (January 1998): 18–30.

Edmond, Rod. *Representing the South Pacific: Colonial Discourse from Cook to Gauguin*. Cambridge: Cambridge University Press, 1997.

Ellis, Jason W., Swaralipi Nandi, and Masood A. Raja. *The Postnational Fantasy: Essays on Postcolonialism, Cosmopolitics and Science Fiction*. Jefferson, NC: McFarland, 2011.

Eng, David L. *The Feeling of Kinship: Queer Liberalism and the Racialization of Intimacy*. Durham, NC: Duke University Press, 2010.

———. "Transnational Adoption and Queer Diaspora." *Social Text* 21, no. 3 (2003): 1–37.

———, Judith Halberstam, and José Esteban Muñoz. "What's Queer about Queer Studies Now?" *Social Text* 23, no. 3 (2005): 1–17.

Esch, Elizabeth Durham. "Fordtown: Managing Race and Nation in the American Empire, 1925–1945." PhD diss., New York University, 2003.

Fausto-Sterling, Anne. "Gender, Race, and Nation: The Comparative Anatomy of 'Hottentot' Women in Europe: 1815–1817." In *Deviant Bodies: Critical Perspectives on Dif-*

ference in Science and Popular Culture, edited by Jennifer Terry and Jacqueline Urla, 19–48. Bloomington: Indiana University Press, 1995.

Ferreira Furtado, Júnia. "Tropical Empiricism: Making Medical Knowledge in Colonial Brazil." In *Science and Empire in the Atlantic World*, edited by James Delbourgo and Nicholas Dew, 127–51. New York: Routledge, 2008.

Firestone, Harvey. *Men and Rubber: The Story of Business*. Garden City, NY: Doubleday, 1926.

Fisher, Mark. *Capitalist Realism: Is There No Alternative?* Zero Books, 2009.

Fortun, Michael. *Promising Genomics: Iceland and DECODE Genetics in a World of Speculation*. Berkeley: University of California Press, 2008.

Foucault, Michel. *The Archaeology of Knowledge*. Translated by A. M. Sheridan Smith. London: Tavistock Publications, 1972.

———. *Security, Territory, and Population: Lectures at the Collège de France, 1977–1978*. Edited by Michel Senellart. Translated by Graham Burchell. New York: Palgrave-MacMillan. 2007.

———. *"Society Must Be Defended": Lectures at the Collège de France, 1975–1976*. Translated by David Macey, edited by Mauro Bertani and Alessandro Fontana. New York: Picador, 2003.

Fowler, Edward. *San'ya Blues: Laboring Life in Contemporary Tokyo*. Ithaca, NY: Cornell University Press, 1996.

Franklin, Sarah. *Dolly Mixtures: The Remaking of Genealogy*. Durham, NC: Duke University Press, 2007.

Freedman, Carl Howard. *Critical Theory and Science Fiction*. Hanover, NH: University Press of New England, 2000.

Freeman, Elizabeth. *Time Binds: Queer Temporalities, Queer Histories*. Durham, NC: Duke University Press, 2010.

Fregoso, Rosa Linda. *MeXicana Encounters: The Making of Social Identities on the Borderlands*. Berkeley: University of California Press, 2003.

Freyre, Gilberto. *The Masters and the Slaves: A Study in the Development of Brazilian Civilization*. 1933. Translated by Samuel Putnam. Berkeley: University of California Press, 1986.

Friedman, Hal M. "The Beast in Paradise: The United States Navy in Micronesia, 1943–1947." *Pacific Historical Review*. 52, no. 2 (1993): 173–95.

———. *Governing the American Lake: The US Defense and Administration of the Pacific, 1945–1947*. East Lansing: Michigan State University Press, 2007.

Gates, Henry Louis, Jr. *The Signifying Monkey: A Theory of Afro-American Literary Criticism*. New York: Oxford University Press, 1988.

Gibson-Graham, J. K. *A Postcapitalist Politics*. Minneapolis: University of Minnesota Press, 2006.

Gier, Jean Vengua, and Calra Alicia Tejeda. "An Interview with Karen Tei Yamashita." *Jouvert* 2, no. 2 (1998).

Gill-Peterson, Julian. "The Value of the Future: The Child as Human Capital and the Neoliberal Labor of Race." *WSQ: Women's Studies Quarterly* 43, nos. 1 and 2 (Spring/Summer 2015): 181–96.

Gilmore, Ruth Wilson. *Golden Gulag: Prisons, Surplus, Crisis, and Opposition in Globalizing California*. Berkeley: University of California Press, 2007.

Gilroy, Paul. *The Black Atlantic: Modernity and Double Consciousness*. Cambridge, MA: Harvard University Press, 1993.

Glave, Dianne D., and Nalo Hopkinson. "An Interview with Nalo Hopkinson." *Callaloo* 26, no. 1 (2003): 146–59.

Gómez-Peña, Guillermo. "Border Brujo: A Performance Poem (from the Series 'Documented/Undocumented')." *TDR* 35, no. 3 (1991): 48–66.

———. *The New World Border: Prophecies, Poems and Loqueras*. San Francisco: City Lights, 1996.

Gopinath, Gayatri. *Impossible Desires: Queer Diasporas and South Asian Public Cultures*. Durham, NC: Duke University Press, 2005.

Gordon, Avery. *Ghostly Matters: Haunting and the Sociological Imagination*. Minneapolis: University of Minnesota Press, 1997.

Grandin, Greg. *Fordlandia: The Rise and Fall of Henry Ford's Forgotten Jungle City*. New York: Metropolitan, 2009.

Green, Eric D., and Mark S. Guyer. "Charting a Course for Genomic Medicine from Base Pairs to Bedside." *Nature* 470, no. 7333 (2011): 204–13.

Gruesz, Kirsten Silva. "The Mercurial Space of 'Central' America: New Orleans, Honduras, and the Writing of the Banana Republic." In *Hemispheric American Studies*, edited by Caroline F. Levander and Robert S. Levine. New Brunswick, NJ: Rutgers University Press, 2008.

Guttman, Herbert. *The Black Family in Slavery and Freedom, 1750–1925*. New York: Pantheon, 1976.

Hacking, Ian. *The Taming of Chance*. Cambridge: Cambridge University Press, 1990.

Halberstam, Judith. *In a Queer Time and Place: Transgender Bodies, Subcultural Lives*. New York: New York University Press, 2005.

Hammonds, Evelyn Brooks. "Toward a Genealogy of Black Female Sexuality: The Problematic of Silence." In *Feminist Genealogies, Colonial Legacies, Democratic Futures*, edited by M. Jacqui Alexander and Chandra Talpade Mohanty, 170–82. New York: Routledge, 1997.

Hara, Kimie. *Cold War Frontiers in the Asia-Pacific: Divided Territories in the San Francisco System*. New York: Routledge, 2007.

Haraway, Donna J. "SF: Science Fiction, Speculative Fabulation, String Figures, So Far." *Ada: A Journal of Gender, New Media, and Technology*, no. 3 (2013).

———. *Simians, Cyborgs, and Women: The Reinvention of Nature*. New York: Routledge, 1991.

———. "Situated Knowledges: The Science Question in Feminism and the Privilege of Partial Perspective." *Feminist Studies* 14, no. 3 (1988): 575–99.

———. "The Virtual Speculum in the New World Order." *Feminist Review* 55 (Spring, 1997): 22–72.

———. *When Species Meet*. Minneapolis: University of Minnesota Press, 2008.

Harney, Stefano, and Fred Moten. *The Undercommons: Fugitive Planning and Black Study*. Wivenhoe, NY: Minor Compositions, 2013.

Hartouni, Valerie. *Making Life Make Sense: New Technologies and the Discourses of Reproduction.* Minneapolis: University of Minnesota Press, 1996.
Harvey, David. *The Condition of Postmodernity: An Enquiry into the Origins of Cultural Change.* Oxford: Blackwell, 1989.
———. *The Limits to Capital.* New York: Verso, 2006.
Henry-Labordère, Pierre. *Analysis, Geometry, and Modeling in Finance: Advanced Models in Option Pricing.* Boca Raton, FL: CRC, 2009.
Herzog, Werner, dir. *Aguirre, Der Zorn Gottes.* Leipzig: Kinowelt, 1972.
———, dir. *Fitzcarraldo.* Leipzig: Kinowelt, 1982.
Ho, Karen Zouwen. *Liquidated: An Ethnography of Wall Street.* Durham, NC: Duke University Press, 2009.
Ho, Tamara. "Larissa Lai's 'New Cultural Politics of Intimacy': Animal. Asian. Cyborg." "Speculative Life," special issue, *Social Text: Periscope: Critical Perspectives on Contemporary Issues* (2012).
Hoagland, Ericka, and Reema Sarwal, eds. *Science Fiction, Imperialism and the Third World: Essays on Postcolonial Literature and Film.* Jefferson, NC: McFarland, 2010.
hooks, bell. *Black Looks: Race and Representation.* Boston: South End Press, 1992.
Hopkinson, Nalo. "Introduction." *So Long Been Dreaming: Postcolonial Science Fiction and Fantasy.* Edited by Nalo Hopkinson and Uppinder Mehan, 7–9. Vancouver: Arsenal Press, 2004.
———. *Midnight Robber.* New York: Grand Central, 2000.
Hopkinson, Nalo, and Alondra Nelson. "Making the Impossible Possible: An Interview with Nalo Hopkinson." *Social Text* 20, no. 2 (2002): 97–113.
Hopkinson, Nalo, and Uppinder Mehan, eds. *So Long Been Dreaming: Postcolonial Science Fiction and Fantasy.* Vancouver, BC: Arsenal Pulp, 2014.
Invisible Committee. *The Coming Insurrection.* Los Angeles: Semiotext(e), 2009.
Jameson, Fredric. *Archaeologies of the Future: The Desire Called Utopia and Other Science Fictions.* London: Verso, 2005.
———. "Future City." *New Left Review* 21 (May-June 2003): 65–79.
Kang, Laura. "The Uses of Asianization: Figuring Crises, 1997–98 and 2007–?" "Race, Empire, and the Crisis of the Subprime," edited by Paula Chakravartty and Denise da Silva, special issue, *American Quarterly* 64, no. 3 (2012): 411–36.
Kaplan, Amy. *The Anarchy of Empire in the Making of U.S. Culture.* Cambridge, MA: Harvard University Press, 2002.
———. "Where Is Guantánamo?" *American Quarterly* 57, no. 3 (2005): 831–58.
Kay, Lily. *Who Wrote the Book of Life? A History of the Genetic Code.* Palo Alto, CA: Stanford University Press, 2000.
Keller, Evelyn Fox. *The Century of the Gene.* Cambridge, MA: Harvard University Press, 2000.
Kim, Jodi. *Ends of Empire: Asian American Critique and the Cold War.* Minneapolis: University of Minnesota Press, 2010.
Klein, Naomi. *The Shock Doctrine: The Rise of Disaster Capitalism.* Toronto, ON: Knopf Canada, 2007.
Knight, Frank. *Risk, Uncertainty and Profit.* Boston: Houghton Mifflin, 1921.

Knorr Cetina, Karin, and Alex Preda. *The Sociology of Financial Markets.* Oxford: Oxford University Press, 2004.

Koepnick, Lutz P. "Colonial Forestry: Sylvan Politics in Werner Herzog's *Aguirre* and *Fitzcarraldo.*" Special issue on German film history. Edited by David Bathrick and Eric Rentscheler. *New German Critique*, no. 60 (1993): 133–59.

Kopinak, Kathryn. "Environmental Implications of New Mexican Industrial Investment: The Rise of Asian Origin Maquiladoras as Generators of Hazardous Waste." *Asian Journal of Latin American Studies* 15, no. 1 (2002): 91–120.

Kuczynski, Alex. "Her Body, My Baby: My Adventures with a Surrogate Mom." *New York Times Magazine*, November 28, 2008. 42–49, 64, 74, 78.

La Berge, Leigh Claire. "The Rules of Abstraction: Methods and Discourses of Finance." *Radical History Review*, no. 118 (2014): 93–112.

Lacan, Jacques. "The Split between the Eye and the Gaze." 1964. In *The Four Fundamental Concepts of Psychoanalysis*, translated by Alan Sheridan, 67–78. New York: Norton, 1978.

Lai, Larissa. "Future Asians: Migrant Speculations, Repressed History & Cyborg Hope." *West Coast Line* 38, no. 2 (2004): 168–75.

———. *Salt Fish Girl: A Novel.* Toronto, ON: Dundurn, 2002.

Lai, Paul. "Stinky Bodies: Mythological Futures and the Olfactory Sense in Larissa Lai's *Salt Fish Girl.*" "Alien/Asian," edited by Stephen Sohn, special issue, MELUS 33, no. 4 (2008): 167–87.

Lakoff, Andrew. "The Generic Biothreat, or, How We Became Unprepared." *Cultural Anthropology* 23, no. 3 (2008): 399–428.

Landon, Brooks. *Science Fiction after 1900: From the Steam Man to the Stars.* New York: Twaynes, 1997.

Latimer, Heather. "Bio-Reproductive Futurism: Bare Life and the Pregnant Refugee in Alfonso Cuaron's *Children of Men.*" *Social Text* 29, no. 3 (2011): 51–72.

Latour, Bruno. *We Have Never Been Modern.* 1991. Translated by Catherine Porter. Cambridge, MA: Harvard University Press, 1993.

Latour, Bruno, and Steve Woolgar. *Laboratory Life: The Construction of Scientific Facts.* Princeton, NJ: Princeton University Press, 1979.

Lau, Estelle. *Paper Families: Identity, Immigration Administration, and Chinese Exclusion.* Durham, NC: Duke University Press, 2007.

Le Guin, Ursula K. "American SF and the Other." *Science Fiction Studies* 2, no. 3 (1975): 208–10.

Lee, Erika. *At America's Gates: Chinese Immigration during the Exclusion Era, 1882–1943.* Chapel Hill: University of North Carolina Press, 2003.

———. "Enforcing the Borders: Chinese Exclusion along the U.S. Borders with Canada and Mexico, 1882–1924." *The Journal of American History* 89, no. 1 (2002): 54–86.

Lee, Rachel C. *The Americas of Asian American Literature: Gendered Fictions of Nation and Transnation.* Princeton, NJ: Princeton University Press, 1999.

——— and Sau-ling Cynthia Wong, eds. *Asian America.Net: Ethnicity, Nationalism, and Cyberspace.* New York: Routledge, 2003.

Lefanu, Sarah. *In the Chinks of the World Machine: Feminism and Science Fiction*. London: Women's Press, 1988.

———. *Feminism and Science Fiction*. Bloomington: Indiana University Press, 1989.

Lefebvre, Henri. *The Production of Space*. Translated by Donald Nicholson-Smith. Oxford: Blackwell, 1991.

Lévi-Strauss, Claude. *Tristes Tropiques*. Paris: Plon, 1955.

Liew, Sonny. *Box of Things: Mementoes from a Dusty City*. Press Kit for *Malinky Robot*. Printed and distributed by Sonny Liew, 2012.

Liew, Sonny. *Malinky Robot: Collected Stories and Other Bits*. New York: Image Comics, 2011.

Lim, Bliss Cua. *Translating Time: Cinema, the Fantastic, and Temporal Critique*. Durham, NC: Duke University Press, 2009.

Lim, Eng-Beng. "Glocalqueering in New Asia: The Politics of Performing Gay in Singapore." *Theatre Journal* 57, no. 3 (2005): 383–405.

Linger, Daniel Touro. *No One Home: Brazilian Selves Remade in Japan*. Stanford, CA: Stanford University Press, 2001.

Lipsitz, George. *The Possessive Investment in Whiteness: How White People Profit from Identity Politics*. Philadelphia, PA: Temple University Press, 1998.

LiPuma, Edward, and Benjamin Lee. *Financial Derivatives and the Globalization of Risk*. Durham, NC: Duke University Press, 2004.

Lowe, Lisa. *Immigrant Acts: On Asian American Cultural Politics*. Durham, NC: Duke University Press, 1996.

———. *The Intimacies of Four Continents*. Durham, NC: Duke University Press, 2015.

———. "Utopia and Modernity" *Rethinking Marxism* 13, no. 2 (2001): 10–18.

——— and David Lloyd. "Introduction." In *The Politics of Culture in the Shadow of Capital*. Eds. Lisa Lowe and David Lloyd. Durham, NC: Duke University Press, 1997. 1–32.

Lubin, Alex. "Welcome to Albuquerque." *American Studies Association Annual Meeting Program: Back Down to the Crossroads: Integrative American Studies in Theory and Practice*. Albuquerque, NM: American Studies Association, 2008.

Luciano, Dana and Mel Y. Chen. "Introduction: Has the Queer Ever Been Human?" "Queer Inhumanisms," special issue, GLQ 21, nos. 2–3 (2015): 182–207.

Lye, Colleen. *America's Asia: Racial Form and American Literature, 1893–1945*. Princeton, NJ: Princeton University Press, 2005.

———. "The Literary Case of Wen Ho Lee." *Journal of Asian American Studies* 14, no. 2 (2011): 249–82.

MacKenzie, Donald A., Fabian Muniesa, and Lucia Siu, eds. *Do Economists Make Markets? On the Performativity of Economics*. Princeton, NJ: Princeton University Press, 2007.

Mahbubani, Kishore. *The New Asian Hemisphere: The Irresistible Shift of Global Power to the East*. New York: PublicAffairs, 2008.

Manalansan, Martin F., IV. "Feeling Our Way through the Crises: Embodied Belongings and Asian American Studies." Keynote address at "Acts of Elaboration: A Symposium on Asian American Studies in the Northeast," Boston College, May 29, 2009.

———."Queering the Chain of Care Paradigm." *The Scholar & Feminist Online* 6, no. 3 (2008).

———. "Race, Violence, and Neoliberal Spatial Politics in the Global City." *Social Text* 23, no. 3 (2005): 141–55.

Marez, Curtis. *Drug Wars: The Political Economy of Narcotics*. Minneapolis: University of Minnesota Press, 2004.

Martin, Randy. *The Empire of Indifference: American War and the Financial Logic of Risk Management*. Durham, NC: Duke University Press, 2007.

———. *The Financialization of Daily Life*. Philadelphia, PA: Temple University Press, 2002.

Marx, Karl. *Capital: A Critique of Political Economy, Vol. III. The Process of Capitalist Production as a Whole*. Edited by Frederick Engels. Translated by Ernest Untermann. Chicago: Charles H. Kerr, 1909.

Masco, Joseph. *Nuclear Borderlands: The Manhattan Project in Post-Cold War New Mexico*. Princeton, NJ: Princeton University Press, 2006.

McClanahan, Annie. "Future's Shock: Plausibility, Preemption, and the Fiction of 9/11." *symploke* 17, no. 1 (2009): 41–62.

McClintock, Anne. *Imperial Leather: Race, Gender, and Sexuality in the Colonial Conquest*. New York: Routledge, 1995.

Mehan, Uppinder. "The Domestication of Technology in Indian Science Fiction Short Stories." *Foundation* 74 (Autumn 1998): 54–66.

Melzer, Patricia. *Alien Constructions: Science Fiction and Feminist Thought*. Austin: University of Texas Press, 2006.

Mercer, Kobena. *Welcome to the Jungle: New Positions in Black Cultural Studies*. London: Routledge, 1994.

Milburn, Colin. "Modifiable Futures: Science Fiction at the Bench." *Isis* 101, no. 3 (2010): 560–69.

Mitchell, Rob, and Cathy Waldby. "National Biobanks: Clinical Labour, Risk Production, and the Creation of Biovalue," *Science, Technology, and Human Values* 35, no. 3 (2010): 330–55.

Morrison, Toni. *Beloved*. New York: Plume, 1988.

Mulvey, Laura. "Afterthoughts on 'Visual Pleasure and Narrative Cinema' Inspired by *Duel in the Sun*." *Framework* 15–17 (Summer 1981): 12–15.

Morley, David and Kevin Robins. "Techno-Orientalism." In *Spaces of Identity: Global Media, Electronic Landscapes, and Cultural Boundaries*, 147–73. London: Routledge, 1995.

Muñoz, José Esteban. *Cruising Utopia: The Then and There of Queer Futurity*. New York: New York University Press, 2009.

———. *Disidentifications: Queers of Color and the Performance of Politics*. Minneapolis: University of Minnesota Press, 1999.

Nag, Rajat M. "The Asian Century: Plausible but not Preordained." Speech. School of Public Policy and Management, Tsinghua University, Beijing, People's Republic of China, June 20, 2011.

Nakamura, Lisa. *Cybertypes: Race, Ethnicity, and Identity on the Internet*. New York: Routledge, 2002.

Nancy, Jean-Luc. *The Creation of the World, or Globalization*. Albany: State University of New York Press, 2007.

Nelson, Alondra, ed. "Afrofuturism." Special issue, *Social Text* 20, no. 2 (2002).

Newman, Karen. *Fetal Positions: Individualism, Science, Visuality*. Stanford, CA: Stanford University Press, 1997.

Nigg, Joseph. *Sea Monsters: A Voyage around the World's Most Beguiling Map*. Chicago: University of Chicago Press, 2013.

Nguyen, Mimi Thi. *The Gift of Freedom: War, Debt, and Other Refugee Passages*. Durham, NC: Duke University Press, 2012.

——— and Thuy Linh N. Tu, eds. *Alien Encounters: Popular Culture in Asian America*. Durham, NC: Duke University Press, 2007.

O'Brien, Patty. *The Pacific Muse: Exotic Femininity and the Colonial Pacific*. Seattle: University of Washington Press, 2006.

Okihiro, Gary. "Afterword: Toward a Black Pacific." In *AfroAsian Encounters: Culture, History, Politics*, edited by Heike Raphael-Hernandez and Shannon Steen, 313–30. New York: New York University Press, 2006.

Ong, Aihwa. "An Analytics of Biotechnology and Ethics at Multiple Scales." In *Asian Biotech: Ethics and Communities of Fate*, edited by Aihwa Ong and Nancy N. Chen, 1–54. Durham, NC: Duke University Press, 2010.

———. *Flexible Citizenship: The Cultural Logics of Transnationality*. Durham, NC: Duke University Press, 1999.

———. *Neoliberalism as Exception: Mutations in Citizenship and Sovereignty*. Durham, NC: Duke University Press, 2006.

Palumbo-Liu, David. *Asian/American: Historical Crossings of a Racial Frontier*. Stanford, CA: Stanford University Press, 1999.

Park, Jane Chi Hyun. *Yellow Future: Oriental Style in Hollywood Cinema*. Minneapolis: University of Minnesota Press, 2010.

Parrinder, Patrick. *Learning from Other Worlds: Estrangement, Cognition, and the Politics of Science Fiction and Utopia*. Durham, NC: Duke University Press, 2001.

Patel, Geeta. "Ghostly Appearances." In *Secularisms*, edited by Janet R. Jakobsen and Ann Pellegrini, 226–46. Durham, NC: Duke University Press, 2008.

———. "Risky Subjects: Insurance, Sexuality, and Capital." *Social Text* 24, no. 4 (2006): 25–65.

Peard, Julyan G. *Race, Place, and Medicine: The Idea of the Tropics in Nineteenth-Century Brazilian Medicine*. Durham, NC: Duke University Press, 1999.

Pease, Donald E. *The New American Exceptionalism*. Minneapolis: University of Minnesota Press, 2009.

Penley, Constance, and Andrew Ross, eds. *Technoculture*. Minneapolis: University of Minnesota Press, 1991.

——— and Donna Haraway. "Cyborgs at Large: Interview with Donna Haraway." *Social Text*, nos. 25–26 (1990): 8–23.

Poovey, Mary. *Genres of the Credit Economy: Mediating Value in Eighteenth- and Nineteenth-Century Britain*. Chicago: University of Chicago Press, 2008.

Pratt, Lloyd. *Archives of American Time: Literature and Modernity in the Nineteenth Century*. Philadelphia: University of Pennsylvania Press, 2010.

Pratt, Mary Louise. *Imperial Eyes: Travel Writing and Transculturation*. 2nd ed. London: Routledge, 2008.

Puar, Jasbir K. "Coda: The Cost of Getting Better: Suicide, Sensation, Switchpoints." GLQ 18 no. 1 (2011): 149–58.

———. "Ecologies of Sex, Sensation, and Slow Death." *Social Text*, November 22, 2010. http://socialtextjournal.org/periscope_article/ecologies_of_sex_sensation_and_slow_death/.

———. *Terrorist Assemblages: Homonationalism in Queer Times*. Durham, NC: Duke University Press, 2007.

Raley, Rita. *Tactical Media*. Minneapolis: University of Minnesota Press, 2009.

Ramírez, Catherine. "Afrofuturism/Chicanafuturism: Fictive Kin." *Aztlán* 33, no. 1 (2008):185.

Rauch, Molly. "Fruit Salad." *Nation*, March 2, 1998, 28–31.

Riesman, Abraham. "The Vulture Transcript: Alfonso Cuarón on *Children of Men*." *Vulture*. January 6, 2017.

Rivera, Alex, dir. *Sleep Dealer*. Los Angeles: Maya Entertainment, 2008.

———, dir. "The Visible Border." *The Borders Trilogy*. Part 3. New York: SubCine.com, 2002.

———, dir. *Why Cybraceros?* United States, 1997. Vimeo (https://vimeo.com/46513267) and described on the artist's website (http://alexrivera.com/project/why-cybraceros/).

Rivera, Lysa. "Future Histories and Cyborg Labor: Reading Borderlands Science Fiction after NAFTA." *Science Fiction Studies* 39, no. 3 (2012): 415–36.

Roach, Joseph. *Cities of the Dead: Circum-Atlantic Performance*. New York: Columbia University Press, 1996.

Roberts, Adam. *Science Fiction*. 2nd ed. London: Routledge, 2006.

Roberts, Dorothy. *Killing the Black Body: Race, Reproduction, and the Meaning of Liberty*. New York: Pantheon Books, 1997.

Rodríguez, Ileana. *Transatlantic Topographies: Islands, Highlands, Jungles*. Minneapolis: University of Minnesota Press, 2004.

Rofel, Lisa. *Desiring China: Experiments in Neoliberalism, Sexuality, and Public Culture*. Durham, NC: Duke University Press, 2007.

Roh, David S., Betsy Huang, and Greta A. Niu, eds. *Techno-Orientalism: Imagining Asia in Speculative Fiction, History, and Media*. New Brunswick, NJ: Rutgers University Press, 2015.

Romero, Fernando. *Hyper-Border: The Contemporary U.S.-Mexico Border and Its Future*. New York: Princeton Architectural Press, 2008.

Roof, Judith. *The Poetics of DNA*. Minneapolis: University of Minnesota Press, 2007.

Rose, Nikolas S. *The Politics of Life Itself: Biomedicine, Power, and Subjectivity in the Twenty-First Century*. Princeton, NJ: Princeton University Press, 2007.

Rosenberg, Jordana, and Britt Rusert. "Framing Finance: Rebellion, Dispossession, and the Geopolitics of Enclosure in Samuel Delany's *Neverÿon* Series." *Radical History Review*, no. 118 (2014): 64–91.

Rutledge, Gregory E., and Nalo Hopkinson. "Speaking in Tongues: An Interview with Science Fiction Writer Nalo Hopkinson." *African American Review* 33, no. 4 (1999): 589–601.

Sadowski-Smith, Claudia. "Reading across Diaspora: Chinese and Mexican Undocumented Immigration across U.S. Land Borders." In *Globalization on the Line: Culture, Capital, and Citizenship at U.S. Borders*, edited by Claudia Sadowski-Smith, 69–97. New York: Palgrave, 2002.

Saldaña-Portillo, María Josefina. "In the Shadow of NAFTA: *Y tu mama tambien* Revisits the National Allegory of Mexican Sovereignty." *American Quarterly* 57, no. 3 (2005): 751–77.

———. *The Revolutionary Imagination in the Americas and the Age of Development*. Durham, NC: Duke University Press, 2003.

Saldívar, José David. *Border Matters: Remapping American Cultural Studies*. Berkeley: University of California Press, 1997.

Saldívar, Ramón. "Imagining Cultures: The Transnational Imaginary in Postrace America." *Journal of Transnational American Studies* 4, no. 2 (2012): 1–18.

Scheper-Hughes, Nancy. "Parts Unknown: Undercover Ethnography of the Organs-Trafficking Underworld." *Ethnography* 5, no. 1 (2004): 29–73.

Schiebinger, Londa. *Plants and Empire: Colonial Bioprospecting in the Atlantic World*. Cambridge, MA: Harvard University Press, 2004.

Schmidt Camacho, Alicia R. *Migrant Imaginaries: Latino Cultural Politics in the U.S.-Mexico Borderlands*. New York: New York University Press, 2008.

Schwartz, Marie Jenkins. *Birthing a Slave: Motherhood and Medicine in the Antebellum South*. Cambridge, MA: Harvard University Press, 2010.

Scott, James C. *Seeing Like a State: How Certain Schemes to Improve the Human Condition Have Failed*. New Haven, CT: Yale University Press, 1998.

Sedgwick, Eve Kosofsky. *Touching Feeling: Affect, Pedagogy, Performativity*. Durham, NC: Duke University Press, 2003.

Shaviro, Steven. "Capitalist Monsters." *Historical Materialism* 10, no. 4 (2002): 281–90.

Sheldon, Rebekah. "Somatic Capitalism: Reproduction, Futurity, and Feminist Science Fiction." *Ada: A Journal of Gender, New Media, and Technology*, no. 3 (2013).

Slaughter, Sheila. "Beyond Basic Science: Research University Presidents' Narratives of Science Policy." *Science, Technology, and Human Values* 18, no. 3 (1993), 278–302.

Smith, Terry. "Visual Regimes of Colonization: Aboriginal Seeing and European Vision in Australia." In *Visual Culture Reader*, edited by Nicholas Mirzoeff, 483–94. 2nd ed. London: Routledge, 2003.

Soja, Edward W. *Thirdspace: Journeys to Los Angeles and Other Real-and-Imagined Places*. Cambridge, MA: Blackwell, 1996.

Soluri, John. *Banana Cultures: Agriculture, Consumption, and Environmental Change in Honduras and the United States*. Austin: University of Texas Press, 2005.

Song, Min Hyoung. "Becoming Planetary." *American Literary History* 23, no. 3 (2011): 555–73.

Spillers, Hortense J. "Mama's Baby, Papa's Maybe: An American Grammar Book." *Diacritics* 17, no. 2 (1987): 65–81.

Squier, Susan Merrill. *Liminal Lives: Imagining the Human at the Frontiers of Biomedicine.* Durham, NC: Duke University Press, 2004.

Stabile, Carol A. "Shooting the Mother: Fetal Photography and the Politics of Disappearance." *Camera Obscura* 10, no. 1 (1992): 178–205.

Stacey, Jackie. *The Cinematic Life of the Gene.* Durham, NC: Duke University Press, 2010.

Stepan, Nancy Leys. *"The Hour of Eugenics": Race, Gender, and Nation in Latin America.* Ithaca, NY: Cornell University Press, 1991.

———. *Picturing Tropical Nature.* Ithaca, NY: Cornell University Press, 2001.

———. "Race, Gender, Science and Citizenship." *Gender and History* 10, no. 1 (1998): 26–52.

Stephan, Paula E. *How Economics Shapes Science.* Cambridge, MA: Harvard University Press, 2012.

———. "Human Genomes: Public and Private." Special issue, *Nature* 409, no. 6822 (2001): 745.

——— and Sharon G. Levin. "Property Rights and Entrepreneurship in Science." *Small Business Economics* 8, no. 3 (June 1996): 177–88.

Sterling, Bruce. "CATSCAN 5: Slipstream." *SF Eye* 5 (July 1989), 4.

———."Slipstream 2." *Science Fiction Studies* 38, no. 1 (2011): 6–10.

Stocking, George Ward, and Myron W. Watkins. *Cartels in Action: Case Studies in International Business Diplomacy.* New York: Twentieth Century Fund, 1946.

Stoler, Ann Laura. *Race and the Education of Desire: Foucault's History of Sexuality and the Colonial Order of Things.* Durham, NC: Duke University Press, 1995.

Striffler, Steve, and Mark Moberg, eds. *Banana Wars: Power, Production and History in the Americas.* Durham, NC: Duke University Press, 2003.

Sturken, Marita. *Tangled Memories: The Vietnam War, the AIDS Epidemic, and the Politics of Remembering.* Berkeley: University of California Press, 1997.

Sunder Rajan, Kaushik. *Biocapital: The Constitution of Postgenomic Life.* Durham, NC: Duke University Press, 2006.

———, ed. *Lively Capital: Biotechnologies, Ethics, and Governance in Global Markets.* Durham, NC: Duke University Press, 2012.

Suvin, Darko. "Estrangement and Cognition." In *Strange Horizons*, November 24, 2014. http://strangehorizons.com/non-fiction/articles/estrangement-and-cognition/#ps.

———. *Metamorphoses of Science Fiction: On the Poetics and History of a Literary Genre.* New Haven, CT: Yale University Press, 1979.

Tadiar, Neferti X. M. "Life-Times of Disposability within Global Neoliberalism." *Social Text* 31, no. 2 (2013): 19–48.

Tal, Kalí. "'That Just Kills Me': Black Militant Near-Future Fiction." *Social Text* 20, no. 2 (2002): 65–91.

Tan, Charles, ed. *Lauriat: A Filipino-Chinese Speculative Fiction Anthology.* Maple Shade, NJ: Lethe, 2012.

Thacker, Eugene. *The Global Genome: Biotechnology, Politics, and Culture.* Cambridge, MA: MIT Press, 2005.

Thaler, Ingrid. *Black Atlantic Speculative Fictions: Octavia E. Butler, Jewelle Gomez, and Nalo Hopkinson.* New York: Routledge, 2010.

Thomas, Sheree R., ed. *Dark Matter: A Century of Speculative Fiction from the African Diaspora*. New York: Grand Central Publishing, 2000.

———, ed. *Dark Matter: Reading the Bones*. New York: Warner Books, 2004.

Thompson, Charis. *Making Parents: The Ontological Choreography of Reproductive Technologies*. Cambridge, MA: MIT Press, 2005.

Tsing, Anna Lowenhaupt. *Friction: An Ethnography of Global Connection*. Princeton, NJ: Princeton University Press, 2005.

Tucker, Richard P. *Insatiable Appetite: The United States and the Ecological Degradation of the Tropical World*. Berkeley: University of California Press, 2000.

Twine, France Winddance. *Racism in a Racial Democracy: The Maintenance of White Supremacy in Brazil*. 1997. New Brunswick, NJ: Rutgers University Press, 2001.

Ty, Eleanor Rose. *Unfastened: Globality and Asian North American Narratives*. Minneapolis: University of Minnesota Press, 2010.

Uncertain Commons. *Speculate This!* Durham, NC: Duke University Press, 2013.

Vasconcelos, José. *The Cosmic Race*. 1925. Translated and annotated by Didier T. Jaén. Baltimore, MD: Johns Hopkins University, 1997.

Van Duzer, Chet. *Sea Monsters on Medieval and Renaissance Maps*. London: The British Library, 2013.

Vora, Kalindi. "Indian Transnational Surrogacy and the Disaggregation of Mothering Work." *Anthropology News* 50, no. 2 (2009): 9–12.

Waldby, Catherine and Robert Mitchell. *Tissue Economies: Blood, Organs, and Cell Lines in Late Capitalism*. Durham, NC: Duke University Press, 2006.

Washington, Harriet A. *Medical Apartheid: The Dark History of Medical Experimentation on Black Americans from Colonial Times to the Present*. New York: Anchor, 2007.

Ward, Douglas Turner. *Happy Ending and Day of Absence: Two Plays*. New York: The Third Press, 1966.

Watson, Jini Kim. *The New Asian City: Three-Dimensional Fictions of Space and Urban Form*. Minneapolis: University of Minnesota Press, 2011.

Weinstein, Barbara. *The Amazon Rubber Boom, 1850–1920*. Stanford, CA: Stanford University Press, 1983.

Wolmark, Jenny. *Aliens and Others: Science Fiction, Feminism, and Postmodernism Jenny Wolmark*. Iowa City: University of Iowa Press, 1994.

Wood, Christopher. *The Bubble Economy: Japan's Extraordinary Speculative Boom of the '80s and the Dramatic Bust of the '90s*. New York: Atlantic Monthly Press, 1992.

Woodward, Kathleen M. *Statistical Panic: Cultural Politics and the Poetics of the Emotions*. Durham, NC: Duke University Press, 2009.

Wynter, Sylvia. "Unsettling the Coloniality of Being/Power/Truth/Freedom: Towards the Human, After Man, Its Overrepresentation—An Argument." *CR: The New Centennial Review* 3, no. 3 (Fall 2003): 257–337.

Yamashita, Karen Tei. *Through the Arc of the Rain Forest: A Novel*. Minneapolis, MN: Coffee House Press, 1990.

———. *Tropic of Orange: A Novel*. Minneapolis, MN: Coffee House, 1997.

Yoneyama, Lisa. *Hiroshima Traces: Time, Space, and the Dialectics of Memory*. Berkeley: University of California Press, 1999.

INDEX

Abu Ghraib, 92, 94
Agamben, Giorgio, 6
Agent Orange, 57, 69, 184n43
Akanksha Infertility Clinic, 80, 86
Alexander, M. Jacqui: on the criminalization of queer sex, 113
alien: abduction as trope, 54, 161; and the border, 57, 62, 67, 70–71; currency, 1; flora and fauna in the Amazon, 26; "illegal alien orange scare," 59; Japanese "as unfeeling aliens," 125; migrants as, 67; "Octomom" as, 87–89; in *Through the Arc of the Rain Forest*, 30–32, 35, 37, 49
Alta Summit, 154, 156, 159
Amazon: as speculative space, 30, 33, 36, 38, 45, 49. *See* rainforest
Amazons, 26
anamorphosis, 93–95, 99
Anansi (trickster spider), 108
Andrews, Arlan. *See* SIGMA
Anzaldúa, Gloria: on frontiers and borders, 21
Arau, Sergio. *See Day without a Mexican, A*
Area 51, 77–78
Arizmendi, Yareli. *See Day without a Mexican, A*
Ashitey, Claire Hope, 91, 100
Asian Century, 119–25, 166
Asian Development Bank (ADB), 5, 122–24, 162, 190n7
Asian Development Fund, 124
Asian migration to Latin America, 67–68

assisted reproductive technologies (ART), 81, 87–89, 103, 160
Association of Southeast Asian Nations (ASEAN), 122–23
Atomic Bomb Casualty Commission, 155
Austin, J. L., 158

Balsamo, Anne: on reproductive technologies and discipline, 89
Barad, Karen, 35, 65, 161
Battlestar Galactica, 53
Baudrillard, Jean: on emergency simulation, 53; *Simulacra and Simulation*, 182n9
Bear, Greg. *See* SIGMA
Beaumont, Matthew: on science fiction's use of the anamorphic image, 187n25
Bell, Derrick: "The Space Traders," 54, 113
benevolence, guise of, 28, 37, 39, 42–45, 113
Benford, Gregory: on "hard" science fiction, 14
Benjamin, Walter: and the "Angel of History," 17, 176n61; "homogeneous empty time," 19, 39
Bergson, Henri: on duration, 33
Berlant, Lauren: "cruel optimism," 22, 143, 145, 169–70; notion of the impasse, 19
Bikini Atoll, 147, 160, 167
biopolitics: 80, 90
Black Atlantic, The (Gilroy), 107
Black Lives Matter, 100–102
Black Star Line, 107
Blade Runner (Scott), 125

Bloch, Ernst, 6
Bogues, Anthony: on the human, 97
borderlands, narratives of futurity at the U.S.-Mexico, 54; and the notions of homeland and nation, 65; "nuclear" (Masco), 77–78; remapping of the, 60–61, 67, 70, 184n36; in *Tropic of Orange*, 55. *See also* borders
borders, 21; border wall, 62; flexibility of, 55, 57, 60, 63, 66, 70; Internal Security Act of 1950 (a.k.a., the McCarran Act), 78; "nuclear borderlands" (Masco), 77; Secure Border Initiative (G. W. Bush), 61; as testing ground for surveillance and military technologies, 54, 57–58; Tropic of Cancer as border, 65
Borders Trilogy (Rivera), 71
British Rubber Restoration Act (a.k.a., the Stevenson Plan), 38, 180n28
Buck v. Bell (1927 Supreme Court case), 86. *See also* eugenics; sterilization campaigns
Bush, George H. W.: and the U.S. invasion of Panama, 59
Bush, George W.: Secure Border Initiative, 62; War on Terror, 72, 78
Butler, Judith: on drag, 160
Butler, Octavia, 9, 104–5

Camacho, Julia, 67
Capitalocene, 22
cartography: counter-cartography, 49; imperialist, 11, 65–66; revisionist (Yamashita), 61, 70; utopian, 184n36. *See also* maps
Celebration, FL (Disney-planned town), 150, 166
Census Bureau: and the "imperative to be counted," 6
Chakrabarty, Dipesh: on "the waiting room of history," 5–7, 130
Chakravartty, Paula and Denise Ferreira da Silva: on the "racial logic of global financial capitalism," 153
chance: staying open to, 170; the "taming of," 11, 133

Chang, Jason Oliver, 67
Chang, Konrad, 67
Chesnutt, Charles, 114
Children of Men (Cuarón), 21, 81–84, 88–100, 117–18
Chilean "grape scare" of 1989, 58–60
Chin, Vincent: murder of, 49–50
Chinese Exclusion Act of 1882, 67
Chuh, Kandice: on citizenship, 18
citizenship, 88, 129; flexible, 124, 129; global (financial), 8; and justice (Chuh), 18; and "Octomom," 90; and race, 84; statistical (Currah and Stryker), 6
clone: Dolly the sheep, 150, 197n57; and the subaltern, 146, 160
cognitive estrangement (Suvin), 13
collaboration: cross-ethnic (in *Tropic of Orange*), 55; in *Midnight Robber*, 105; of SIGMA and the Department of Homeland Security, 51–53; transnational (in *Sleep Dealer*), 74
colonization: of the future, 11–12, 73; of Southeast Asia, 44; temporal, 28
compound interest, 7
Cook-Deegan, Robert: on the connection between the HGP and atomic bomb effects, 154–55
Cooper, Melinda, 157, 166
creolization: as survival technique in *Midnight Robber*, 109
Crick, Francis. *See* Watson, James and Francis Crick
crisis: everyday (in *Malinky Robot*), 143; simulation, 53
Cuarón, Alfonso: *Children of Men*, 91–100, 117–18; *Y Tu Mamá También*, 92–93
Currah, Paisley, 6
cyborg: Japanese as, 125; labor, 71; manifesto (Haraway), 15
cybracero, 71, 74

Dark Winter (2001 smallpox attack simulation), 52–53

da Silva, Denise Ferreira. *See* Chakravartty, Paula and Denise Ferreira da Silva
da Silva, Luiz Inácio Lula, 3
datafication, 4, 158, 170
Davis, Angela, 102–3
Davis, Dana Ain: on "Octomom" Nadya Suleman, 87–88
Day of Absence (Ward), 54
Day without a Mexican, A (Arau and Arizmendi), 54, 113
"Day without Immigrants, A," 54
dead capital (de Soto), 46
de Certeau, Michel, 75–76, 135
Delany, Samuel, 9, 15–17, 19, 104, 167, 168–69
Deng Xioping, 123
derivatives, 1–5, 12, 16, 78, 156
Derrida, Jacques, 16, 172n2
Dery, Mark, 104
de Soto, Hernando: on "dead capital," 46
diasporic movement, 17, 106–7, 111; "queer diaspora" (Eng), 164
difference: as asset, 31–32; as marking "how ancient the alphabet of our bodies" (Lai), 167; punishing (in *Salt Fish Girl*), 198n72; racial, 42; spotting the, 141
disaster: capitalism, 51, 78, 157; fiction of, 52
discourse: speculation as, 168–70
dividual (Deleuze), 149
Dolly the sheep, 150, 197n57. *See also* clone
double consciousness, 110
Douglass, Frederick, 107, 114
Downes v. Bidwell (1901 Supreme Court case), 56, 58
drag: as example of gender performativity (Butler), 160; genetic (Franklin), 149, 159, 160, 167, 197n57; temporal (Freeman), 160–61, 167
Drysdale, Peter: on the Asian Century, 122–23
Du Bois, W. E. B., 9, 107; use of the "veil" concept, 110
Dunmire, Patricia: on preemption and policy, 52–53

Ebbet, Charles Clyde: *Lunch atop a Skyscraper*, 138, 141
econometrics, 4, 149
economies of exchange, alternative: in *Malinky Robot*, 135
Edelman, Lee: on "reproductive futurism," 98, 142
Electronic Disturbance Theater, 55
emergency: coalitions in times of, 83; detention clauses, 78; discourses of, 78; filmmaking (Arizmendi), 54; simulations of, 52–53
"empire-building corporation" (Ford), 48
Eng, David: on queer diaspora, 164
Esch, Elizabeth, 42–43
eugenics, 42–43, 50, 86–88, 100, 102, 159
Everett, Anna, 104, 115
exception, conditions of, 72
exceptionalism: via difference, 31–32; U.S., 54, 77
extrapolation, 166, 170; Cuarón's (re: *Children of Men*), 94; economic, 2–4, 151, 157; through excavation, 27–28, 30–37, 45
exuberance: irrational, 120, 141–42, 169–70, 194n13; queer, 145

fantasy: colonial fantasy of mastery over the technology of looking (Mercer), 98; of deliverance from a subsistence economy through becoming a hacker, 183n18; of flight, 135; in Ford's ventures in Brazil, 26, 39, 45; genre of, 13, 28, 104; imperialist fantasies of the tropics, 29–30, 34, 48; neoliberal fantasy of a seamless world unified under the sign of global capitalism, 8; racialized fantasies of a neocolonialist capitalism, 181n36; of rendering laborers docile, 44; of risk and terror at the border, 76–77; U.S. and European fantasies of Japan in techno-Orientalism, 124, 126–27; Western fantasy of Asia as supplementary and disposable, 128
feminist science studies, 2, 35, 65, 84

Ferreira Furtado, Júnia: "tropical empiricism," 33–34
fictitious capital (Marx), 2, 49
finance: as "capitalism's imagination" (Haiven), 4
Findlay, David, 109
Fisher, Mark, 13, 16–17
fish radio-autograph, 146
Fitzcarraldo (Herzog), 25, 29, 178n1
flexible: accumulation, 57, 145; borders, 57, 70; citizenship, 20, 124, 129; construction of Singaporeans, 130; future, 13, 62; status of "foreign" vs. "domestic," 56; system of speculative capital as, 12; temporalities, 19
Food and Drug Administration, 5
Ford, Henry. *See* Fordlândia
Fordlândia, 20, 26–29, 38–49
foreign: feigned foreignness (in *Children of Men*), 95; foreign vs. domestic, 32, 56–57; students/professionals in Singapore, 129
forgetting: "culture of amnesia" in the U.S. (Sturken), 28; imperialist practices of, 49, 70; selective (of Hiroshima and Nagasaki by NHGRI), 155. *See also* memory
Foucault, Michel: on biopower, 158–59; on discourse, 168–69; on heredity, 158; and "the population," 103
Franklin, Sarah: on "genetic drag," 159–60, 197n57
Freeman, Elizabeth: on temporal "drag" as a productive obstacle, 161; temporally regulated laboring bodies, 19
Fregoso, Rosa Linda: on *Lone Star* (Sayles), 187n32
Freyre, Gilberto: on "racial democracy" in Brazil, 42–43
future: colonization of, 5, 11–12, 73, 169; as contested terrain, 143; "creative sabotage of" (Cooper), 166; Future•Singapore initiative, 127–30, 133; in the present, 7; as "queerness's domain" (Muñoz), 6; and scientific research, 148–51; as speculative space, 53; writing bodies into, 149, 167, 169
Future•Singapore initiative, 127–30

futurism: Afro, Asian, and Chican@, 10; reproductive, 98, 116, 118, 142
futurity, 2–23, 15, 19; Asian, 120–27, 143, 145, 167; genomic, 150–51, 158, 160; in *Midnight Robber*, 81–82, 106, 112, 116; neoliberal, 149; policy from ideological, 52–53; politics of (in *Sleep Dealer*), 73; profit-driven, 27; queer, 6, 169, 106; reproductive, 81, 87, 88–89, 99, 116, 138, 141–42; Singaporean, 130, 133, 142; transpacific, 164, 166–67

Gandhi, Rajiv, 123
Garner, Margaret, 102–3
Garvey, Marcus: Black Star Line, 106–7
Gates, Bill, 108
Gates, Henry Louis, Jr., 104, 109, 115
Gauguin, Paul: and Tahiti, 31, 179n15
gaze: anamorphic, 93–94; cinematic, 76, 93–94, 99; colonial, 31, 178n1; policing, 76
gene therapy, 150, 159–60
genetic mutation, 148, 150, 153, 159; vs. modification, 151, 160; vs. regeneration, 151, 154, 156, 158–59
Gibson, William, 108, 124
Gilmore, Ruth Wilson: on racism, 84
Gilroy, Paul: image of the ship in *The Black Atlantic*, 107; survival via alternative technologies, 115
Glave, Diane, 107–8
Global North/South, 5, 42, 46, 50, 62, 72, 80, 82, 84, 99–100, 102, 111
god: "the god trick" (Haraway), 2, 15; "voyeur-god" perspective (de Certeau), 75–76
Gómez-Peña, Guillermo, 64, 184n36
good life, 138, 141, 143, 145
Gordon, Avery: on haunted texts, 37–38, 82; "memory as haunting," 152; "repetition-as-displacement," 156
Grandin, Greg, 27, 181n36
Granny Nanny of the Maroons, 108
"grape scare." *See* Chilean "grape scare" of 1989
Great Pacific Garbage Patch, 147

Greenspan, Alan, 120, 122, 169
griot tradition: in Hopkinson's *Midnight Robber*, 110
Greenfield Village (historic theme park), 48
Guantánamo Bay, 78, 94–95

Hacker, Marilyn, 16
Hacking, Ian, 11
Haiven, Max: on capitalism, 4
Halberstam, Jack: on queer subcultures, 18–19
Haraway, Donna, 15, 35; "virtual speculum," 97
Harvey, David, 11
hauntology, 172n2; in *Children of Men*, 92–95, 99; in Guantánamo, 95; haunted future, 120; haunted Pacific, 147; haunted texts, 37; haunting as analytic device through which to read science fiction, 186n19; haunting Pacific, 167; haunting as "transformative recognition" (Gordon), 89; necropolitical, 88; and quantum entanglements, 65, 161; in *Salt Fish Girl*, 150, 152
Heidegger, Martin, 6
Herzog, Werner, 25, 29–30, 178n1
Highlights (magazine), 141
Hiroshima and Nagasaki, 146–48, 160; and genomics, 153–55, 167. *See also* Manhattan Project
Hochschild, Arlie, 80
homeland security, 21, 77; Department of Homeland Security, 51–53, 71, 78
hope: in *Children of Men*, 91–92, 97–99; over experience, 169; and home in Singapore, 129; in LaRue's "Living Conditions in the Amazon Valley," 42; in *Malinky Robot*, 133, 135; in *Midnight Robber*, 118. *See also* Ashitey, Claire Hope; optimism
Hopkinson, Nalo: *Midnight Robber*, 82–84, 89–91, 104–18; on "postcolonial speculative fiction" 9
Hu-DeHart, Evelyn, 67
Human Genome Project (HGP), 148–50, 153–60
HyperContexts: in *Tropic of Orange*, 66, 70

idleness: forms of (in *Malinky Robot*), 133
imperialism: of British and Dutch in Asia, 39, 123–24; neoliberalism as a particularly American form of capitalist, 127; temporal and gustatory, 39; by the United Fruit Company, 61; U.S. "imperialism-without-colonies" (McClintock), 174n36; of U.S. in Asia, 123–24, 147–48, 166; of U.S. in Brazil, 38–39; of U.S. in Puerto Rico, 56
industrialized farming, 96
Internal Security Act of 1950 (a.k.a., the McCarran Act), 78
International Monetary Fund (IMF), 122, 127
invisible labor, 81, 120, 124: and the "Supermarket Slave Trail," 166–67; supporting scientific enterprises, 19–20; in transnational surrogacy, 79–87; in *Tropic of Orange*, 69
"irrational exuberance," 120, 141–42, 169–70, 194n13

James, C. L. R., 7
James, P. D., 21, 82
Jameson, Fredric: on perpetual renovation, 171n4; on "spectrality," 94
Japanese-Brazilian immigration, 36–37

Kang, Laura: and the "Asianization" of financial crises, 127
Kaplan, Amy: on the foreign vs. the domestic, 56–58, 95
Kim, Jodi: on wartime targets as objects of state knowledge, 155
King, Rodney, 61
Klein, Naomi, 51, 78, 100
Knight, Frank: on uncertainty, 5, 173n17
Koepnick, Lutz P.: on the colonial gaze in Herzog's *Fitzcarraldo* and *Aguirre*, 178n1
Kuczynski, Alex, 79–81

La Condamine, Charles-Marie de, 26, 28–29, 42

INDEX - 221

Lai, Larissa: *Salt Fish Girl*, 148–54, 160–66, 169
Lai, Paul: on smelliness in *Salt Fish Girl*, 198n72. *See also* smelliness
Lakoff, Andrew: on "imaginative enactment," 52
LaRue, Carl, 26, 42–44, 48
Latimer, Heather: on reproductive politics in *Children of Men*, 100
Latour, Bruno: and the "dirty underbelly" of the laboratory, 128
Lee, Benjamin. *See* LiPuma, Edward and Benjamin Lee
Lee, Erika, 67
Lee, Rachel, 34
Lee Hsien Loong, 142
Lefanu, Sarah: on "the plasticity of science fiction," 175n41
Lévi-Strauss, Claude: *Tristes Tropiques*, 31
Liew, Sonny: *Malinky Robot*, 130–45
Lipsitz, George: on California's Proposition 187, 59–60
LiPuma, Edward and Benjamin Lee, 1, 3, 16
Lloyd, David, 17, 27
Los Alamos, 77, 185n51
Los Angeles riots (1992), 56, 61
L'Ouverture, Toussaint, 112
Lowe, Lisa, 17–18, 27, 125
Lubin, Alex: on "transcontinental crossroads," 77
Luciano, Dana: "chronobiopolitics," 19; "queer inhumanisms" (Luciano and Chen), 149
Ludwig, Daniel, 29

Mahbubani, Kishore, 119–23
Malinky Robot (Liew), 130–45
Manalansan, Martin: on "queer love," 112
Manhattan Project, 154–56
maps: fantastical, 11–12, 174n33; of North, Central, and South America, 184n36
maquiladora system, 35, 54, 58, 63, 71–72
Marez, Curtis: on drug traffic and state power, 59

Martin, Randy: on risk management, 182n11
-maru (Japanese suffix: cycle or circle), 36
Marx, Karl: on predatory lending, 2; "reproductive labor," 80
McClintock, Anne: the "imperialism-without-colonies" of the U.S., 174n36
Mehan, Uppinder, 9, 110
memory: counter-memory, 104, 115; genetic, 160; as haunting (Gordon), 152; in *Salt Fish Girl*, 152; in *Sleep Dealer*, 74–75; transgenerational genetic, 160; Yamashita's speculative fictions as technologies of, 28, 60, 68. *See also* forgetting
Mentos: and the 2012 effort to increase birth rate in Singapore (National Night), 142
Mercer, Kobena, 98; on Mapplethorpe and the fetishizing of black skin, 188n35
metaphor: and DNA, 158; financial growth and gendered, agricultural, 128; "metaphorical literacy" (Gates, Jr.), 104, and technology, 107
Midnight Robber (Hopkinson), 81–84, 104–18
Milburn, Colin: on science and science fiction, 151
modernity, 10–11; Asian, 126; birth of, 97; brought to the jungle, 26, 41, 44; "counterculture of modernity" (Gilroy), 115; and racism, 19, 27; technoscientific, 29; and temporality, 19, 39
Monsanto, 150, 167
Morley, David and Kevin Robins: on techno-Orientalism, 124–25. *See* techno-Orientalism
Morrison, Toni: *Beloved* (1987), 96–97, 102–3; and Angela Davis, 103
Mosley, Walter, 9, 104
Muñoz, José: on the horizon of potentiality, 6–7
mutation: Department of Energy's interest in detecting, 154; rebranded as regeneration, 158–59; in *Salt Fish Girl*, 22, 151–53, 160, 163, 169; in *Through the Arc of the Rain Forest*, 30–32, 36. *See also* genetic mutation

NAFTA, 56–57, 59–61, 71
Nagasaki. *See* Hiroshima and Nagasaki
National Day (Singapore), 130, 142. *See also* National Night (Singapore)
National Human Genome Research Institute (NHGRI), 149, 154–57, 166
National Night (Singapore), 142. *See also* Mentos
Nelson, Alondra, 104
neoliberalism: American, 124, 127; in Asia, 120, 122, 124–25, 128–30; and cartography, 184n36; in *Children of Men*, 90; "chronobiopolitics" of neoliberal futurity, 19; and its fantasies, 8–10; and "free" trade, 14, 28, 55–57, 60, 62, 67, 71; in *Malinky Robot*, 132, 138, 145; neoliberal economic policy, 20–21; neoliberal financialization, 4; neoliberal pluralism, 18; and racial and colonial subjugation (Chakravartty and Ferreira da Silva), 153; in *Salt Fish Girl*, 164; in *Sleep Dealer*, 71–72; and transnational circulations of commodified bodies, 84
Nilsson, Lennart, 99
Niven, Larry. *See* SIGMA
North American Free Trade Agreement. *See* NAFTA
notional figure, 1–2, 172n1
not yet, the, 2, 5–7, 23
novela (Brazilian soap opera), 31

Obayashi Global, 138
O'Brien, Patty: on Gauguin's Tahiti, 179n15
Octomom. *See* Suleman, Nadya ("Octomom")
One Hundred Years of Solitude (Marquez): and the banana, 62
Ong, Aihwa: on "flexible citizenship," 124; on "technopreneurialism," 129
Operation Blockade/Hold the Line (El Paso, TX), 60
Operation Gatekeeper (San Diego, CA), 60
Oppenheimer, Robert, 78
optimism: and the Asian century, 122; over and against "better judgment," 169–70; cruel (Berlant), 143, 170; about genomics' potential, 156, 166; in *Malinky Robot*, 133, 145; Singapore as a place of, 22, 145. *See also* hope
oranges: and the foreign/domestic relationship of Puerto Rico to the U.S., 56; history of, 61–62; as migrant subject, 57, 61; in *Tropic of Orange*, 56–57, 59–66, 69. *See also* Agent Orange; Rauch, Molly; Simpson, O. J.

Pacific Ocean: and building on sand, 119; as occupied, 166–67; as testing ground, 147–48
Pacific Proving Ground, 148
paraliterature, 15–16, 20, 169
Peas, Donald: on the "fantasmatic representation of a nuclear holocaust in the anterior future," 155; and the "symbolic drama" of the homeland, 55
Penderecki, Krzysztof: "Threnody for the Victims of Hiroshima," 92
Philips Norelco, 125–28
Planned Parenthood, 101–2
population regulation, 6
Pournelle, Jerry. *See* SIGMA
Pratt, Mary Louise: on imperialist cartographers, 65; on La Condamine's expedition report, 26; and the "mapping of progress," 11
prisons, private, 3
privacy: as most precious commodity (in *Midnight Robber*), 112
privatization, 7; of care, 88; of corporate interests and military defense, 73; culture of, 59; of food, 163; of the future, 23; of genetic material, 164; in *Sleep Dealer*, 73; of social reproduction, 164; and speculative fiction, 20; of water, 75
progress narratives, 10–11; Benjaminian, 17, 39; of Henry Ford, 26, 28, 169; and the HGP, 150; "*Ordem e Progresso*" (motto on Brazil's flag), 41; of racial discrimination, 105; of technofutures, 112
property: "portraits of property," 11; transformation of genes into, 158; transformation of land into, 46–47

Proposition 187 (California, 1994), 54, 59–60
Proposition 209 (California, 1996), 60
pseudoscience, 34, 43
Puar, Jasbir, 169; on "regenerative productivity," 159–60
public health, 6, 82

Rai, Amit: on an "ecology of sensations," 165
rainforest: agency of, 30, 45, 47; chaotic diversity of, 178n1; resilience of, 26; spectacularization of, 29; as speculative space, 33, 36. See also Amazon; Yamashita, Karen Tei
Ramayana (epic poem), 110–11, 189n57
Ramírez, Catherine: on enjoying science fiction, 171n3
Rauch, Molly: on oranges, 61
Reagan, Ronald: War on Drugs, 56
reality television: in *Sleep Dealer*, 75–76. See also Trump, Donald
rebellion: at Fordlândia, 39–40, 45
regeneration: genomic, 148, 150, 155, 157; in *Salt Fish Girl*, 151
reparative practices (Sedgwick), 132–35
return of the repressed: the alien invader as, 37; "dreaming sickness" in *Salt Fish Girl* as (Gordon), 152
risk, 5–6, 12–13: at the border, 53–55, 76; and fruit, 59; the future parceled into portions of, 77; and the HGP, 155–57; management, 21, 78, 170, 182n11; society, 72
Rivera, Alex: Borders Trilogy, 71; *Sleep Dealer*, 55, 71–77; *Why Cybraceros?*, 71
Roach, Joseph: on surrogation, 85
Roberts, Dorothy: on the limits of reproductive liberty, 102–3
Rofel, Lisa: on neoliberalism in China, 130
Roof, Judith: on textual metaphors and DNA, 158–59
Rutledge, Gregory, 104

Sadowski-Smith, Claudia: on the Chinese Exclusion Act of 1882, 67
Salazar, Rubén, 69

Saldaña-Portillo, María Josefina: on the fantasy of deliverance from a subsistence economy through becoming a hacker, 183n18; on NAFTA's "fictions of development," 60; on the oscillation between central and peripheral, 93
Salt Fish Girl (Lai), 148–54, 160–66, 169
Sanchez, Rosaura and Beatrice Pita: *Lunar Braceros*, 55
Sanger, Frederick, 154
Sanger, Margaret, 101–2
Sayles, John: *Lone Star*, 187n32
science, 10–11; entrepreneurial approach to, 148–51, 155–56, 195n15, 197n47; feminist science studies, 2, 35, 65, 84; and imperialist enterprises, 28; and invisible labor, 19–20, 81; and myth, 78; and neocolonial enterprises, 37; plasticity of (Lefanu), 175n41; and racism, 43; regenerative medical, 157–60; reproductive, 153; and science fiction, 10, 13–15, 77, 106, 118, 151, 169, 186n19; and speculation, 8; and the war on drugs, 59; "word science" (signifying), 109. See also pseudoscience; technoscience
science fiction: and the anamorphic image, 187n25; antipositivist, 12–17; capitalism's reliance on fantastical representations of space and time as, 49; "discovery" of rubber as, 26; hard, 14; in the national interest, 51–53, 71, 73, 78; and "Octomom," 81–89; "overwhelming whiteness" of (Ramírez), 171n3; and race, 9, 84, 104; and science, 10, 13–15, 77, 106, 118, 151, 169, 186n19; and the trope of colonization, 189n48
Scott, Ridley. See *Blade Runner* (Scott)
securitization: financial, 3–5, 21–22, 52–55, 156; genetic, 87, 155, 157, 164; military, 78, 147–48, 156, 169; security state, 53, 72, 155; in *Simulacra and Simulation*, 182n9; in *Sleep Dealer*, 73, 77
Sedgwick, Eve Kosofsky: reparative practices, 132
Sensenbrenner Bill (California), 54
SIGMA, 51–53, 71

signification: as survival technique, 109, 115
signifying, 115
Simpson, O. J., 57, 61, 69
Sims, J. Marion: experimentation on slave women, 103, 153
Simulacra and Simulation (Baudrillard), 182n9
simulation: of birth in *Children of Men*, 99–100; "scenario-based exercises," 52–53; *Simulacra and Simulation* (Beaudrillard), 182n9
Singapore: reinvention of (Future•Singapore), 127–30
skyscraper: as global sign for financial growth, 119–21; *Lunch atop a Skyscraper* (Ebbets), 141; in *Malinky Robot*, 133–35, 138, 140f
Sleep Dealer (Rivera), 55, 71–77
slipstream, 151, 195n17
smelliness: in *Malinky Robot*, 133; in *Salt Fish Girl*, 152–53, 162, 198n72
sousveillance. *See* surveillance
"Space Traders, The" (Bell), 54, 113
spectacle, 72, 76, 178n1; "consumer spectacles" (Ford), 41
spectatorship, dynamics of, 77, 95
speculative fiction, 8–20; the Asian Century as, 122; La Condamine's expedition report as, 26; LaRue's scouting report as, 44; as narrative of futurity, 50; as survival technique (in *Midnight Robber*), 109; as a technology, 28, 70, 115
Squier, Susan Merrill: on regenerative medicine, 157
Stepan, Nancy Leys: on scientific autonomy, 15; on the tropicalist representations of the rainforest, 34, 179n19
sterilization campaigns: in the Global South, 42; in Puerto Rico, 86; in the U.S., 43, 88, 90, 102
Sterling, Bruce: on "slipstream," 195n17
Stoler, Ann Laura, 27
strategic trust, 147–48
Stryker, Susan, 6
student loans: as financial speculation, 75
Sturken, Marita: "culture of amnesia," 28

Sturtevant, Alfred, 154
Subramaniam, Banu, 159
Suleman, Nadya ("Octomom"), 81–82, 88–90
Surrogacy (Regulation) Bill (née Assisted Reproductive Technologies Bill), 80
surrogacy, transnational, 79–87
surrogation (Roach), 85
surveillance: by "citizen-detectives," 72; medical, 99; and the pregnant body, 82; sousveillance (surveillance from below), 61; state, 55, 94; technologies at the border, 53–54, 57, 60, 62–63, 71
survival literature, 26
Suvin, Darko: on science fiction, 13

Tal, Kalí: on science fiction and black people, 104
Tate, Greg, 104
Tavener, John, 97
Teatro Amazonas opera house, 29
technology: of biocapitalization, 83; border, 57, 71; in *Children of Men*, 90, 92, 96; of control, 113; diasporic movement as, 17, 107, 111; and the drug war, 59; of haunting, 93; liberation narrative of, 84; of looking, 98, 187n30; of memory, 28, 60, 68; and metaphor/myth, 107–8; in *Midnight Robber*, 90, 106–9, 112, 115; of perspective, 97; of reproduction, 81, 99; of rhetoric, 54; speculative fiction as, 70; the state's use of, 77, 94; of visibility, 69. *See also* assisted reproductive technologies (ART); techno-Orientalism; technoscience
techno-Orientalism, 124–27, 132–33, 145, 160
technoscience, 11, 15, 19, 29, 41, 106, 108, 120, 126, 156
Thomas, Sheree, 9, 104
Through the Arc of the Rain Forest (Yamashita), 27–37, 45–50
time, 17–19; experiencing (reparative vs. paranoid modalities), 132–33; fantasies of smooth, continuous, 126; at Fordlándia, 26, 39–41; in *Midnight Robber*, 113–16; "out

INDEX - 225

time (*continued*)
of joint," 1, 19, 172n2; in *Salt Fish Girl*, 149, 160–61, 167; travel, 28; wasted (in *Malinky Robot*), 133

traffic jam: in *Tropic of Orange*, 60, 63–64, 67

Trans-Pacific Partnership, 120, 167

travel writing: and the mapping of progress, 11; as scientific knowledge production, 42

trickster tradition: in *Midnight Robber*, 108–9, 114–15

Tristes Tropiques (Lévi-Strauss), 31

trolls, Internet, 100–101

Tropic of Orange (Yamashita), 55–70

Trump, Donald, 3

trust territories: 147; Trust Territory of the Pacific Islands (TTPI), 148

Tsing, Anna Lowenhaupt: on friction as an integral component of movement, 191n21

Tubman, Harriet, 117

Tucker, Richard: on greed and leaf blight, 45, 181n37

Turner, Frederick Jackson: on frontiers and borders, 21

Ty, Eleanor, 67

Underground Railroad, 117

United Nations, 123, 147–48

utopia, 6–7, 125

Vora, Kalindi: on transnational Indian surrogacy, 86

Walker, Sage. *See* SIGMA

"Walking in the City" (de Certeau), 75–76, 135

Ward, Douglas Turner: *Day of Absence*, 54

War of the Worlds (Welles), 52

War on Drugs, 56, 59, 72

War on Terror, 72, 78

Watson, James and Francis Crick, 154, 158

Welles, Orson: and the imaginative enactment of an emergency in *War of the Worlds*, 52

Why Cybraceros? (Rivera), 71

Woodward, Kathleen: on rendering data into fiction or statistical narrative, 4

World Bank, 5, 122

Wynter, Sylvia: on humanism, 98, 102

x-ray: at the border, 58, 71; in fish radio-autographs, 146

Yamashita, Karen Tei: *Through the Arc of the Rain Forest*, 27–37, 45–50; *Tropic of Orange*, 55–70

Žižek, Slavoj: on *Children of Men*, 93, 100

www.ingramcontent.com/pod-product-compliance
Lightning Source LLC
Chambersburg PA
CBHW071817230426
43670CB00013B/2483